The First Book of

The Norton Utilities®

Joseph Wikert

SAMS

A Division of Macmillan Computer Publishing
11711 North College, Carmel, Indiana 46032 USA

This book is dedicated to my entire family.

International Standard Book Number: 0-672-27308-X
Library of Congress Catalog Card Number: 90-62683

Product Manager: *Marie Butler-Knight*
Acquisitions Editor: *Richard K. Swadley*
Manuscript Editor: *Faithe Wempen*
Cover Artist: *Held & Diedrich Design*
Illustrators: *Don Clemons, Tom Emrick*
Production Assistance: *Claudia Bell, Brad Chinn, Denny Hager, Marj
Hopper, Diana Moore*
Proofreaders: *Bruce Steed, Betty Kish*
Indexer: *Hilary Adams*
Technical Reviewer: *C. Herbert Feltner*

Printed in the United States of America

Contents

Introduction, xi

iii

1   *An Introduction to the Norton Utilities, 1*

Picking Up Where DOS Left Off, 1
    System Requirements, 2
Unpacking the Utilities, 2
Installing the Utilities, 3
    Hard Disk Installation, 3
    Floppy Disk Installation, 4
Summarizing the Utilities, 5
    BE: Batch Enhancer, 7
    CALIBRAT: Calibrate, 7
    DISKEDIT: Disk Editor, 7
    DISKMON: Disk Monitor, 7
    DISKREET: Diskreet, 8
    DISKTOOL: Disk Tools, 8
    FILEFIND: File Find, 8
    FILEFIX: File Fix, 8
    FILESAVE: File Save, 8
    IMAGE: Image, 8
    NCACHE-F and NCACHE-S: Norton Cache, 9
    NCC: Norton Control Center, 9
    NCD: Norton Change Directory, 9
    NDD: Norton Disk Doctor II, 9
    NORTON: Norton Integration, 9
    SFORMAT: Safe Format, 10

SPEEDISK: Speed Disk, 10
SYSINFO: System Information, 10
UNERASE: UnErase, 10
UNFORMAT: UnFormat, 10
WIPEINFO: Wipe Info, 11
Utility Integration, 11
Using Menus, 15
Utility Help, 16
Help Within a Utility, 16
Utility Syntax Help, 17
What You Have Learned, 18

2 *DOS and Utility Basics, 19*

What is DOS?, 19
Microprocessors, 20
PC Memory, 22
RAM vs. ROM, 22
TSRs, 23
PC Disks, 23
More to Come..., 24
SYSINFO: System Information, 25
The System Menu, 25
The Disks Menu, 28
The Memory Menu, 28
The Benchmarks Menu, 31
The Report Menu, 34
NCC: Norton Control Center, 34
Cursor Size, 35
DOS Colors, 36
Palette Colors, 37
Video Mode, 38
Keyboard Speed, 40
Mouse Speed, 41
Serial Ports, 42
Watches, 44
Country Info, 46
Time and Date, 47
What You Have Learned, 49

iv

3 *Using Norton File Utilities, 51*

File Attributes and FILEFIND, 52

Setting and Clearing File Attributes, 54
Modifying File Attributes from the Command
Line, 56
Clearing all Attributes, 56
Filtering File Selections, 57
Measuring File Size and Disk Space for Backup, 57
Determining File Size and Disk Space with
FILEFIND, 58
Determining Target Fit from the Command
Line, 61
Date/Time Stamps, 62
Using FILEFIND to Set Date/Time Stamps, 62
Setting Date/Time Stamps from the Command
Line, 63
Using the Default Date and Time, 64
Clearing the Date and Time, 64
Quickly Recovering an Erased File, 64
UNERASE: The Inside Story, 65
What To Do If UNERASE Fails..., 67
Preserving Deleted Files with FILESAVE, 68
Recovering Files from the TRASHCAN, 70
Purging Files from the TRASHCAN, 71
Repairing Special Files, 72
The FILEFIX Solution, 72
Removing a File Permanently, 74
Removing Files with WIPEINFO, 75
What You Have Learned, 77

V

4 *Enhancing Your Batch Files, 79*

Automation: The Key to Batch Files, 79
Creating a Batch File, 80
A Simple Batch File, 81
Batch File Parameters, 83
Looping within a Batch File, 85
Conditional Execution (IF and GOTO), 86
Interactive Batch Files, 87
BE: Batch Enhancer, 88
The CLS Subcommand, 91
The SA Subcommand, 91
The WINDOW Subcommand, 92
The ROWCOL Subcommand, 93
The ASK Subcommand, 94

The ERRORLEVEL Variable, 94
The BOX Subcommand, 95
The BEEP Subcommand, 95
The DELAY Subcommand, 96
What You Have Learned, 96

5   *Managing Your Disks with the Utilities, 99*

Directories and Tree Structures, 99
NCD: Norton Change Directory, 101
    NCD Speed Search, 102
    NCD Function Keys, 103
    Volume Label Maintenance, 107
Recovering a Deleted Directory, 108
Finding Your Way Through the Forest, 111
    FILEFIND Revisited, 111
    Searching for Text with FILEFIND, 113
What You Have Learned, 115

6   *Maintaining Your Hard Disk Drive, 117*

Understanding Disk Structures, 117
    Bits, Bytes, Sectors and Clusters, 118
    Tracks and Cylinders, 118
Disk Areas, 121
    Boot Record, 121
    Root Directory, 121
    File Allocation Table (FAT), 121
    Data Area, 123
Obtaining Disk Information, 123
    Disk Summary, 123
    Disk Characteristics, 124
    Partition Tables, 125
Formatting Disks, 126
    SFORMAT: The Safe Format Alternative, 127
Preserving Important Disk Information, 131
    Maintaining a Good "Image", 131
Recovering Data from an Accidentally Formatted
    Disk, 132
    Analyzing an UNFORMATted Disk, 134
Wiping Files from a Disk, 135
Diagnosing and Correcting Disk Problems, 137
    Surface Test Configuration, 140

vi

Other Disk Doctor Options, 142
Undoing NDD Repairs, 144
What You Have Learned, 145

7 *Advanced Disk Management, 147*

Viruses and Disk Protection, 148
Monitoring Disk Activity, 148
Disk Monitor Options, 150
Disk Light, 151
Parking Your Hard Disk, 151
Miscellaneous Disk Tools, 152
Using DISKTOOL to Make a Disk Bootable, 153
Backtracking after a Disk RECOVERy, 154
Reviving a Defective Diskette, 155
Marking Clusters, 156
Using a Rescue Diskette, 156
Protecting Sensitive Files, 157
Encrypting Files, 157
Encryption Options, 159
Decrypting Files, 160
Using the Disk Editor, 161
A Note on Hexadecimal Notation, 162
Working with the Hexadecimal/ASCII View, 163
Selecting Other Views and Objects, 165
Manually UNERASEing Files, 167
Optimizing Disk Performance, 171
Using SPEEDISK, 171
Using a Disk Cache, 173
Using CALIBRAT, 174
What You Have Learned, 177

8 *Introducing the Commander, 179*

What the Commander Provides, 180
Installing the Commander, 182
Starting the Commander, 184
The Commander Interface, 185
Selecting Items, 187
Using the Keyboard, 188
Using a Mouse, 188
Configuring the Commander for Your System, 189
Using the Panels, 190

Changing Drives, 193
Sorting Your Files, 193
Narrowing Down the List, 193
Getting Help, 194
Leaving the Commander, 196
What You Have Learned, 196

9   *Managing Files and Disks with the Commander, 197*

Managing Your Files, 198
Finding Files (Alt-F7), 198
Selecting and Unselecting Files, 199
Copying Files (F5), 203
Renaming Files (F6), 205
Moving Files (F6), 206
Deleting Files (F8), 207
Setting File Attributes, 208
Viewing a File's Contents (F3), 210
Editing Files (F4), 211
Managing Your Disks and Directories, 214
The Norton Commander Directory (NCD)
Tree, 214
Making Directories (F7), 216
Deleting Directories (F8), 216
Running Applications from the Commander, 217
Creating a Menu for Running Your
Applications, 217
The Point-and-shoot Feature, 219
What You Have Learned, 220

10   *Communicating with the Commander, 221*

Using Commander Link, 221
Connecting the Two Computers, 222
Transferring Files, 224
Terminating the Link, 225
Using Commander Mail, 225
Basic Requirements, 225
Setting Up Commander Mail, 226
The Commander Mail Screen, 229

viii

Creating a Message, 231
Sending and Receiving Messages, 232
Checking Your In Box, 232
What You Have Learned, 233

11   *Using the Norton Backup, 235*

An Ounce of Prevention, 235
Getting Started, 236
Keyboard and Mouse Use, 237
Installing the Norton Backup, 237
Configuring the Norton Backup for Your
System, 239
Running the Norton Backup, 242
Getting Help When You Need It, 243
Exiting the Program, 245
The Basic Backup, 245
Selecting the Backup Drives, 247
Selecting the Backup Type, 248
Selecting Backup Options, 249
Selecting Files To Back Up, 251
Starting the Basic Backup, 254
Advanced Backup, 256
Advanced Backup Options, 257
Advanced File Selection, 259
The Basic Restore, 260
Selecting the Drives To Restore To
and From, 262
What Is a Catalog?, 262
Selecting Catalog Files, 263
Retrieving and Rebuilding a Catalog, 265
Selecting Restore Options, 266
Selecting Files To Restore, 267
Starting the Basic Restore, 269
The Start Verify Option, 270
Advanced Restore, 270
Advanced Restore Options, 271
Advanced File Selection, 273
Preparing Setup Files for PreSet Backup or
Restore, 273
Creating a Setup File, 273
Changing a Setup File, 274
Installing a Setup File for Others, 275
PreSet Level Backup and Restore, 275

The PreSet Backup, 276
The PreSet Restore, 277
Using Macros with the Norton Backup, 279
Recording a Macro, 279
Playing a Macro, 280
What You Have Learned, 281

Index, 283

Introduction

Who This Book Is For

Congratulations on your purchase of one of the fine software packages from Peter Norton Computing, Inc.! This book explains how to use the following Norton products:

The Norton Utilities Version 5.0

The Norton Commander Version 3.0, and

Norton Backup Version 1.1.

If you're just starting out with any of these popular products you'll appreciate the way topics are covered in *The First Book of The Norton Utilities*—this book takes you by the hand and leads you step-by-step through all the fundamental features of each software package. As a more knowledgeable user, you will appreciate the way important operations are summarized with Quick Steps in this book.

Conventions Used in This Book

As you read through *The First Book of The Norton Utilities* you'll notice certain conventions we've used to make the book easier for you to use. Any text that you should type in is shown in special computer type like this. Also, certain operations require depression of two keys simultaneously. For example, the expression Alt-C tells you to press the Alt and C keys simultaneously to perform a command.

 Quick Steps

1. Look for these lists of step-by-step instructions for frequently used procedures. The first column will tell you something to do.

   The second column will tell you the results of your actions.

Tip: Helpful tips, notes, and shortcuts are included in tip boxes throughout this book.

---

xii

Caution: Cautionary notes, also in boxes, warn of possible dangers.

Acknowledgments

I would like to thank Kraig Lane with Peter Norton Computing, Inc. for all his assistance throughout the development of *The First Book of The Norton Utilities*. Thanks also to Richard Swadley, Marie Butler-Knight, Joe Kraynak, and Herb Feltner for all their contributions to this book.

Trademarks

All terms mentioned in this book that are known to be trademarks or service marks are listed below. In addition, terms suspected of being trademarks or service marks have been appropriately capitalized. SAMS cannot attest to the accuracy of this information. Use of a term in this book should not be regarded as affecting the validity of any trademark or service mark.

Clipper is a registered trademark of Nantucket, Inc.

Commander Mail, Commander Link, and The Norton Editor are trademarks of Peter Norton Computing, Incorporated.

COMPAQ is a registered trademark of COMPAQ Computer Corporation.

CompuServe is a registered trademark of CompuServe Incorporated.

dBASE, dBASE II, dBASE III, dBASE IV, and MultiMate are registered trademarks of Ashton-Tate.

dBXL is a trademark of WordTech Systems, Inc.

DESQview is a trademark of Quarterdeck Office Systems.

FoxBASE is a registered trademark of Fox Software, Inc.

IBM is a registered trademark of International Business Machines Corporation.

Lotus, 1-2-3, and Symphony are registered trademarks of Lotus Development Corporation.

MCI logo and MCI Mail are registered service marks of MCI Communications Corporation.

Mosaic Twin is a registered trademark of Mosaic Software, Inc.

MS Word, MS-DOS, MS Works, MS Windows Write, and Excel are trademarks of Microsoft Corporation.

The Norton Backup is a registered trademark of Peter Norton Computing, Incorporated. The Norton Commander is a registered trademark of Peter Norton Computing, Incorporated.

The Norton Utilities, Norton Disk Doctor, WipeFile, WipeDisk, and UnErase are registered trademarks and Speed Disk, Disk Monitor, Calibrate, Diskreet, and WipeInfo are trademarks of Peter Norton Computing, Incorporated.

PC Paintbrush is a registered trademark of ZSoft Corporation.

Quattro and Paradox are registered trademarks of Borland International, Inc.

R:BASE is a registered trademark of Micorim, Inc.

Reflex is a registered trademark of Borland/Analytica, Inc.

Software Carousel is a registered trademark of SoftLogic Solutions.

VP-Planner Plus is a registered trademark of Paperback Software International.

xiii

WordPerfect is a registered trademark of WordPerfect Corporation.

WordStar Pro and WordStar 2000 are registered trademarks of WordStar International, Inc.

Words & Figures is a registered trademark of Lifetree Software, Inc.

XyWrite is a registered trademark of XYQUEST, Inc.

An Introduction to the Norton Utilities

In This Chapter

- ▶ *Unpacking and installing the utilities*
- ▶ *What the utilities are and what they do*
- ▶ *Utility integration*
- ▶ *How to get help*

This first chapter explains how the Norton Utilities can simplify your life as a PC user. We'll begin by looking at what's included in the Norton Utilities version 5.0 package and then we'll discuss the installation steps for both hard and floppy disk systems. We will briefly discuss each utility in general, then take a close look at the NORTON utility integration program.

Picking Up Where DOS Left Off

As a PC user you have encountered situations where DOS was not as friendly as you might expect. For example, what about the potentially dreadful DEL command? Have you ever accidentally deleted a very important file? As far as DOS is concerned, once you've deleted a file, it's gone for good—there is no DOS command to recover a deleted file. Fortunately, as an owner of the Norton Utilities, you now have access to tools for solving this and many other DOS-related shortcomings.

System Requirements

The Norton Utilities will run on any IBM PC or 100% compatible PC running DOS 2.0 or later (including DOS 4.xx with large hard disk partitions) with a minimum of 512K of available RAM. The Utilities support the popular display configurations including Hercules, CGA, EGA, and VGA. Although a hard disk is not required, one is recommended. (As you will see in the "Installing the Utilities" section, installation and execution to/from a floppy disk can be rather awkward.) In short, if your computer runs DOS, it will probably run the Norton Utilities! Now let's explore the contents of the Norton Utilities 5.0 package.

2

Unpacking the Utilities

You should find these items listed when you open your Norton Utilities 5.0 package:

> 6 5-1/4" floppy diskettes
> 3 3-1/2" floppy diskettes
> *The Norton Utilities Version 5.0 User's Guide*
> *The Norton Utilities Version 5.0 Disk Explorer*

Peter Norton Computing, Inc. is generous with floppy diskettes—not too many software packages include both 5-1/4" and 3-1/2" diskettes for your convenience. Since both the 5-1/4" and 3-1/2" sets contain the same files, you can choose to install with either set, depending on the kind(s) of floppy drive(s) your PC's configuration includes. If your system has both 5-1/4" and 3-1/2" drives, you might want to use the 3-1/2" set because less disk swapping will be required.

Installing the Utilities

Those of you with floppy disk-based PCs (no hard disk) will probably find the installation process more cumbersome than those with hard disk-based systems. Let's take a look at the hard disk installation first.

Hard Disk Installation

The Norton Utilities distribution diskettes are sequentially numbered for identification. For example, the 5-1/4" diskettes are identified as "Installation Disk 1," "Disk 2," "Disk 3," "Disk 4," and "Disk 5." Find the "Installation Disk" of either set (5-1/4" or 3-1/2," depending upon your floppy disk drive configuration), insert it in drive A:, type `A:INSTALL`, and press Enter. This command starts the Utilities' INSTALL program, shown in Figure 1.1.

3

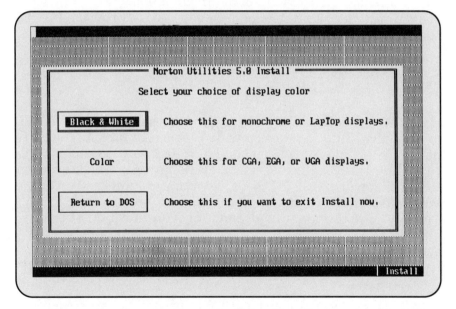

Figure 1.1   Use the Norton Utilities Install program to install the Norton Utilities on your computer.

Follow the directions displayed by INSTALL to swap disks, configure the Utilities for your system, etc. The INSTALL program is very easy to use, since it provides helpful explanations throughout the installation process. One of the benefits of INSTALL is that it gives you the option of replacing the DOS FORMAT program with Norton's Safe Format (SFORMAT) utility. I highly recommend that you let INSTALL make this replacement, because SFORMAT is an excellent utility and much more user-friendly than FORMAT. (See chapter 6 for a complete explanation of SFORMAT.) A typical installation using INSTALL takes about 10 minutes.

In earlier versions of the Norton Utilities (before version 5.0), you could use DOS' COPY command to place the Utilities on your hard disk rather than using INSTALL. Many of the utilities in version 5.0 are in a special compressed format on the distribution disks, so you *must* use INSTALL to decompress them onto your hard disk. The INSTALL program also performs several extra useful operations like creating a Norton Utilities directory, tailoring the Utilities for your system, etc.

After you've installed the Norton Utilities, be sure to read the READ.ME file in the utilities directory. The READ.ME file contains important information which doesn't appear in the Norton Utilities documentation. Use DOS' TYPE command to list the READ.ME file and pause for each screenful of information (i.e. `TYPE READ.ME | MORE`). If you have a printer connected to your PC, you can use the command `COPY READ.ME PRN:` to print a copy of READ.ME.

Floppy Disk Installation

If your PC has no hard disk, you might still be able to use INSTALL to place the Utilities on a floppy disk. You will probably want to install the Utilities on a bootable floppy disk so you don't have to swap disks to access them. (A bootable floppy disk contains special system files which your PC needs to start up, or "pull itself up by the bootstraps.") But how much space is available on a bootable floppy? The answer to this question depends on a few other questions:

1. What version of DOS is on the bootable floppy?
2. What size floppy disk are you using (i.e. 360KB, 720KB, 1.2MB, or 1.44MB)?
3. Besides DOS, how many other programs/utilities are already on the bootable floppy disk?

Use DOS' DIR command to determine how much space is available on your bootable floppy before trying to use INSTALL. (DIR displays the total number of bytes free at the bottom of a directory listing.) Run INSTALL as described above for hard disk installation (except the Utilities disks should be placed in drive B:

and you should type `B:INSTALL`). Select the `Partial Install` button when INSTALL displays the Installation Type screen shown in Figure 1.2; this will display the File Selection screen in Figure 1.3.

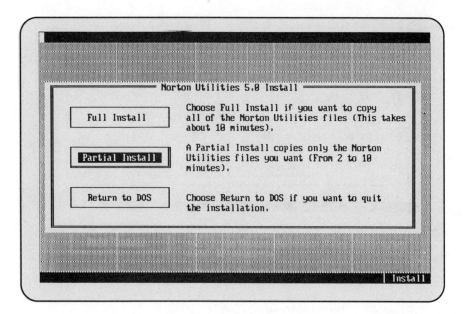

Figure 1.2 *Choose the type of installation you wish to do with the Installation Type screen.*

Use the space bar to select or deselect the utilities you wish to install, and note the total size of the selected files at the bottom of the screen, as shown in Figure 1.3. You can select and deselect different files to determine exactly which utilities will fit on your bootable disk. After you've selected all the utilities which will fit on your bootable disk, press Enter to continue the installation process.

If you can't fit all the utilities you need on one bootable disk, you can use the same steps outlined above to create another floppy disk containing the remaining utilities.

Summarizing the Utilities

Table 1.1 lists all the Norton Utilities and tells where to look in this book for a detailed explanation of each of them.

5

```
┌──────────────────── Norton Utilities 5.0 Install ────────────────────┐
             Select the files you would like to install

        [ ] Batch Enhancer          [ ] Norton Control Center
        [x] Calibrate               [ ] Norton Change Directory
        [x] Disk Editor             [ ] Norton Disk Doctor II
        [x] Disk Monitor            [x] Norton
        [x] Diskreet                [x] Shadow RAM loader
        [x] Disk Tools              [ ] Safe Format
        [x] File Find               [ ] Speed Disk
        [x] FileFix                 [ ] System Information
        [x] File Save               [x] UnErase
        [x] Image                   [x] UnFormat
        [x] Norton Cache Fast       [x] WipeInfo
        [x] Norton Cache Small      [x] Help Files

   Total Size of Selected Files:   1,986,000 bytes

          ┌─────────────────┐        ┌─────────────────┐
          │    Continue     │        │   Return to DOS │
          └─────────────────┘        └─────────────────┘

                                                        │ Install │
```

Figure 1.3   The Installation File Selection screen lets you choose which utilities to install.

6

Table 1.1   A Summary of the Norton Utilities

Program File Name	Utility Name	Covered in Chapter
BE	Batch Enhancer	4
CALIBRAT	Calibrate	7
DISKEDIT	Disk Editor	7
DISKMON	Disk Monitor	7
DISKREET	Diskreet	7
DISKTOOL	Disk Tools	7
FILEFIND	File Find	3, 5
FILEFIX	FileFix	3
FILESAVE	File Save	3
IMAGE	Image	6
NCACHE-F and NCACHE-S	Norton Cache Fast and Norton Cache Small	7
NCC	Norton Control Center	2
NCD	Norton Change Directory	2
NDD	Norton Disk Doctor II	6

Program File Name	Utility Name	Covered in Chapter
NORTON	Norton	1
SFORMAT	Safe Format	6
SPEEDISK	Speed Disk	7
SYSINFO	System Information	2
UNERASE	UnErase	3, 7
UNFORMAT	UnFormat	6
WIPEINFO	WipeInfo	3, 6

Now that you know what's provided with version 5.0 of the Norton Utilities, let's take a look at the features of each utility.

BE: Batch Enhancer

BE adds a great deal of flexibility to the already-powerful DOS batch file feature. If you are tired of dull and dreary batch files, you will enjoy using BE to enhance them with color, pop-up windows, sound, and more. Perhaps the most important benefit of BE, however, is that it lets you easily create interactive menu-driven batch files.

CALIBRAT: Calibrate

The CALIBRAT utility performs several tests on your PC's hard disk. This powerful utility also has the ability to rewrite the data on your hard disk to improve the disk's efficiency and performance.

DISKEDIT: Disk Editor

This utility allows you to locate, view, and edit virtually all areas of a disk. You can also use DISKEDIT to learn more about important DOS system files and the layout of DOS disks.

DISKMON: Disk Monitor

The DISKMON utility lets you monitor all disk activity on your system, and can prevent computer "viruses" from destroying the contents of your hard disk.

7

DISKREET: Diskreet

Use the DISKREET utility to prevent others from viewing the contents of your personal/private files. DISKREET encodes files with password protection so only you can decode and understand them.

DISKTOOL: Disk Tools

Norton's DISKTOOL utility is actually several tools in one! DISKTOOL lets you perform several disk-related functions including making a disk bootable, reviving a defective diskette, saving/restoring important system configuration information, and more.

FILEFIND: File Find

As its name implies, the FILEFIND utility helps you find files which may be located anywhere on your disk; but that's only part of FILEFIND's functionality. DOS maintains a set of file attributes and a time and date stamp for every file on a disk. In addition to other useful operations, FILEFIND can easily modify a file's attributes and time/date stamp.

FILEFIX: File Fix

FILEFIX is an intelligent file repair tool that can fix damaged Lotus 1-2-3, Symphony, or dBASE data files. FILEFIX builds a new copy of the damaged file containing as much recoverable data as possible.

FILESAVE: File Save

This utility is a powerful tool that can prevent deleted file data from being overwritten so that files can be recovered long after they are deleted.

IMAGE: Image

Use IMAGE to prepare for an inadvertent file erasure or disk format. IMAGE writes important disk information to a special file which is used by Norton's file recovery utilities (UNERASE and UNFORMAT).

NCACHE-F and NCACHE-S: Norton Cache

The Norton Cache utility expedites disk operations by maintaining frequently-accessed disk data in a fast memory buffer. The cache utility is easily tailored for any PC configuration. NCACHE-S is a "small" cache which doesn't require much memory to use. NCACHE-S is not as fast, however, as NCACHE-F (for "fast" cache). Use NCACHE-S if your PC doesn't have enough memory to use NCACHE-F.

NCC: Norton Control Center

NCC provides a centralized function for setting and adjusting everything from DOS' display colors to your keyboard's repeat rate. This utility also allows you to configure up to four serial ports, set your PC's time/date, and more.

9

NCD: Norton Change Directory

This utility is Norton's answer to DOS' cryptic CHDIR command which changes the active directory. It is easy to forget where a subdirectory is located, especially when you have subdirectories off of subdirectories (for example, C:\UTILITY\SHELLS\NU). NCD offers a graphical representation, or tree structure, of your disk's directory layout as well as a speed search option to quickly locate a specific entry.

NDD: Norton Disk Doctor II

The NDD utility can diagnose and even correct many common disk problems. NDD is the first utility you should consult when you encounter problems with unreadable and damaged files.

NORTON: Norton Integration

Later in this chapter, you will see how the NORTON utility provides a menu from which all the other Norton utilities may be executed. NORTON doesn't just provide access to the other utilities though—it also provides detailed help including syntax for each utility and help with common DOS errors.

SFORMAT: Safe Format

SFORMAT is a powerful utility that provides a safe and fast means to format hard and floppy disks. As noted in the previous installation section, you can (and should) let the INSTALL program replace DOS' FORMAT with Norton's SFORMAT. SFORMAT offers an easy-to-use menu feature for selecting different format modes.

SPEEDISK: Speed Disk

Disks develop inefficient unused areas, or become "fragmented," as a result of writing, changing, and deleting files. Fragmented hard disks are a common cause of poor PC performance. Use SPEEDISK to unfragment and optimize your hard disk with one of several different optimization methods.

10

SYSINFO: System Information

The System Information utility is perhaps best known for calculating common benchmarks for PC performance comparison. This utility also provides PC configuration details, including microprocessor, memory, video, and disk drive information.

UNERASE: UnErase

This cornerstone of the Norton Utilities allows you to quickly and easily recover accidentally-deleted files. The sooner you run UNERASE after deleting a file, the better your chances are of complete data recovery.

UNFORMAT: UnFormat

UNFORMAT is a lifesaver for the "Oops, I just formatted the wrong disk!" syndrome. UNFORMAT recovers as many files as possible from an accidentally-formatted disk. Be sure to use the IMAGE utility (discussed earlier) regularly to assist UNFORMAT in its recovery process.

WIPEINFO: WipeInfo

With all of Norton's wonderful data recovery utilities (for example, UNFORMAT and UNERASE), you may be wondering how to actually remove data from a disk. Norton's WIPEINFO utility overwrites all data in a file or disk so that it cannot be recovered—this is an important utility to use when working with confidential files. Use WIPEINFO with extreme caution, because even the most powerful Norton utilities cannot recover data from a disk after WIPEINFO is run.

Utility Integration

Now that you've been briefly introduced to each of the Norton Utilities, let's take a closer look at NORTON, the utility integration tool which provides a friendly interface to all of the other utilities.

11

 Running the NORTON Utility Integration Tool

1. Type the command NORTON.
2. Press Enter.   This starts the
                               NORTON utility
                               (Figure 1.4)   □

> **Tip:** If the message "Bad command or file name" is displayed after typing NORTON and pressing Enter, you may have incorrectly installed the Utilities. The INSTALL program can (and should) be used to place the Utilities' directory in your AUTOEXEC.BAT file's PATH statement (for example, PATH=C:\NORTON5). This permits you to run any of the utilities from any directory/subdirectory. However, you must reboot your PC after installation for this change to the AUTOEXEC.BAT file to take effect.

The screen in Figure 1.4 is divided into three sections. The left side of Figure 1.4 shows a list of several of the Norton Utilities split into categories like Recovery and Speed. Press the down-arrow key to highlight the Disk Doctor II entry. The right side of the screen now provides a description of Norton's Disk Doctor (NDD) utility, includ-

```
┌─────────────────────────────────────────────────────────────┐
│  Configure   Advise   Quit!                         F1=Help   │
│ ╔═══════════════ The Norton Utilities 5.0 ═══════════════════╗│
│ ║  ┌──── Commands ────┐   ┌──────── Description ────────────┐║│
│ ║  │                  │   │                                 │║│
│ ║  │ ── RECOVERY ──   │   │ Norton Disk Doctor II           │║│
│ ║  │ Disk Doctor II   │   │ NDD [d:][d:]... [SWITCHES]       │║│
│ ║  │ Disk Editor      │   │                                 │║│
│ ║  │ Disk Tools       │   │ Automatically detects and corrects│║│
│ ║  │ File Fix         │   │ physical and logical disk errors.│║│
│ ║  │ File Save        │   │                                 │║│
│ ║  │ Image            │   │ SWITCHES                         │║│
│ ║  │ UnErase          │   │ /QUICK    Just test System Area  │║│
│ ║  │ UnFormat         │   │ /COMPLETE Test System and Data Areas│║│
│ ║  │                  │   │ /R:file   Write a report to 'file'│║│
│ ║  │ ── SPEED ──      │   │ /RA:file  Append a report to 'file'│║│
│ ║  │ Calibrate        │   │ /X:d      Exclude drive from testing│║│
│ ║  │ Norton Cache     │   │ /FORMAT   Format physically bad track│║│
│ ║  │ Speed Disk       │   │                                 │║│
│ ║  └──────────────────┘   └─────────────────────────────────┘║│
│ ║  ┌────┐                                                     ║│
│ ║  │NDD │                                                     ║│
│ ║  └────┘                                                     ║│
│ ╚═════════════════════════════════════════════════════════════╝│
│  Press Enter to run a command, or F10 to activate menu │ Norton Utilities │
└─────────────────────────────────────────────────────────────┘
```

Figure 1.4   NORTON provides easy access to many utilities.

ing syntax and usage. The bottom line of Figure 1.4 contains the letters NDD and a blinking cursor. Press the down arrow key a few times and notice three things:

1. The next utility name down the list on the left side of the screen is highlighted each time the down arrow key is pressed,
2. a description of the newly-highlighted utility on the left side of the screen is shown on the right side of the screen, and
3. the bottom line of the screen changes to show the program name of the highlighted utility.

For example, the screen in Figure 1.5 shows what is displayed when I highlight System Info (Note: The list of utilities on the left side of the screen in Figure 1.4 scrolls up/down when you reach the bottom/top of the exposed portion of the list. The SYSINFO utility appears at the very end of the unexposed portion of the utilities list.).

You can run any of the other utilities within NORTON by selecting them, entering any necessary parameters, then pressing Enter. Select SYSINFO (as shown in Figure 1.5) and press Enter to run SYSINFO and display the System Summary screen in Figure 1.6.

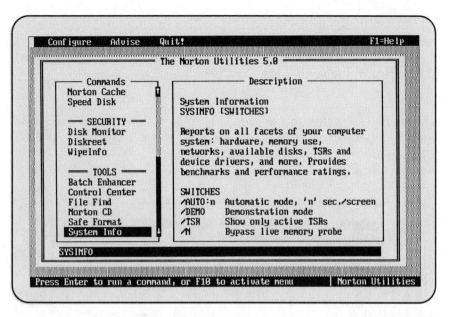

Figure 1.5   SYSINFO can be selected from the NORTON screen.

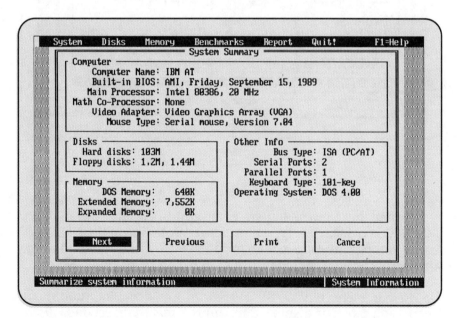

*Figure 1.6   The System Summary screen is the first
SYSINFO screen displayed.*

We will examine SYSINFO specifics in chapter 2, so for now, press Esc twice to return to the screen in Figure 1.5. We did not specify any parameters when we ran SYSINFO above. As you can see in Figure 1.5, the syntax for SYSINFO is:

```
SYSINFO [switches]
```

where the "switches" are either /AUTO:n, /DEMO, /TSR, or /N as described below in the same panel. Now let's run SYSINFO with a /DEMO parameter by selecting SYSINFO (Figure 1.5) and typing /DEMO as shown in Figure 1.7.

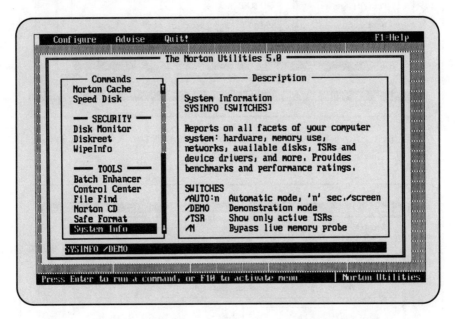

Figure 1.7   NORTON provides a command line to enter parameters.

Notice that the /DEMO parameter appears at the bottom of the SYSINFO screen as you type it in. The bottom line of the NORTON screen is a pseudo-DOS command line—it will display and allow you to edit the highlighted utility's name and parameters. Now you can press Enter to run SYSINFO with the /DEMO parameter. The /DEMO parameter tells SYSINFO to run in a demonstration mode where each screen is displayed for approximately 10 seconds. Press Esc to return to the NORTON utility.

14

Using Menus

Most of the Norton utilities include pull-down menus which offer access to additional utility features and settings. Press the Alt key when the NORTON screen in Figure 1.4 is displayed to pull down the NORTON Configure menu (Figure 1.8). (NOTE: If your PC is configured with a mouse, you can pull down a menu by positioning the mouse cursor over the menu name (for example, `Configure`) and pressing the mouse button.)

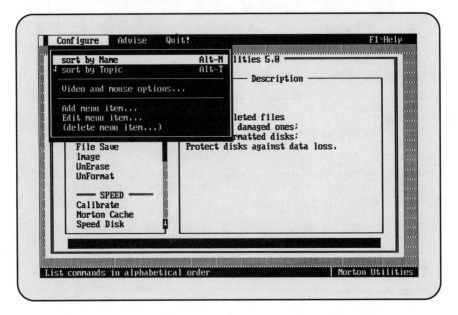

Figure 1.8   The Configure menu is one of 3 pull-down menus available to customize the program.

At the NORTON Configure menu, press the down-arrow key twice to highlight the `Video and mouse options...` selection and press Enter to get Figure 1.9.

The dialog box shown in Figure 1.9 lets you set up the Norton Utilities for your PC's video and mouse configuration. Use the arrow keys to move the blinking cursor from one selection to another, and press the space bar to activate a selection. Finally, press Enter to save your configuration settings for the Norton Utilities.

<figure>
```
  Configure   Advise   Quit!                              F1=Help

                     The Norton Utilities 5.0
                     Video and Mouse Options

       Screen Colors              Graphics Options
       ( ) Laptop                 (•) Standard
       (•) Black and white        ( ) Graphical controls
       ( ) Monochrome             ( ) Graphical controls
       ( ) Color                      and mouse pointer
       ( ) Alternate color            (requires EGA/VGA)


       Screen Options             Mouse Options
       [x] Zooming boxes          [ ] Left-handed mouse
       [ ] Solid background       [x] Fast mouse reset


                  Save            Cancel


  Customize program settings                      Norton Utilities
```
</figure>

*Figure 1.9   Use the Video and Mouse Options dialog box
to set mouse and display options.*

The NORTON utility also includes an Advise menu which offers easy-to-read suggestions for solving common disk problems and other DOS-related errors.

Utility Help

The Norton Utilities offer two different types of on-screen help: help within a utility and utility syntax help.

Help Within a Utility

The help screen in Figure 1.10 is displayed if you press F1 while the NORTON screen is displayed (Figure 1.4).

The screen in Figure 1.10 describes many of the NORTON features we already discussed. Use the up- or down-arrow keys to scroll through the help screen and learn more specifics about the NORTON utility. Most of the Norton utilities display a help screen when the F1 key is pressed. These help screens provide information

Figure 1.10   NORTON's Help screens provide general information about the program, as well as specific help for each utility.

about how to use the utility, special keys, and other important points. If you require help within a utility and you don't feel like reaching for the documentation, press F1 and you might find what you need!

Utility Syntax Help

It's convenient to have help within a utility via the F1 key. But what if you can't remember a utility's syntax and you don't want to hunt through the documentation? The answer is simple: type in the utility name with a question mark parameter and press Enter. For example, if you want to see SYSINFO's syntax, type SYSINFO ? and press Enter (Figure 1.11).

The help information in Figure 1.11 might look familiar to you. This same information was displayed in the NORTON utility for SYSINFO (see Figure 1.5). The ? help feature is handy when you want to quickly see a utility's syntax without running NORTON or thumbing through documentation.

```
C:\NORTON5>sysinfo ?
System Information, Norton Utilities 5.0, Copyright 1990 by Peter Norton

     SYSINFO [switches]

Switches
     /AUTO:n    Automatically cycle through all information screens
     /DEMO      Cycle through benchmark tests only
     /TSR       Print list of TSR programs to standard output
     /N         Suppress Memory Scan
     /SOUND     Beep between CPU tests
     /SUMMARY   Print SysInfo Summary screen

C:\NORTON5>
```

Figure 1.11   When you type ? after a command, NORTON shows you the proper syntax for the command.

What You Have Learned

In this chapter you learned some Norton Utilities fundamentals. You also learned:

▶ If your computer runs DOS, it will also run the Norton Utilities.

▶ It is fairly easy to install the Norton Utilities to either a floppy or hard disk-based PC—Norton's INSTALL program is very user-friendly.

▶ The NORTON utility is a handy tool which provides information about (and easy access to) all the other utilities.

▶ The Norton Utilities offer two different types of on-screen help: help within a utility (using F1) and utility syntax help (using the ? parameter).

DOS and Utility Basics

In This Chapter

- ▶ *Understanding DOS and PC hardware*
- ▶ *Obtaining configuration data with SYSINFO*
- ▶ *Configuring PC attributes with NCC*

This chapter explains some DOS and PC hardware fundamentals. You will need to understand these concepts before you can appreciate all the information the Norton Utilities can provide.

This chapter will also introduce you to two special utilities, SYSINFO and NCC, which provide operations which are either difficult or impossible to perform via DOS. Most of the Norton Utilities can be classified as either file utilities or disk utilities, but these two do not fall into either of these categories.

What Is DOS?

Your PC's hardware does not directly understand the commands you type at your keyboard. When you enter the command `DIR C:*.*`, the command must be translated by an interface so your PC's hardware can understand it. The primary interface between you and your hardware is the Disk Operating System, or DOS, for short.

Regardless of whether your PC is floppy or hard disk-based, it relies on DOS to perform fundamental operations. DOS is simply a collection of special tools which allow you to copy, delete, and rename files, format disks, view directories, etc. But although DOS provides a multitude of useful commands, many of them are cryptic and cumbersome to use; that is one of the reasons the Norton Utilities are so popular.

There have been several different versions of DOS distributed since the original DOS for the IBM PC. To see which version of DOS your PC is running, type the VER command at the DOS prompt and press Enter. VER is another of DOS' many built-in tools. When I run DOS' VER command, it indicates my PC is running MS-DOS Version 3.30. The "MS" in MS-DOS stands for Microsoft, the company which developed and distributes the DOS package I use.

A more recent version of DOS, 4.x, allows very large hard disk partitions. (Hard disk partitions are discussed later in this chapter in the DOS Disks section.) DOS 4.x also offers a built-in DOS "shell," which substitutes a graphic command interface for the traditional DOS command line (for example, c\>). Chapters 8, 9, and 10 of this book cover a very popular DOS shell, the Norton Commander. I feel that the Commander is a much more powerful shell than the one available with DOS 4.x, and I think you will agree after reading these chapters and testing the Commander's abilities.

DOS relies on many different components of your PC to do its job. Let's take a look at what I feel is the most important of these components, the microprocessor.

Microprocessors

The microprocessor is the "brains" of your PC and is often referred to as a Central Processing Unit, or CPU, because it controls virtually all processing within the computer.

Like DOS, there have been several different models of micro-processors used in PCs since the IBM PC was introduced. The original IBM PC featured the Intel 8088, an 8-bit microprocessor. The 8088 did a pretty good job of managing most processing needs but it soon became apparent that additional horsepower would be required to handle more sophisticated software. The next generation of PCs, the IBM PC-XTs and compatibles, also used the Intel 8088 microprocessor and featured hard disks.

As software packages became more elegant and complex, the 8088 had to give way to the faster, more powerful 80286 microprocessor. The 80286 is the microprocessor found in IBM PC ATs and compatibles. Besides offering faster throughput than 8088s, the 80286 family of microprocessors was the first to allow multitasking on PCs. Multitasking means the computer can run two or more programs, or tasks, concurrently. This multitasking feature allows products like Microsoft Windows and Quarterdeck's DESQview to run more than one application at a time.

But even the fastest 80286s are not quick enough to handle the more processor-intensive programs like graphics design and 3-D modeling applications. These power-hungry programs require the 80386, a 32-bit microprocessor. The 80386 can process larger pieces of data than any of its predecessors, and offers more sophisticated multitasking capabilities than the 80286.

> ▶ **Note:** A microprocessor's speed is expressed in megahertz, or MHz, for short. The original IBM PC's microprocessor ran at 4.77 MHz. Today you can purchase an 80386-based PC running at 16, 20, 25, or even 33 MHz.

The 80386's cousin, the 80386SX, is sort of a cross between the 80286 and 80386 CPUs. The 80386SX has many of the same features as the 80386; the primary difference between the two is in the size of data they can exchange with external devices. If you think of this data exchange as a highway, you could say the 80386 offers a 4-lane expressway and the 80386SX is restricted to a 2-lane country road, like the 80286. In more technical terms, the 80386 uses a 32-bit data bus whereas the 80386SX and 80286 microprocessors use a 16-bit data bus.

It seems that every day brings a newer, faster microprocessor. Several PC manufacturers are now distributing 80486-based systems, which blow the socks off the fastest 80386 PCs.

What about the older 80286/8088 computers? Are they obsolete and totally useless in today's computer marketplace? Absolutely not! The vast majority of PC users do not need the horsepower of an 80486, or even an 80386. Further, new applications are being written every day which run on all types of IBM compatible PCs, regardless of the CPU.

With this microprocessor knowledge under your belt, let's now take a look at the types of memory your PC uses to store and manipulate data.

PC Memory

The smallest piece of data a computer can store is called a **bi**nary digit, or bit. A binary digit is either a one or a zero—no other values are allowed. A bit is very similar to a light switch, which also has two possible states: on or off. When a bit holds a value of one, we can say that the bit is **on**. Alternatively, a bit which is **off** holds a value of zero.

The amount of memory in your PC is expressed in bytes; one byte is made up of 8 bits. Large amounts of memory are expressed in kilobytes (or K, for short). One K of memory equals 1,024 bytes. For example, if your PC has 640K of memory, it can store up to 640 x 1,024 (655,360) bytes.

There are actually two different types of memory in your PC: RAM and ROM.

RAM vs. ROM

RAM is short for Random Access Memory, which means your PC can access different RAM locations without having to traverse every location in between. Actually, your PC can access both RAM and ROM in a random manner so this is not what differentiates the two.

ROM is an acronym for Read Only Memory. Your PC can read from ROM memory but it cannot write to ROM. The primary difference between RAM and ROM is that data can be read from and/ or written to RAM; the information held in ROM is fixed and cannot be overwritten. In addition, RAM is sometimes referred to as volatile memory. That is, the information stored in RAM is lost when you turn your PC off. In contrast, the contents of ROM are not lost or changed when you turn off your computer. Most ROM chips contain important programs which control fundamental device operations on your PC (for example, disk drive reads/writes).

When someone says a PC has 640K of memory, they are usually referring to the amount of RAM. Your PC uses RAM to hold your applications programs and their data while the programs are active. Although microprocessors can address 1 or more megabytes (one megabyte (Mb) equals 1,048,576 bytes) of memory, MS-DOS only provides access to a total of 640K of RAM. That is why it is so common to find PCs with a total of 640K of RAM.

If DOS can only access 640K, why do so many PCs come with 1 or more megabytes of RAM? This additional memory is generally referred to as either expanded or extended memory. There are several different applications available today which allow you to take advantage of this additional memory. For instance, Quarterdeck's DESQview program allows you to run several applications simultaneously (multitasking) using expanded or extended memory.

TSRs

TSR is an abbreviation for Terminate-and-Stay-Resident. Once a TSR program has been loaded, it becomes almost invisible until you press a special key to use it. This special key or key combination is also called a *hot key*.

TSRs are executed from the DOS command line like any other program. Once a TSR is loaded, it requires a portion of DOS' 640K of accessible RAM to remain resident. Although each TSR may only take up a few K of RAM, when several TSRs are loaded the 640K pool may be significantly reduced. That is when you will start running into problems executing non-TSR programs which require almost all of DOS' 640K of memory.

23

Fortunately, there are several commercially-available utilities which allow you to place your TSRs in expanded or extended memory rather than DOS' 640K of RAM. Some TSRs offer this option as a standard feature so you do not need to purchase a special utility to free up DOS' RAM space.

Now let's take a look at another PC storage medium, disks.

PC Disks

There are several brands and models of disk drives on the market. Table 2.1 shows storage information about the 4 most popular floppy disk types.

> ⊘ **Caution:** You can utilize the full capacity of both double- and high-density diskettes in a high-density disk drive, but when working with different density diskettes *do not format double-density diskettes in a high-density drive.* This could cause corrupted or unreadable data on your diskettes.

Table 2.1   Floppy Disk Specifications

Disk Size	Type	Storage Capacity
5-1/4"	Double-sided Double-density	360K bytes
5-1/4"	Double-sided High-density	1.2 megabytes
3-1/5"	Double-sided Double-density	720K bytes
3-1/5"	Double-sided High-density	1.4 megabytes

In the early days of PCs, data storage was limited to slow, low-density floppy disks. The door was opened for hard disk-based PCs when DOS 2.0 and the IBM PC-XT architecture were introduced. The original PC hard disks stored from 5 to 30 megabytes of data. Today's hard disks are much faster than those earlier models and offer up to several hundred megabytes of storage in one unit.

If you are using DOS 2.x or 3.x, you are limited to a maximum hard disk partition size of 32 megabytes. When you partition a hard disk via DOS' FDISK command, you are telling DOS how to configure the disk as one or more logical drives. Although you only have one physical hard disk in your PC, you can have DOS treat it as several logical disks (for example, C, D, and E). For example, if you have a 100 megabyte hard disk, you could use FDISK to partition it as follows:

Logical Drive	Size (in megabytes)
C:	32
D:	32
E:	32
F:	4

Version 4.0 of DOS allows unlimited logical disk partition sizes. With DOS 4.0, the 100 megabyte disk above can be set up via FDISK as one 100 megabyte partition.

More to Come . . .

Disks and disk formats are fairly complex subjects, and we have only scratched the surface so far. More advanced disk concepts, as well as the disk-based Norton Utilities, are covered in Chapters 5, 6, and 7.

SYSINFO: System Information

We briefly discussed SYSINFO in Chapter 1, and you saw how it can be invoked from the NORTON utility. Now let's use our newfound DOS and hardware knowledge to see exactly what SYSINFO reports. SYSINFO may also be invoked directly from the DOS prompt as shown in the following Quick Steps.

Q Using SYSINFO to Obtain System Information

1. At the DOS prompt, type the command **SYSINFO** and press Enter.

   The System Summary screen is displayed (Figure 2.1).

2. Press Enter.

   The Video Summary screen is displayed.

3. Press Enter.

   The Hardware Interrupts screen is displayed.

4. Keep pressing Enter to browse through the rest of SYSINFO's screens. When you want to leave SYSINFO, press Esc twice or select the Quit menu.

25

SYSINFO provides five types of information: System, Disks, Memory, Benchmarks, and Report. If you keep pressing Enter to view the next screen, all the System menu screens are displayed first, followed by all the Disks menu screens, etc. These five also correspond to pull-down menus at the top of each screen. If you don't want to display all the SYSINFO screens, you can quickly jump from one SYSINFO screen to any other one by using the pull-down menus.

The System Menu

The System menu consists of six selections: System Summary, Video Summary, Hardware Interrupts, Software Interrupts, Network Information, and CMOS Status.

Figure 2.1   The System Summary screen contains general system information.

System Summary

The System Summary screen (Figure 2.1) provides details about your computer system, including disk/memory size and other interesting facts. The screen is split into four areas: Computer, Disks, Memory, and Other Info. Most of the information displayed is self-explanatory, but I would like to make note of a couple of important items.

The second line in the Computer section, "Built-in BIOS:", indicates the date of my PC's Basic Input/Output System (BIOS) ROM. The BIOS provides an interface to your PC's hardware for input/output activities. The BIOS date could be important if you are having problems running certain programs on your PC—check with your PC dealer to determine if your BIOS is out-of-date and needs upgraded.

The System Summary screen is also an excellent reference for quickly determining a PC's configuration. For example, in Figure 2.1 you can see that my PC is an 80286-based model with a 42 megabyte hard disk and a 1.2 megabyte floppy disk drive. Further, I have a monochrome monitor, a mouse, and a 101-key keyboard.

Video Summary

The Video Summary screen (Figure 2.2) shows information about your PC's video configuration. This information includes details about your PC's display adapter, character specifics, and video memory.

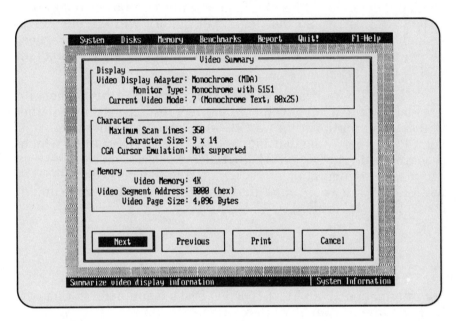

Figure 2.2   The Video Summary screen reports your PC's video configuration.

Hardware Interrupts and Software Interrupts

The next two SYSINFO screens provide information about hardware and software interrupts. An interrupt causes the microprocessor to stop what it is currently doing and perform some special task. The interrupt information provided on these screens is useful for programmers writing sophisticated applications.

Network Information

The Network Information screen is accessible only if your PC is connected to a Novell network. This screen reports miscellaneous network and network user details.

27

CMOS Status

The last SYSINFO screen in the System category, the CMOS Values screen, provides specifics about your PC's memory and hard/floppy disk drives.

CMOS is an abbreviation for Complementary Metal-Oxide Semiconductor. CMOS RAM chips require less power than non-CMOS RAM chips, so that the small battery within your PC is enough to preserve their contents even after the computer is turned off. Your PC's hardware configuration information is stored in CMOS memory.

The CMOS Values screen shows the contents of this memory in a readable form. If any invalid or incorrect results are shown in the CMOS Status portion of the CMOS Value screen, you should consult your PC owner's manual and or run the SETUP utility which accompanied your PC. (NOTE: SETUP is not a Norton Utility—it is a hardware configuration utility which should have been delivered with your PC. If you cannot find your SETUP utility, you should contact your PC dealer.)

The Disks Menu

For information about The SYSINFO Disks menu, refer to Chapter 6—Maintaining Your Hard Disk Drive.

The Memory Menu

The Memory menu contains four selections: Memory Usage Summary, TSR Programs, Memory Block List, and Device Drivers.

Memory Usage Summary

The screen in Figure 2.3 is displayed when the Memory Usage Summary option is selected from the Memory menu.

The Memory Summary screen in Figure 2.3 displays information about the various types of memory in your PC. This memory information is reported in three categories: DOS Usage, Overall, and BIOS Extensions.

The **DOS Usage** section in Figure 2.3 shows the amount of memory used by and accessible to DOS. The total amount of memory reported by DOS is then split into two areas: memory used by DOS

```
 System  Disks  Memory  Benchmarks  Report  Quit!      F1=Help
                        Memory Summary
 ┌ DOS Usage ───────────────────────────────────────────────┐
 │  DOS reports 639 K-bytes of memory:                       │
 │     284 K-bytes used by DOS and resident programs         │
 │     355 K-bytes available for application programs        │
 │                                                           │
 │ ┌ Overall ─────────────────────────────────────────────┐ │
 │  A search for active memory finds:                        │
 │     640 K-bytes main memory     (at hex 00000-0A000)      │
 │      64 K-bytes display memory   (at hex 0B000-0C000)     │
 │     384 K-bytes extended memory  (at hex 10000-16000)     │
 │       0 K-bytes expanded memory                           │
 │                                                           │
 │ ┌ BIOS Extensions ─────────────────────────────────────┐ │
 │  ROM-BIOS Extensions are found at hex paragraphs:         │
 │  F000                                                     │
 └───────────────────────────────────────────────────────────┘

   ┌────────┐   ┌──────────┐   ┌───────┐   ┌────────┐
   │  Next  │   │ Previous │   │ Print │   │ Cancel │
   └────────┘   └──────────┘   └───────┘   └────────┘

 Summarize system memory usage              │ System Information
```

*Figure 2.3   The Memory Summary screen shows how your
PC's memory is being utilized.*

29

and resident programs (for example, TSRs), and memory available
for application programs.

In the **Overall** section of Figure 2.3, SYSINFO reports the total
size and location of four memory areas: main memory, display
memory, extended memory, and expanded memory.

The **main memory** total is generally equal to the amount of DOS
memory reported above. (One exception to this rule is if you are
using an application switcher like SoftLogic Solutions' Software Carousel which lets you keep several applications loaded
in memory simultaneously.)

The amount of **display memory** reported by SI depends on
what type of video adapter (CGA, EGA, VGA, etc.) you are
using.

The amount of **expanded/extended memory** should reflect the
total expanded or extended memory installed on your PC.

The **BIOS Extensions** section in Figure 2.3 indicates the memory
locations of any ROM BIOS extensions (for example, special add-on
boards).

TSR Programs

The TSR Programs screen shown in Figure 2.4 lists information about any active TSR applications.

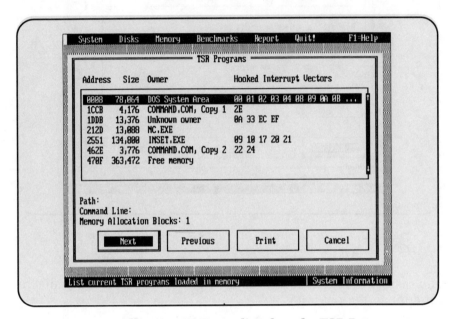

Figure 2.4   All active TSRs are listed on the TSR Programs Screen.

You can use the up- and down-arrow keys to scroll through the TSR list and obtain additional information about each application. This additional information includes the TSR's directory path (for example, c:\MYTSRS), the command line used to invoke it (for example, ATSR.EXE), and how much memory it occupies.

Memory Block List

The DOS Memory Blocks screen is displayed when the Memory Block List option is selected from the Memory menu. This screen displays information about DOS memory allocation, including the memory size, owner, and type (data, environment, or program).

Device Drivers

Device drivers are applications which allow DOS to recognize and interface with special hardware devices, such as a mouse. The

Device Drivers screen lists memory locations, names, and descriptions for all device drivers currently loaded in your PC.

The Benchmarks Menu

Norton's System Information (SI) utility, SYSINFO's predecessor, was perhaps best known for its benchmark (i.e. PC performance comparison) reporting.

SYSINFO continues in the tradition of SI by providing very interesting benchmark data. If you are an old SI user, you will probably be surprised at the results that SYSINFO reports— SYSINFO's benchmark numbers are significantly *lower* than those previously reported by SI. SI tended to overstate benchmark results, and the SYSINFO comparisons are more realistic. The Benchmark menu offers four comparison selections: CPU speed, Hard disk speed, Overall performance index, and Network performance speed.

CPU Speed

The CPU Speed screen (Figure 2.5) shows the CPU benchmark results of the PC being tested, along with the results of three other computers: a Compaq 386/33MHz, an IBM AT 286/8MHz, and an IBM XT 88/4.77MHz.

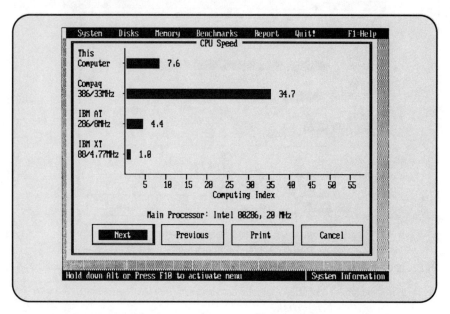

Figure 2.5   Microprocessor benchmark results are reported on the CPU Speed screen.

The CPU Speed information shown in Figure 2.5 is fairly easy to interpret. The IBM XT 88/4.77MHz computer listed is an IBM PC XT with an 8088 microprocessor running at 4.77 MHz. SYSINFO's benchmark calculations show a comparison of the PC being tested to the IBM PC XT. Figure 2.5 reports a 1.0 CPU rating for the IBM XT 88/4.77MHz computer and a 4.4 rating for the IBM AT 286/8MHz computer. So according to SYSINFO, the IBM AT's (286/8MHz) microprocessor is 4.4 times as fast as the IBM XT's (88/4.77 MHz) microprocessor. Further, the Compaq's (386/33MHz) microprocessor is 34.7 times as fast as the IBM XT's (88/4.77 MHz) microprocessor.

The CPU rating for "This Computer" shown at the top of Figure 2.5 is for my PC. As you can see, the SYSINFO CPU speed rating for my PC is 7.6, which places it in between the performance of an IBM AT 286/8MHz and a Compaq 386/33MHz. The bottom of Figure 2.5 also shows that my PC has an Intel 80286 microprocessor running at 20 MHz.

32   Disk Speed

The SYSINFO Disk Speed screen shown in Figure 2.6 compares the performance of my PC's hard disk with a Compaq 386 disk, an IBM AT disk, and an IBM XT disk.

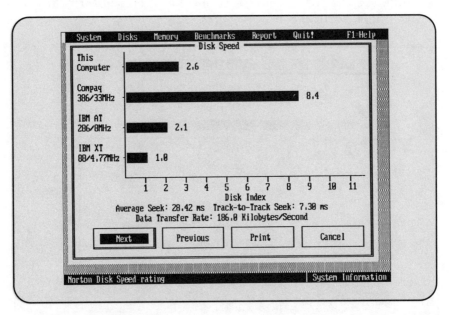

Figure 2.6   The Disk Speed screen shows the benchmark results for you PC's hard disk.

The speed rating for the IBM XT's disk in Figure 2.6 is 1.0. Since the IBM AT's disk speed rating is 2.1, we can say that the AT's disk is 2.1 times as fast as the XT's disk. Further, the Compaq's disk is 8.4 times as fast as the XT's disk. SYSINFO reports my PC's disk speed to be 2.6, which ranks it slightly faster than an IBM AT's disk. The Disk Speed screen in Figure 2.6 also reports other technical disk statistics, including average seek time, track-to-track seek time, and data transfer rate.

Overall Performance Index

The performance values reported in the CPU Speed and Disk Speed screens (Figures 2.5 and 2.6) are averaged and presented in the Overall Performance Index screen (Figure 2.7).

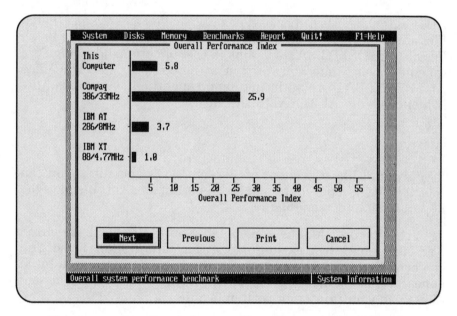

Figure 2.7   Results of the overall performance benchmark are reported on the Overall Performance Index Screen.

Once again, your PC's performance is compared against the performance of a Compaq 386, an IBM AT, and an IBM XT.

Network Performance Speed

The Network Performance Speed screen is the last screen displayed in the SYSINFO Benchmarks area. This screen reports network read/write throughput values if your PC is connected to a Novell network.

The Report Menu

The Report menu allows you to view a couple of special files and print a SYSINFO report.

View CONFIG.SYS

CONFIG.SYS is an important file, containing configuration information for special devices or device drivers used with your PC (for example, an extended memory driver or a mouse driver). The View CONFIG.SYS option in the Report menu lets you look at the contents of your CONFIG.SYS file.

View AUTOEXEC.BAT

AUTOEXEC.BAT is a special type of file called a *batch file*. (Batch files are thoroughly discussed in Chapter 4—Enhancing Your Batch Files.) AUTOEXEC.BAT contains the set of commands which are executed every time you turn on or reboot your PC. The View AUTOEXEC.BAT option in the Report menu lets you look at the contents of your AUTOEXEC.BAT file.

Print Report

If you would like a printout of all SYSINFO's statistics, you can select the Print report option in the Report menu. This displays the Report Options screen (Figure 2.8).

The Report Options screen lets you construct customized SYSINFO reports by choosing among each of the options listed. You can even specify a report header and/or special notes you want to appear at the bottom of the report. The SYSINFO report can be sent directly to your printer, or written to a file.

NCC: Norton Control Center

The other utility we will discuss in this chapter allows you to control and configure several attributes of your PC. The Norton Control Center (NCC) provides an easy interface for configuring display, keyboard, mouse, serial port, and other functions.

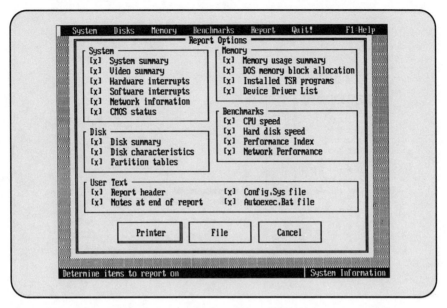

Figure 2.8   You can customize your SYSINFO report with Report Options Screen.

35

Q Running Norton Control Center (NCC)

1. At the DOS prompt, type the command N C C.

2. Press Enter.   The Norton Control Center screen is displayed (Figure 2.9).

As you can see in Figure 2.9, the Norton Control Center provides access to 10 different items: Cursor Size, DOS Colors, Palette Colors, Video Mode, Keyboard Speed, Mouse Speed, Serial Ports, Watches, Country Info, and Time and Date.

Cursor Size

Through the NCC interface (Figure 2.9) you can modify your cursor's appearance. You configure your cursor size by specifying two values: where the cursor starts and where it ends. The range of possible start/end values depends on your video adapter (CGA, EGA, etc.). The values on my Hercules monochrome system range from 0 to 13.

Figure 2.9 *Norton Control Center (NCC) screen provides access to 10 customizable items.*

Q Setting the Cursor Size

1. Press Tab.

   This deactivates the left panel (Select Item) of Figure 2.9 and makes the right panel (Cursor Size) active.

2. Press the up- or down-arrow key to move the cursor to the desired Start position, and press Tab.

   This sets the starting position of the cursor.

3. Press the up- or down-arrow key to move the cursor to the desired End position, and press Enter.

   This sets the cursor size and reactivates the Select Item panel (Figure 2.9).

DOS Colors

NCC's DOS Colors option allows you to set the text color, background attributes, and border color for DOS screens.

Setting the DOS Colors

1. Press the down-arrow key to highlight the DOS Colors selection and press Enter. Or, press the D key.

    This selects the DOS Colors option and displays the screen in Figure 2.10.

2. Press the up- or down-arrow key to select the desired text color.

3. Press the space bar to toggle between the available text options of Blinking, Bright, or Normal.

3. When you are satisfied with your selection, press Tab to move to the background attributes selection.

4. Press the space bar to toggle between the available background options of Blinking, Bright, or Normal.

5. When you are satisfied with your background selection, press Tab to move to the Border Color selection.

6. Press the up- or down-arrow keys to select the desired border color, and press Enter.

    This ends the DOS Color selection process reactivates the Select Item panel in Figure 2.9.   □

37

Palette Colors

If your PC is equipped with either an EGA or VGA monitor, you can use the Palette Colors selection to specify the 16 colors available for display use.

 Setting the Palette Colors

1. Press the down-arrow key to highlight the Palette Colors selection and press Enter. Or, press the P key.

    This selects the Palette Colors option and displays screen in Figure 2.11.

2. Press the up- or down-arrow key to select the desired palette color.

This scrolls through the 16 available palette colors.

3. Press Tab and select the Change box at the bottom of the screen and press Enter (Figure 2.11).

The Change Color Dialog box is diaplayed.

4. Press the up- or down-arrow keys to select the desired color, and press Enter.

This selects the new palette color and returns you to the Palette Color selection panel. Select OK to reactivate the left panel in Figure 2.9.   □

38

Figure 2.10   You can change your DOS color settings with the DOS Colors Selection screen.

Video Mode

The Video Mode feature allows you to select which video mode to use if your monitor supports more than one mode. As you experiment with different display modes, you will find that the compressed characters used in a compact mode (for example, 50 line EGA display) are sometimes difficult to read—most people stay with the default 25 line mode.

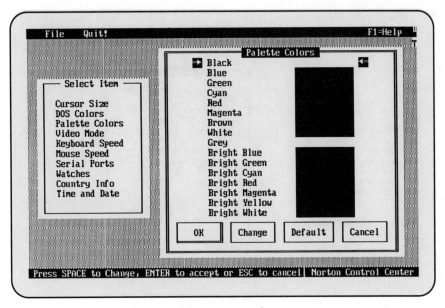

Figure 2.11   The Palette Colors Selection screen lets you customize your colors.

Setting the Video Mode

1. Press the down-arrow key to highlight the Video Mode selection and press Enter. Or, press the V key.

   This selects the Video Mode option and displays the screen in Figure 2.12.

2. Press the up- or down-arrow key to highlight the desired Display Lines value. Press Tab.

3. Press Tab to move to the Display Mode selection.

4. Press the up- or down-arrow key to toggle between the Black and White and Color mode options. Press the space bar to select the desired mode.

5. Press Enter.

   This ends the Video Mode selection process and reactivates the Select Item panel in Figure 2.9.

*Figure 2.12   You can set up your monitor to operate in any of
its available modes using the Video Mode Selection screen.*

Keyboard Speed

If your PC's microprocessor is an 80286, 80386, or 80486, you can
use the Keyboard Speed utility to alter two keyboard characteristics:
keyboard repeat rate and the *delay before auto repeat*. The keyboard
repeat rate is the number of times a depressed key will repeat per
second. The delay before auto repeat is the amount of time to wait
after a key is pressed and held down before it will automatically
repeat.

Setting the Keyboard Speed

1. Press the down-arrow key to
highlight the Keyboard Speed
selection and press Enter. Or,
press the K key.

   This selects the Keyboard
Speed option and displays
the screen in Figure 2.13.

2. Press the left-arrow key
(slower rate) or right- arrow
key (faster rate) to move the
keyboard repeat rate indicator
to the desired setting.

40

3. Press Tab.

The cursor moves to the auto repeat selection area of the screen.

4. Press the left-arrow key (longer delay) or right-arrow key (shorter delay) to move the delay before auto repeat indicator to the desired setting.

5. Press Enter when you are satisfied with the keyboard rate settings.

This ends the Keyboard Rate selection process and reactivates the Select Item panel in Figure 2.9. □

Figure 2.13   Use the Keyboard Speed screen to change your keyboard's speed and repeat rate.

Mouse Speed

If your PC is configured with a mouse, you can use NCC to set the mouse's sensitivity value. A high sensitivity value causes slight mouse movement to result in broad cursor movement. On the other hand, a low sensitivity value causes substantial mouse movement to result in slight cursor movement.

Setting the Mouse Speed

1. Press the down-arrow key to highlight the `Mouse Speed` selection and press Enter. Or, press the M key.

   This selects the Mouse Speed option and displays the screen in Figure 2.14.

2. Press the left-arrow key (lower sensitivity) or right arrow key (higher sensitivity) to move the Mouse Sensitivity indicator to the desired setting.

3. Press Enter.

   This ends the Mouse Rate selection process and reactivates the left panel in Figure 2.9. □

Figure 2.14   Change the sensitivity of mouse movement with the Mouse Speed screen.

Serial Ports

A port is an outlet on your PC which provides a plug-in interface for various peripheral devices (such as a mouse, modem, printer, etc.). Your PC probably has several different ports, including serial and parallel ports. Typical serial devices include a mouse, modem, or serial printer—a parallel printer is generally the only device you would ever see connected to a parallel port.

NCC allows you to specify communications protocol for each of your PC's serial ports. This communications protocol includes: baud rate, parity, number of data bits, and number of stop bits.

Q Configuring Serial Ports

1. Press the down arrow key to highlight the Serial Ports selection and press Enter. Or, press the S key.

   This selects the Serial Ports option and displays the screen in Figure 2.15.

2. Press the up- or down-arrow key to select a communications port (COM1, COM2, etc.) to configure.

3. Press Tab to move to the Baud selection area.

4. Press the up- or down-arrow key to move to a different baud rate. Then press the space bar to select that baud rate.

5. Press Tab to move to the Stop Bits selection area.

6. Press the up- or down-arrow key to move to a different stop bits value. Then press the space bar to select that value.

7. Press Tab to move to the Parity selection area.

8. Press the up- or down-arrow key to move to a different parity value. Then press the space bar to select that value.

9. Press Tab to move to the Data Bits selection area.

10. Press the up- or down-arrow key to move to a different data bits value. Then press the space bar to select that value.

43

11. Press Enter.

This ends the Serial Ports selection process and reactivates the Select Item panel in Figure 2.9. □

44

Figure 2.15 *The Serial Ports screen displays and lets you modify the current serial port configuration.*

Watches

As you probably know, your PC has an internal clock which keeps track of the current time and date. The DOS TIME and DATE commands allow you to display and/or set the clock's time and date. The Norton Utilities take timekeeping one step further. The NCC utility offers four independent stopwatches for tracking elapsed times. These stopwatches allow you to easily determine how long it took a program to run, a batch file to execute, etc.

Using the Stopwatches

1. Press the down-arrow key to highlight the Watches selection and press Enter. Or, press the W key.

This selects the Watches option and displays the screen in Figure 2.16.

2. Press the up- or down-arrow key to highlight the desired watch. Then press the space bar to select it.

3. Press Tab.
         This moves the cursor to the bottom of the Watches screen.

4. Press the left- or right-arrow key to select the Start, Reset, or Pause box at the bottom of the Watches screen (NOTE: The Start box is replaced by the Pause box if an active watch is selected).

5. Press Enter to execute your selection, and then press Escape.
         This starts, pauses, or resets the selected watch and reactivates the left panel in Figure 2.9. ☐

45

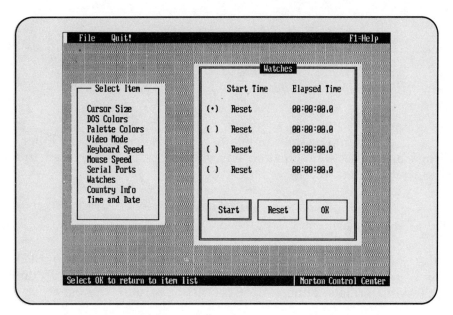

Figure 2.16 The Watches screen provides access to four separate stopwatches.

The Norton stopwatches also offer another, more useful method of tracking time. You can run NCC with a command line parameter to start or stop a specific watch without having to go through all the

NCC menus and screens. When you type the command NCC /START:1 and press Enter, NCC resets and starts stopwatch #1 and displays the information shown in Figure 2.17.

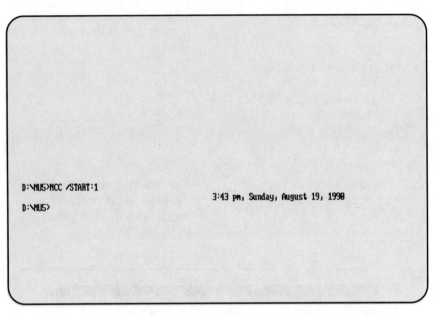

D:\NU5>NCC /START:1

3:43 pm, Sunday, August 19, 1990

D:\NU5>

Figure 2.17   You can also start, stop, or pause a stopwatch from the command line.

If you then type the command NCC /STOP:1 and press Enter, you can see how much time has elapsed since you started the stopwatch (Figure 2.18).

Country Info

The Country Info selection in NCC allows you to configure your PC for use in foreign countries. With Country Info you can set up the following formats: Time, Date, Currency, List, and Numbers.

> **Note:** Before you can use this feature, you must run the utility NLSFUNC from the DOS command line. Refer to *The Waite Group's MS-DOS Bible, 3rd Ed.* for a detailed explanation of the NLSFUNC command.

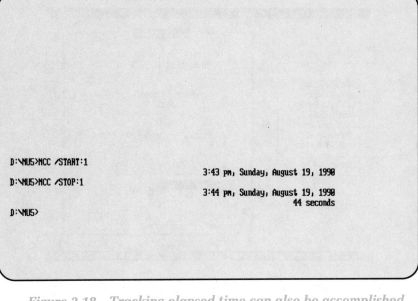

D:\NU5>NCC /START:1

3:43 pm, Sunday, August 19, 1990

D:\NU5>NCC /STOP:1

3:44 pm, Sunday, August 19, 1990
44 seconds

D:\NU5>

Figure 2.18   Tracking elapsed time can also be accomplished from the command line.

47

Q Setting Country Formats

1. Press the down-arrow key to highlight the Country Info selection and press Enter. Or, press the I key.

   This selects the Country Info option and displays the screen in Figure 2.19.

2. Press the up- or down-arrow key to select the desired country, and press Enter.

   This sets the country formats, ends the Country Info selection process, and reactivates the left panel in Figure 2.9.   □

Time and Date

The NCC Time and Date selection offers a visually-pleasing alternative to DOS' TIME and DATE functions.

**Figure 2.19   Reconfigure a PC for a different country
using the Country Info screen.**

48

Setting the System Time and Date

1. Press the down-arrow key to highlight the Time and Date selection and press Enter. Or, press the T key.

   This selects the Time and Date option and displays the screen in Figure 2.20.

2. Enter the current month, day, and year in numeric format (for example, 03 13 90 for March 13, 1990).

   If you want to set the system time only, skip this step and press Enter.

3. Enter the current hour, minutes, and second (for example, 08 23 59).

   If you do not want to set the system time, press Enter and skip step #4.

4. Enter either A or P (for A.M. or P.M.) and press Enter.

   This ends the Time and Date selection process and reactivates the left panel in Figure 2.9.

```
┌─────────────────────────────────────────────────────────┐
│  File   Quit!                                    F1=Help  │
│                                                           │
│                          ┌──── Time and Date ────┐        │
│      ┌─ Select Item ─┐   │      ┌─ Date ─┐        │        │
│      │               │   │      │ 3-19-90│        │        │
│      │ Cursor Size   │   │      └────────┘        │        │
│      │ DOS Colors    │   │                        │        │
│      │ Palette Colors│   │      ┌─ Time ─┐         │        │
│      │ Video Mode    │   │      │3:54:13 pm│       │        │
│      │ Keyboard Speed│   │      └────────┘        │        │
│      │ Mouse Speed   │   │                        │        │
│      │ Serial Ports  │   │  Use + and - to change │        │
│      │ Watches       │   │  highlighted field     │        │
│      │ Country Info  │   │                        │        │
│      │ Time and Date │   │  ┌─ OK ─┐  ┌─ Cancel ─┐│        │
│      └───────────────┘   │  └──────┘  └──────────┘│        │
│                          └────────────────────────┘        │
│                                                           │
│  Select OK to accept, or CANCEL to discard │ Norton Control Center │
└─────────────────────────────────────────────────────────┘
```

Figure 2.20   Use NCC's Time and Date screen to set your system's time and date.

49

What You Have Learned

In this chapter you learned about DOS and a few of the important hardware components within your PC. You also learned:

▶ The System Information (SYSINFO) utility provides information about DOS, hardware configuration, memory layout, and benchmark results.

▶ SYSINFO's benchmark calculations show a comparison of your PC to an IBM PC-XT.

▶ The Norton Control Center (NCC) provides an easy interface for configuring display, keyboard, mouse, serial port, and other functions.

Using Norton File Utilities

In This Chapter

▶ *Using FILEFIND to simplify file operations*
▶ *Quickly recovering an erased file*
▶ *Preserving deleted files*
▶ *Repairing special files*
▶ *Removing files from a disk*

This chapter explains many of the Norton Utilities features which compensate for DOS' file-handling shortcomings. One of these utilities, FILEFIND, is quite useful for many of your everyday PC tasks. If you are concerned with file security on your PC, you will definitely want to examine the WIPEINFO utility, which goes beyond the DEL command for file erasure.

Lotus 1-2-3, Symphony, and dBASE users will be pleased to know that version 5.0 of the Norton Utilities offers a FILEFIX utility which is intelligent enough to know how to repair damaged data files for these popular business applications.

But for most PC users, no one Norton utility may be as important as UNERASE, which can resurrect previously-deleted files. When teamed up with the FILESAVE utility, UNERASE provides the capability to recover files long after they have been deleted.

File Attributes and FILEFIND

DOS maintains special status information for each file on a disk. This information indicates the state of several important file attributes, including read-only, archive, system, and hidden (see Table 3.1). DOS' ATTRIB command allows you to change a file's read-only and archive attributes, but it does not provide access to the system and hidden attributes. Norton's FILEFIND lets you display, set, or clear any of the four file attributes, including those inaccessible to ATTRIB.

Table 3.1   File Attribute Definitions

Attribute	Meaning
Archive	Indicates whether file has been backed up
Hidden	Indicates whether file is visible via DIR command
Read-only	Indicates whether file can be modified
System	Indicates operating system (DOS) file

Displaying File Attributes Using FILEFIND

1. At the DOS prompt, type FILEFIND and press Enter.

   This starts the FILEFIND utility and displays the FileFind screen in Figure 3.1.

2. Type a file specification in the File Name: field (for example, c:*.*) and press Enter.

   This tells FILEFIND to start looking for all files in C:\. When the desired files are found, a search completion message appears.

3. Press Enter to acknowledge the search completion message.

   This displays the list of files which match the search criteria (Figure 3.2).   ☐

The FILEFIND listing in Figure 3.2 shows all files in the root directory of drive C. The contents of this box can be scrolled by using either the up/down arrow keys or the mouse scroll bar along the right side of the box.

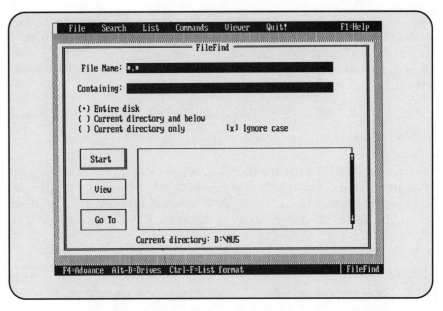

Figure 3.1   *The FileFind screen provides access to several file-handling tools.*

Figure 3.2   *FILEFIND displays a list of files matching the search criteria.*

A file attribute is either on or off. FILEFIND displays a one-character identifier for each attribute which is on. These identifiers appear on the right side of each file line entry. For example, the IMAGE.IDX file has all four attributes turned on: archive (A), read-only (R), system (S), and hidden (H).

Setting and Clearing File Attributes

You can use the Commands menu to set or clear any of the four file attributes. For example, let's clear the archive attribute for all files in C:'s root directory. The Change Attributes dialog box is displayed when you select the Set Attributes option in the Commands menu (Figure 3.3).

Figure 3.3   The Change Attributes dialog box lets you assign 1 or more of the 4 file attributes to any file.

Press the space bar so the "for entire file list" option is selected in the Set Attributes portion of the Change Attributes dialog box. Then press Tab twice, then the space bar, to place an "x" in the Clear column next to the Archive attribute (Figure 3.4).

Press Enter to initiate the file attribute change. When FILEFIND is finished changing the attributes, the summary screen in Figure 3.5 is displayed.

Figure 3.4   You can clear an attribute from a file by placing an "x" in the Clear column.

Figure 3.5   FILEFIND displays a summary of the changes made.

The summary information in Figure 3.5 shows how many files were affected and which attributes were set or cleared.

Modifying File Attributes from the Command Line

FILEFIND also lets you set file attributes directly from the DOS command line if you desire. This technique is a time-saver and lets you avoid all the menu and dialog box selections discussed above. Table 3.2 shows the four file attributes and their corresponding FILEFIND command line identifiers.

Table 3.2   FILEFIND Identifiers

File Attribute	Identifier
Archive	/A
Hidden	/HID
Read-only	/R
System	/SYS

Use a plus sign (+) after the file attribute identifier to turn on an attribute. For example, the command `FILEFIND TEST.TXT /HID+` turns on the hidden attribute for the file TEST.TXT. Place a minus sign (-) after a file attribute identifier to turn off an attribute. For example, `FILEFIND TEST.TXT /R-` turns off TEST.TXT's read-only attribute.

Combinations of identifiers can be used to set or clear several attributes with one command. For example, the command `FILEFIND TEST.TXT /A+/HID+/R-` turns on the archive and hidden attributes and turns off the read-only attribute.

If you run FILEFIND with command line parameters as shown above, you will notice that the summary screen in Figure 3.5 is always displayed when FILEFIND is finished. Use the /BATCH option if you want FILEFIND to skip the summary screen and automatically return to the DOS prompt (for example, `FILEFIND TEXT.TXT /R-/BATCH`).

Clearing all Attributes

Although the command `FILEFIND *.* /A-/HID-/R-/SYS-` clears attributes for all files in the current directory, FILEFIND offers the /CLEAR option as a shortcut alternative. Therefore, `FILEFIND *.* /CLEAR` is equivalent to `FILEFIND *.* /A-/HID-/R-/SYS-` but is much easier to type.

> ▶ **Tip:** DOS' DEL command cannot find hidden/system files and will not delete read-only files. I use FILEFIND with the /CLEAR option to turn off the hidden and read-only attributes so I can delete an entire directory with DEL. FILEFIND can be used with Norton's WIPEINFO utility (discussed later in this chapter) to remove files in directories/subdirectories quickly and easily.

Filtering File Selections

In the previous examples, you have seen how to use the * wildcard character to select specific files for FILEFIND. DOS' ? wildcard character may be used for more restrictive file selections as well. But what if you want to hide *all* archived files in a directory? No combination of * and ? will accomplish this. In this situation, you need to use file attribute identifiers as file filters.

57

The command `FILEFIND C:\*.* /HID` lists all hidden files in C:'s root directory. The /HID identifier in this command acts as an additional file filter for the C:*.* specification. We can use this feature to set or clear file attributes based on the values of other file attributes. For example, here is the command to hide all archived files in the root directory: `FILEFIND C:\*.* /A/HID+`. Since the file selection (C:*.*) is modified by the archive filter (/A), this command turns on the hidden attribute for archive files only.

Measuring File Size and Disk Space for Backup

Backing up data files onto floppy disks is an important routine which should be performed regularly, but which is often skipped for one reason or another. It's not necessary to use a sophisticated utility like Norton Backup to maintain backup copies of your data files; DOS' BACKUP utility works well for this purpose. In addition, many backup operations can be accomplished with DOS' COPY and XCOPY commands. However, Norton does offer some utilities which make the job easier.

The available data storage space on your target disk is an important consideration. Before starting a backup, you must determine whether or not your floppy disk has enough space available to hold the files you wish to copy. Since the DIR command shows file sizes and available disk space, you could use it to decide whether a group of files will fit on a floppy disk, but this solution is not very user-friendly since it requires you to add up the individual file sizes and compare the total to the available space on the floppy. Fortunately, the Norton Utilities offer a more elegant alternative.

Determining File Size and Disk Space with FILEFIND

The FILEFIND utility can be used to report the size of one or more files, and determine whether the files will fit on another disk (i.e. the target floppy disk).

58

Q **Determining Available Disk Space for File Copy**

1. At the DOS prompt, type FILEFIND and press Enter.

This starts the FILEFIND utility and displays the screen in Figure 3.1.

2. Type a file specification in the File Name: field (for example, c:*.*) and press Enter.

This tells FILEFIND to start looking for all files in C:\. When the desired files are found, a search completion message appears.

3. Press Enter to acknowledge the search completion message.

The list of files which match the search criteria (C:*.*) is displayed (Figure 3.2).

4. Press Alt-C, then the down-arrow key twice, then Enter, to select the Target Fit option from the Commands menu.

This displays the Target Fit dialog box shown in Figure 3.6.

5. Press the up- or down-arrow key to select the target drive (for example, A:) and press Enter.

FILEFIND reports whether or not the selected files will fit on the target disk (Figure 3.7). □

The information shown in Figure 3.7 can be split into two areas: summary file information and target disk information.

Figure 3.6   Select the target copy drive with the Target Fit dialog box.

Figure 3.7   The target fit report indicates whether the selected files will fit on the target disk.

Summary File Information

The Summary File Information portion of FILEFIND's Target Fit Report includes a total of the individual file sizes and the total disk space they occupy.

At first, you may wonder why these two figures would differ. After all, if the size of a group of files is X bytes why wouldn't they also occupy X bytes on the disk? To understand the answer to this question, you must first understand how DOS stores files on a disk. Disk storage specifics are discussed in Chapter 6—Maintaining Your Hard Disk Drive, but a brief introduction to one of these concepts— clusters—is provided here to help you understand the information reported by FILEFIND.

DOS' DIR command and Norton's FILEFIND show file sizes in bytes. For example, DIR reports that my AUTOEXEC.BAT file is 832 bytes in size. In order to quickly and easily address an entire disk's data area, DOS works with larger, more manageable chunks of data called *clusters*. A cluster is the smallest block of space DOS will reserve for a file on a disk. The number of bytes in a cluster depends on the size and format of the disk in question. Table 3.3 shows cluster sizes for four most common floppy drive formats.

Table 3.3   Floppy Disk Cluster Sizes

Disk Size	Disk Format	Bytes per Cluster
5-1/4"	360K bytes	1,024
5-1/4"	1.2M bytes	512
3-1/2"	720K bytes	512
3-1/2"	1.4M bytes	512

The number of bytes per cluster for a hard disk depends on the version of DOS in use. I use DOS 3.3, and each cluster on my hard disk consists of 2,048 bytes.

Because it requires only 832 bytes of storage space, my AUTOEXEC.BAT file occupies one cluster on my hard disk. Even though AUTOEXEC.BAT uses only 832 of the 2,048 bytes in that cluster, the remaining 1,216 bytes are not available for another file's use. This unused area in a cluster is referred to as *slack*. The following formula may be used to determine the percent of slack space for one or more files:

$$\% \text{ Slack} = \frac{(\# \text{ Cluster Bytes}) - (\# \text{ Data Bytes})}{(\# \text{ Cluster Bytes})}$$

where *# Cluster Bytes* is the number of bytes allocated for the file(s) and *# Data Bytes* is the number of bytes actually used by the file(s). Using this formula, we can plug in the values for the AUTOEXEC.BAT file on my hard disk:

$$\frac{(1 \text{ Cluster} * 2,048 \text{ Bytes/Cluster}) - (832 \text{ Bytes})}{(1 \text{ Cluster} * 2,048 \text{ Bytes/Cluster})}$$

which simplifies to:

$$\frac{1,216 \text{ Bytes}}{2,048 \text{ Bytes}}$$

or 59% slack.

61

Target Disk Information

The target disk information reported by FILEFIND shows:

1. how much disk space is required for the specified files,
2. how much space is available on the target disk, and
3. whether or not enough disk space is available on the target disk for the specified files.

FILEFIND checks the slack characteristics of both the source and target disks. The disk space requirements in this portion of FILEFIND's report therefore indicate the total number of bytes, including slack, required on the target disk.

Determining Target Fit from the Command Line

If you want to bypass the menus and dialog boxes of FILEFIND, you can specify command line parameters to determine if a set of files will fit on a target disk. For example, the command `FILEFIND C:\*.*` `/TARGET:A` tells FILEFIND to determine if the files in the root directory of C: will fit on the disk in drive A:. When FILEFIND completes this task, the Target Fit Report in Figure 3.7 is displayed.

Date/Time Stamps

The date and time stamps shown in a DIR or FILEFIND listing typically indicate when a file was created or last modified. DOS does not offer a command to easily modify a file's date/time stamp, but fortunately, the Norton Utilities do.

> ▶ **Note:** DOS' COPY command does not change a file's date/time stamp. For example, the command COPY TEST.TXT TESTBACK.TXT creates a new file TESTBACK.TXT with the same date/time stamp as TEST.TXT.

Using FILEFIND to Set Date/Time Stamps

62

The versatile FILEFIND utility provides an easy way to set a file's date/time stamp. Shown in the following Quick Steps is an example of date/time setting using FILEFIND.

Q Setting a File's Date/Time Stamp

1. At the DOS prompt, type FILEFIND and press Enter.

   This starts the FILEFIND utility and displays the screen in Figure 3.1.

2. Type a file specification in the File Name: field (for example, C:\AUTOEXEC.BAT) and press Enter.

   FILEFIND locates the specified file and displays a search completion message.

3. Press Enter to acknowledge the search completion message.

   FILEFIND then displays the list of files which match the search criteria.

4. Press Alt-C, the down-arrow key, and then Enter, to select the Set Date/Time option from the Commands menu.

   The Set Date/Time dialog box shown in Figure 3.8 is displayed.

5. Press Tab, then the space bar.

   This moves the cursor to the "Set the time to:" field and places an x next to it.

6. Press Tab, then enter the current time (for example, 2:00 PM).

   This moves the cursor to the Set the date to:" field and places an x next to it.

7. Press Tab, then the space bar.

8. Press Tab, then enter the current date (for example, 3-30-90) and press Enter.

FILEFIND changes the date/time stamp for the AUTOEXEC.BAT file to the values you specified. ☐

Figure 3.8   Specify the file's new date and time using the Set Date/Time dialog box.

63

Setting Date/Time Stamps from the Command Line

The /D and /T options may be used with FILEFIND to set file date/time stamps from the command line. For example, the command

```
FILEFIND C:\AUTOEXEC.BAT /D03-30-90 /T14:20:00
```

sets the date/time stamp for the AUTOEXEC.BAT file to 3-30-90 2:00 PM.

The preceding example showed you how FILEFIND can set both the date and time, but you can also use this utility to set just one of those values (for example, `FILEFIND C:\AUTOEXEC.BAT /D03-30-90` or `FILEFIND C:\AUTOEXEC.BAT /T14:20:00`). In addition, you can use the DOS wildcard characters in FILEFIND's file specification (for example, `FILEFIND C:\*.* /T14:20:00`).

When setting date/time stamps with FILEFIND from the command line, the date and time formats are mm-dd-yy and hh:mm:ss respectively. The time value is expressed in 24-hour clock format, so 15:20:00 is 3:20 PM. And you can omit leading zeroes, so /D3-3-90 is the same as /D03-03-90.

Using the Default Date and Time

One of the most useful applications for FILEFIND is to have it set a file's date/time stamp to the current date/time. This is accomplished via the /NOW option (for example, FILEFIND C:*.* /NOW). Use DOS' DATE and TIME commands to make sure your PC's internal date and time are correct before using this option.

Clearing the Date and Time

64

In the PC world, the origin of time is 12:00 AM on January 1, 1980 —at least that's as far back as DOS' DATE and TIME commands will let you go. You can use FILEFIND to reset file date/time stamps to 12:00 AM on January 1, 1980 by specifying /D and /T with no date and time values. For example, the command FILEFIND C:*.* /D /T sets the date and time values for all files in C:'s root directory to 12:00 AM, January 1, 1980.

Quickly Recovering an Erased File

So far, you have learned about several of the file-based tools available in the Norton Utilities. These tools allow you to change file attributes, determine whether a set of files will fit on another disk, and more. But for my money, no one file-based utility is as important as Norton's UNERASE.

> ⊘ **Caution:** If you want to recover deleted files from your hard disk and you haven't installed the Norton Utilities **do not** install the utilities now! The Norton installation program copies all the utilities to your hard disk and may overwrite the deleted files you wish to recover. Instead, insert the Norton Utilities Disk 1 into your A: (or B:) drive and substitute A:UNERASE (or B:UNERASE) for UNERASE in the Quick Steps which follow.

The UNERASE utility gives you the ability to easily recover previously-deleted files from your hard or floppy disks.

> ▶ **Note:** When DOS deletes a file, it still remembers all but the first character of the deleted file's name. Unerase displays a question mark (?) as the first character of a deleted file's name. As part of the UNERASE procedure, you must provide unerase with the real first character of the deleted file's name.

Q Recovering Deleted Files

1. At the DOS prompt, type CD and the name of the directory where the deleted file resided (for example, CD C:\WORK) and press Enter.

2. Type UNERASE and press Enter.

   This starts the UNERASE utility and displays the screen in Figure 3.9.

3. Press the up- or down-arrow key to highlight the file you wish to recover (for example, ?axmemo.txt).

4. Press U, and then press Enter.

   This displays the first character dialog box shown in Figure 3.10.

5. Type the first character of the deleted file's name (for example, T).

   This recovers the deleted file.

   □

UNERASE: The Inside Story

One of the DOS DEL command's nicest features is that it does not destroy a file's contents; rather, DEL tells DOS to make the specified file's disk space available for other storage. For example, let's say my file C:\WORK\TAXMEMO.TXT is 950 bytes large and therefore occupies only one cluster on my hard disk (remember, each cluster on my hard disk consists of 2,048 bytes). For additional clarity, let's say that cluster #20 is where C:\WORK\TAXMEMO.TXT resides.

Figure 3.9 *UNERASE lists all erased files in the current directory.*

Figure 3.10 *Specify the first character of the deleted file's name in the first character dialog box.*

The command `DEL C:\WORK\TAXMEMO.TXT` does not affect cluster #20. All the data in C:\WORK\TAXMEMO.TXT still resides on my disk, at cluster #20, even after I use DEL to remove the file. The only thing DEL does is inform DOS that the cluster(s) occupied by the deleted file(s) are now available for use by other files. Although the contents of C:\WORK\TAXMEMO.TXT still exists on my disk, it is now unprotected by DOS and could be overwritten the next time something is copied to the disk.

The UNERASE utility is fairly effective at recovering deleted files because it knows how to analyze unused clusters. Keep in mind that every time you COPY a file, save a file from a word processor, etc. you run the risk of overwriting the unprotected data of a deleted file. Therefore, the chances of recovering an accidentally-deleted file are best if you run UNERASE immediately after the deletion.

What To Do If UNERASE Fails . . .

67

The Prognosis column in Figure 3.9 indicates whether or not UNERASE thinks it can recover the specified files. A "good" prognosis means that UNERASE can probably resurrect the file with no manual intervention. However, a file with a "poor" prognosis may be more difficult to recover. Regardless of the prognosis listed, you should first try the Quick Steps for "Recovering Deleted Files" to recover the deleted file. The message shown in Figure 3.11 is displayed if UNERASE cannot recover the specified file.

There are many reasons why UNERASE may be unable to automatically recover certain files, and most of them can be circumvented manually. So if you encounter a problem automatically recovering a file with UNERASE, don't give up hope! UNERASE offers a manual recovery feature which you may be able to use to reconstruct the deleted file. This advanced feature is covered in Chapter 7—Advanced Disk Management.

> ▶ **Note:** Another important utility, IMAGE, is covered in Chapter 6—Maintaining Your Hard Disk Drive. Regular use of IMAGE can increase UNERASE's ability to recover accidentally-deleted files. Be sure to read about IMAGE in Chapter 6 to see how it can guard against accidental data loss.

Now let's discuss the FILESAVE utility, which can be instrumental in allowing an automatic UNERASE of older deleted files.

```
  File    Search   Options   Quit!                          F1=Help

                    ─── Erased files in C:\DOS ───

         Name          Size     Date     Time    Prognosis

      ?BIII
      ?BRUSH                ─── UnErase ───
      ?D          Unable to automatically recover ?ormat.com
      ?KPLUS         because its data space is being used
      ?NSET                    by another file
      ?ormat
      ?OUSE1       You may attempt to recover the deleted
      ?P            data with a Search or Manual UnErase
      ?P50
      ?PSOUR                                                 age
      ?TIL                    ┌────────┐
      ?U                      │   OK   │
                             └────────┘


            ┌──────┐      ┌──────┐      ┌────────┐
            │ Info │      │ View │      │ UnErase│
            └──────┘      └──────┘      └────────┘

  Select files to UnErase                           │ UnErase
```

Figure 3.11   Sometimes UNERASE may not be able to recover a file.

Preserving Deleted Files with FILESAVE

Although Norton's UNERASE utility can often recover recently-deleted files, it is not always 100% successful. By itself, UNERASE can fully recover only those deleted files which have not been overwritten by other files. Since you never know when a COPY command is going to overwrite a deleted file, you might consider using the FILESAVE utility to extend the life of deleted files. FILESAVE is a TSR utility which can prevent deleted file data from being overwritten so that files may be recovered long after they are deleted.

Using FILESAVE to Protect Deleted File Data

1. At the DOS prompt, type
   FILESAVE and press Enter.

   This starts the FILESAVE utility and displays the initial screen shown in Figure 3.12.

2. Press Enter

   The Choose Drives dialog box is displayed.

3. Use the Tab and space bar keys to specify which drives you want FILESAVE to protect, and press Enter.

This selects drives to protect and updates the initial screen. Notice that the number of drives selected in this step is now indicated in the Status: field next to the Choose drives dialog box.

4. Press the down-arrow key to highlight the File Protection dialog box, and then press Enter.

5. Press Tab three times, enter the maximum amount of deleted file data you wish to retain.

For example, you might enter 1000, which is 1000 Kb or approximately 1 megabyte.

6. Press Enter.

This accepts the default FILESAVE settings, at which all files (*.*) are retained for 5 days, with a maximum of 1 megabyte of deleted file data. The initial screen is redisplayed with updated information.

69

7. Press the down arrow key twice to highlight the Quit box, and press Enter.

This concludes FILESAVE configuration and terminates the utility. Remember that FILESAVE is a TSR, however, so although it has been terminated it is still resident in memory and ready to preserve data each time you delete a file. □

After you complete these Quick Steps, the FILESAVE utility is configured and loaded as a TSR. Each time you delete a file, FILESAVE places the contents of the deleted file in a special directory called TRASHCAN. To ensure that FILESAVE has been properly loaded, use DOS' DIR command to see if a TRASHCAN directory exists on each drive you specified in step #3 of the preceding Quick Steps.

Using the FILESAVE parameter settings as directed in the Quick Steps, the TRASHCAN directory will retain files up to 5 days after they are deleted. We have also specified a size limit for the TRASHCAN directory — no more than 1 megabyte of deleted files will be maintained in the TRASHCAN directory. When this size

```
                                                          F1=Help
┌──────────────────────── FileSave ───────────────────┐
│   FileSave protects you from accidentally deleting files │
│   by automatically holding them for a period of time.    │
│                                                          │
│  ┌────────────────┐   Specify which drives receive protection. │
│  │ Choose drives  │   Status: OFF                        │
│  └────────────────┘                                      │
│                                                          │
│  ┌────────────────┐   Specify which files receive protection.  │
│  │ File protection│   Status: All files (0 KB, 5 days)   │
│  └────────────────┘                                      │
│                                                          │
│  ┌────────────────┐   Permanently delete some or all held files.│
│  │ Purge files    │                                      │
│  └────────────────┘                                      │
│                                                          │
│  ┌────────────────┐   Quit FileSave, activating new settings.  │
│  │      Quit      │                                      │
│  └────────────────┘                                      │
└──────────────────────────────────────────────────────────┘
 Select the item to perform or select QUIT to exit      │ FileSave
```

Figure 3.12   The initial FILESAVE screen lets you configure the utility for your PC.

limit is reached FILESAVE will begin to delete, or purge, the oldest files in the TRASHCAN directory to make room for newly deleted files. You may wish to adjust this size limit based upon the size of your hard disk, how much space is available on your hard disk, how often you delete files, etc.

When you turn your PC off today and turn it back on tomorrow, you don't need to go through the Quick Steps to restart FILESAVE. FILESAVE stores your configuration information in a file called FILESAVE.INI.

To restart FILESAVE with your configuration information, use the /ON option and run FILESAVE /ON from the DOS command line.

FILESAVE also offers an option which uninstalls the utility. The command FILESAVE /OFF disables the utility and removes it from memory. Another command line option, /STATUS, lets you check the current condition of the FILESAVE utility. If you enter the command FILESAVE /STATUS, FILESAVE indicates whether it is enabled or disabled and shows the current configuration settings.

Recovering Files from the TRASHCAN

Norton's UNERASE utility is used to recover deleted files which FILESAVE has saved in the TRASHCAN directory. The UNERASE utility checks to see if a TRASHCAN directory exists on the active drive. If this special directory does exist, UNERASE uses the information in the .SAV and EP.MAP files to quickly and easily recover any deleted files which have been retained.

Purging Files from the TRASHCAN

Once a file has been deleted, it may remain in the TRASHCAN directory for several days, depending upon your FILESAVE configuration. Don't expect the deleted file's name to show up in a directory listing of TRASHCAN, however. When you delete a file, FILESAVE places it in the TRASHCAN directory and gives it a special file name. The deleted files retained in the TRASHCAN directory have a .SAV extension but the rest of their file names are fairly meaningless. A special file in the TRASHCAN directory called EP.MAP is FILESAVE's cross reference between these meaningless file names and the original file names.

71

   When you are certain that you want to delete a file and completely remove it from your disk, you can use FILESAVE's purge feature to erase it. When you select the "Purge files" box in Figure 3.12, the Purge Deleted Files screen in Figure 3.13 is displayed.

Figure 3.13   The Purge Deleted Files screen shows a list of all deleted files which may be purged.

The Purge Deleted Files screen shows a list of the files currently in the TRASHCAN directory. You can use the up- and down-arrow keys to scroll through this list and use the space bar to mark a highlighted file for deletion. After you have marked all the files you wish to purge from the TRASHCAN directory, highlight the Purge box in Figure 3.13 and press Enter to erase the files. Remember that once a file has been purged from the TRASHCAN directory there is no guarantee that you will be able to recover it with UNERASE.

Repairing Special Files

If you use Lotus 1-2-3, Symphony, or dBASE, you will be happy to know that the Norton Utilities include a tool to help you repair corrupt data files for these popular business applications. A data file can become corrupted for one of several reasons, including a malfunctioning disk, a software bug, etc.

The FILEFIX Solution

If you are having problems with a Lotus 1-2-3, Symphony, or dBASE data file, you should consider letting FILEFIX try to repair the damage. FILEFIX creates a new, undamaged version of the data file and leaves the original damaged file intact. The following Quick Steps explain how to repair a Lotus 1-2-3 data file, but the steps are similar for Symphony and dBASE data files.

 Repairing a Lotus 1-2-3 Data File

1. At the DOS prompt, type FILEFIX and press Enter.

   This starts the FILEFIX utility and displays the FILEFIX Type Selection screen in Figure 3.14.

2. Press Enter to accept the 1-2-3 selection highlighted.

   The Choose File to Repair screen is displayed.

3. Press Tab and use the up- and down-arrow keys to select a 1-2-3 file (for example, lotus.wk1) from the list displayed.

   If needed, you can change the active directory/drive using the Dirs/Drives selectors.

4. Press Enter.

The Repair Lotus 1-2-3 File screen is displayed.

5. Press Enter to accept the default fixed file name (fixed.wk1) and recovery mode (full recovery).

The recovery process begins and the Repair Summary screen shown in Figure 3.15 is displayed.

6. Press the left- or right-arrow key to highlight one of the report selection boxes, and press Enter.

Based on your selection, FILEFIX either prints a report, writes a report to a file you specify a report file name on a subsequent screen), or skips the report process. □

Figure 3.14   Select the type of damaged file with the FILEFIX type selection screen.

The FILEFIX utility has the smarts to know what may be wrong with a damaged Lotus 1-2-3, Symphony, or dBASE data file. Since FILEFIX knows the internal structure of these data file types, it can make an educated guess at how to repair the damage. After you use FILEFIX to repair a data file, you should immediately test the repaired data file to see if the damage has been corrected. Do *not* delete the original damaged data file until you are satisfied with the contents of the repaired data file created by FILEFIX.

Figure 3.15   FILEFIX repair results are shown on the repair summary screen.

Removing a File Permanently

Earlier in this chapter, I explained how the UNERASE utility can recover deleted files. Is there any way to actually remove a file from a disk so it cannot be recovered? Although it is convenient to have a recovery feature available, sometimes you really want to delete a file so no one else can see what it contained (for example, personnel records, top secret memos, etc.).

If you COPY enough files to a disk, you may eventually overwrite the unprotected clusters of all deleted files. But this could take a long time (especially if you have a large hard disk partition), and there is no way to guarantee that it would overwrite all the deleted files. If you are *really* determined to obliterate a file you may even consider FORMATting the disk. This approach is a bit drastic and may not work anyway since files can often be recovered from recently-formatted disks (thanks to Norton's UNFORMAT utility!). If you truly need to eradicate a file from a disk you should use Norton's WIPEINFO utility.

Removing Files with WIPEINFO

Norton's WIPEINFO utility overwrites a file's clusters thereby re-moving the file's data from a disk.

⊘   **Caution:** WIPEINFO should be used with extreme cau-tion because it overwrite's a file's data clusters and makes recovery via UNERASE impossible.

Q **Wiping a File from a Disk**

1. Type WIPEINFO and press Enter.

   This starts the WIPEINFO utility and displays the screen shown in Figure 3.16.

2. Press Enter.

   This selects the default Files selection in Figure 3.16 and displays the Wipe Files screen.

3. Type the name of the file to be wiped (for example, JUNK.DOC) and press Enter.

   A warning message is dis-played.

4. Press Enter to acknowledge the warning message.

   The Wiping Files screen is displayed.

5. Press the right-arrow key to select the file, then Enter to wipe the file selected.

   WIPEINFO wipes the file and displays a completion mes-sage.   □

75

WIPEINFO Configuration

WIPEINFO overwrites each byte in every cluster of the specified file with the default value, zero. Therefore, if you look at the clusters previously occupied by JUNK.DOC, all you will see is a bunch of zeros. If you want, you can change this value to any other number. You can also select the number of times you want the file wiped, for extra security. Select the Configure button on the WIPEINFO screen shown in Figure 3.16 to access the Wipe Configuration screen (Figure 3.17).

There are two Wipe options available in WIPEINFO: Fast Wipe and Government Wipe. WIPEINFO was configured with the Fast Wipe option when we eradicated the JUNK.DOC file in the previous Quick Steps. WIPEINFO overwrites each byte in a file one time with the specified value (0). You can change the 0 to another value: press

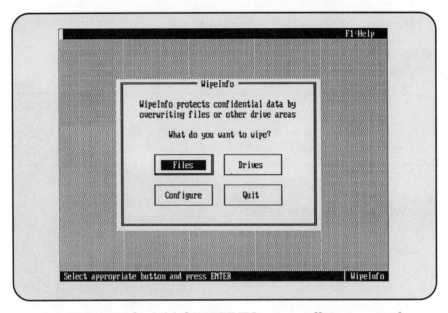

Figure 3.16   The initial WIPEINFO screen allows you to choose the type of wiping you wish to do.

the Tab key to move the cursor to the Fast Wipe default value field, and type a new value. After you change the overwrite value, press Enter to save the new WIPEINFO configuration setting.

If WIPEINFO is used with the Government Wipe option shown in Figure 3.17, each wiped file is overwritten seven times with the following overwrite values:

Overwrite #	Overwrite Value
1	1
2	0
3	1
4	0
5	1
6	0
7	246

The Wipe Configuration screen in Figure 3.17 lets you change the number of times the 1/0 overwrite combination will be performed (the default is 3 times). You can also specify a different overwrite value for the final overwrite (the default value is 246). Press the down-arrow, then the space bar (to place a dot next to the

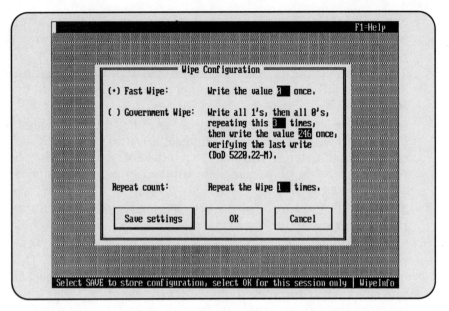

Figure 3.17 Select the desired WIPEINFO settings with the Wipe Configuration screen.

Government Wipe selection) to use the Government Wipe option instead of the Fast Wipe option.

If you are the kind of person who worries whether the refrigerator light goes off when the door closes, you will appreciate the repeat count option shown in Figure 3.17. The default repeat count is 1 but you can tell WIPEINFO to repeat the wipe as many as 999 times! So if you use the Government Wipe option and change the repeat count to 4, each file will be overwritten 28 times (4 x 7 = 28)!

WIPEINFO can also be used to wipe entire disks. We'll see how to use WIPEINFO to eradicate a disk in Chapter 6—Maintaining Your Hard Disk Drive.

What You Have Learned

In this chapter, you learned about Norton's file-related utilities. Specifically, you learned:

▶ DOS maintains a special status indicator for each file on a disk. This status indicates the state of several important file attributes, including: read-only, archive, system, and hidden.

▶ Norton's FILEFIND utility lets you display, set, or clear any of the four file attributes listed above, including those inaccessible to DOS' ATTRIB.

▶ The FILEFIND utility also reports the size of one or more files, and (optionally) determines whether or not the files will fit on another disk.

▶ In order to quickly and easily address an entire disk's data area, DOS works with larger, more manageable chunks of data called *clusters*. A cluster is the smallest block of space DOS will reserve for a file on a disk. The unused area of a cluster is referred to as *slack*.

▶ The FILEFIND utility allows you to set or clear a file's date and time stamp value.

▶ Norton's UNERASE utility gives you the ability to easily recover previously-deleted files from your hard or floppy disks. The chances of recovering an accidentally-deleted file are best if you run UNERASE immediately after the deletion.

▶ FILESAVE is a TSR utility which can prevent deleted file data from being overwritten so that files may be recovered long after they are deleted.

▶ The FILEFIX utility can repair corrupt Lotus 1-2-3, Symphony, and dBASE data files.

▶ Norton's WIPEINFO utility overwrites a file's clusters, thereby removing the file's data from a disk. WIPEINFO overwrites each byte in every cluster of the specified file with the default value, zero.

Enhancing Your Batch Files

In This Chapter

▶ *Using batch files for automation*
▶ *Batch file syntax*
▶ *Improving batch files with BE: Batch Enhancer*

This chapter begins by explaining DOS batch file syntax, and continues with an explanation of Norton's Batch Enhancer (BE) utility. Even if you are a batch file expert, you will appreciate what the Batch Enhancer can do for you—BE can make the simplest batch file look like a sophisticated windowing application.

Automation: The Key to Batch Files

Many PC operations require the same commands to be performed over and over again. For example, I have two subdirectories, WORK\MEMOS and WORK\REPORTS, which contain important work-related files. At the end of each week I have to place the contents of each subdirectory on separate floppy disks for my boss. The DOS commands I execute to perform this operation are shown in Table 4.1.

Table 4.1   DOS Commands for File Backup

DOS Command	Result
`CD WORK\MEMOS`	Moves to the WORK\MEMOS subdirectory
`COPY *.* A:`	Copies the contents of WORK\MEMOS to a floppy disk in the A: drive (when the COPY is complete, I place new floppy in the A: drive.)
`CD ..\REPORTS`	Moves to the WORK\REPORTS subdirectory
`COPY *.* A:`	Copies the contents of WORK\REPORTS to the floppy disk in the A: drive

Using a DOS batch file, I can consolidate all four commands in Table 4.1 into one command.

Creating a Batch File

A batch file is an ASCII text file which contains one or more DOS commands. DOS can get confused if it encounters non-ASCII characters in a batch file. Therefore, you must be careful when determining what text editor to use for writing batch files. Although DOS' EDLIN editor creates ASCII text files, I do not recommend using it—EDLIN is an antiquated, hard-to-use line editor (which means you can only edit one line at a time). Even the most modest shareware editors look fully-featured when compared to EDLIN!

> ▶ **Tip:** Some word processors (for example, Wordstar) offer a non-document mode for creating/modifying ASCII text files. Use the DOS TYPE command (for example, `TYPE AUTOEXEC.BAT`) to see if a file contains only ASCII characters. If TYPE does not beep or display strange symbols, it's a good bet the file consists of ASCII characters only.

If you are looking for a good text editor, I suggest using either the Norton Editor or the built-in editor with the Norton Commander. The Norton Commander's built-in editor cannot handle large files, but you would have to write a very large batch file to exceed its limitations. The Norton Editor can edit virtually any size file, and provides more bells and whistles than the Commander's built-in editor.

A Simple Batch File

When you have selected a text editor, you are ready to start creating batch files. It's not as hard as it sounds; all you have to do is type a list of commands that are to be carried out consecutively. To try it, use your text editor to create a batch file called ONE.BAT using the commands shown in Listing 4-1.

Listing 4.1   ONE.BAT Batch File Listing

```
ECHO OFF
REM This is a simple batch file called ONE.BAT.
REM It performs a DIR of the current directory.
DIR *.*
ECHO ON
REM This is the end of the ONE.BAT batch file.
PAUSE
```

To execute the ONE.BAT batch file, type the command ONE.BAT or just ONE and press Enter (see Figure 4.1).

81

```
BE        EXE    24304   7-17-90    5:00p
CALIBRAT  EXE   124566   7-17-90    5:00p
DISKEDIT  EXE   216730   7-17-90    5:00p
DISKMON   EXE    68798   7-17-90    5:00p
DISKREET  EXE   156918   7-17-90    5:00p
DISKREET  SYS    52886   7-17-90    5:00p
DISKTOOL  EXE   122712   7-17-90    5:00p
FILEFIND  EXE   104708   7-17-90    5:00p
FILEFIX   EXE   137082   7-17-90    5:00p
FILESAVE  EXE    86248   7-17-90    5:00p
IMAGE     EXE    11894   7-17-90    5:00p
NCACHE-F  EXE    49156   7-17-90    5:00p
NCACHE-S  EXE    39672   7-17-90    5:00p
NCC       EXE    96818   7-17-90    5:00p
NCD       EXE    86600   7-17-90    5:00p
ONE       ~BA      173   8-20-90   10:19a
ONE       BAT      178   8-20-90   10:36a
        34 File(s)  14176256 bytes free

D:\NORTON5>REM This is the end of the ONE.BAT batch file.

D:\NORTON5>PAUSE
Strike a key when ready . . .

D:\NORTON5>
```

Figure 4.1   The ONE.BAT batch file displays the content of the current directory.

Each line of the ONE.BAT batch file in Listing 4.1 is an executable DOS statement. Some of the special batch file statements used in ONE.BAT may not be familiar to you, however, so let's discuss each command separately.

The ECHO Command

DOS displays, or echoes, each statement on the screen as it executes a batch file. The ECHO OFF command causes DOS to suppress display of subsequent command lines in a batch file. DOS continues to suppress command line displays until an ECHO ON command is encountered.

The REM Command

You can include comments or notes in a batch file by using the REM command. When DOS encounters a REM command in a batch file, it ignores everything else on that line. The second, third, and sixth lines of ONE.BAT are comment lines. Comment lines can be used to document a batch file's purpose and explain what is happening at a certain point within the batch file.

The ECHO OFF command at the start of ONE.BAT causes DOS to not display the first two comment lines when the batch file is executed. The comment on line 6 of ONE.BAT is displayed when the batch file is executed because the ECHO feature is turned back on at line 5 (ECHO ON).

The DIR Command

You can run an executable program (for example, files with the .EXE or .COM extensions), or a DOS command, in a batch file by specifying the program name/command followed by any required parameters. For example, the DIR command is invoked at the fourth line of ONE.BAT. The next statement in ONE.BAT, ECHO ON, is not performed until DIR finishes execution.

The PAUSE Command

The two lines following the DIR command in Listing 4.1

```
ECHO ON
REM This is the end of the ONE.BAT batch file.
```

turn the ECHO feature back on and note the end of the ONE.BAT batch file. Actually, the next statement, PAUSE, is the last one in ONE.BAT. The PAUSE command causes DOS to suspend execution of a batch file until you press a key. PAUSE is useful for suspending batch file execution while a user reads a screen, inserts a diskette, etc.

Batch File Parameters

You have seen examples of some of the Norton Utilities which use command-line parameters (for example, the /ON in FILESAVE /ON). Many other DOS applications support command-line parameters as well. Since batch files represent a special type of executable file, it should be no surprise that they also support command-line parameters. Our next batch file, TWO.BAT (Listing 4.2) shows how to incorporate command-line parameters in a simple batch file.

Listing 4.2   TWO.BAT with a Parameter

```
ECHO OFF
REM This is a simple batch file called TWO.BAT.
REM It starts up FILESAVE with a user-specified pa-
rameter
FILESAVE %1
ECHO ON
REM This is the end of the TWO.BAT batch file.
PAUSE
```

When you run TWO.BAT, you should include one of the FILESAVE parameters discussed in Chapter 3 (/ON, /OFF, or /STATUS). For example, if you type TWO.BAT /STATUS and press Enter, TWO.BAT will run FILESAVE with a /STATUS parameter, thus showing the status of the FILESAVE TSR. The /STATUS parameter on the TWO.BAT command line is passed to FILESAVE via the %1 operator in the statement FILESAVE %1.

DOS offers nine unique operators for using command-line parameters in batch files: %1 through %9. The leftmost command-line parameter is referred to as %1, the next leftmost parameter is %2, and so on.

> ▶ **Note:** Refer to *The Waite Group's Using PC DOS* for an explanation of how to use the SHIFT command to access more than 9 command-line parameters.

The next batch file, THREE.BAT (Listing 4.3), illustrates how two parameters can be used in a batch file.

Listing 4.3   THREE.BAT with Two Parameters

```
ECHO OFF
ECHO Hello, %2 !
REM This is a simple batch file called THREE.BAT.
REM We start off by greeting the user.
REM Next, THREE.BAT starts up FILESAVE with a
REM user-specified parameter.
REM The batch file concludes with another brief
REM message to the user.
FILESAVE %1
ECHO ON
REM This is the end of the THREE.BAT batch file, %2 !
PAUSE
```

84

When you run THREE.BAT you must specify two parameters: the parameter for FILESAVE and your name. For example, I might try `THREE.BAT /STATUS Joe`

The second line in THREE.BAT displays a greeting to the user. Even though the ECHO feature is turned off by the first line of THREE.BAT, we can use ECHO to display a string of characters on the screen. For example, the statement in Listing 4.3 `ECHO Hello, %2 !` echoes the message "Hello, Joe." regardless of whether ECHO is ON or OFF.

The next-to-last line in THREE.BAT also uses %2: `REM This is the end of the THREE.BAT batch file, %2 !` This statement displays a batch file termination message with the user's name and illustrates two important points:

1. Batch file command-line parameters may be incorporated in remark (REM) statements, and

2. A parameter can be used in as many different statements within a batch file as is necessary.

Looping within a Batch File

Creating a batch file is similar to writing a computer program in a language like C, PASCAL, or BASIC. Computer programming languages offer a means for user input, output, and comments. We have seen how DOS batch files offer these features as well with PAUSE, ECHO, and REM. Another important feature common to programming languages and batch files is the ability to perform the same operation over and over again, or loop. Listing 4.4 illustrates how to use a loop in a batch file.

Listing 4.4   FOUR.BAT with a Looping Construct

```
ECHO OFF
REM This is a simple batch file called FOUR.BAT.
REM FOUR.BAT runs FILESAVE twice...once for each
REM parameter entry in the FOR loop.
FOR %%a IN (ON STATUS) DO FILESAVE /%%a
ECHO ON
```

FOUR.BAT uses a FOR loop to run the FILESAVE utility twice. The syntax of a FOR loop is: `FOR %%x IN (set) DO statement %%x`. In short, this syntax means that the specified "statement" will be executed once with each item listed in "set." Each item in "set" is a parameter for the statement. Therefore, the FOR loop in Listing 4.4 first executes `FILESAVE /ON`, followed by `FILESAVE /STATUS`.

You may wonder why the slash (/) appears before the second %%a and not with the ON and STATUS parameters. We must write the parameters without slashes because DOS strips the slash off the parameters in the FOR loop. So if you try to use: `FOR %%a IN (/ON /STATUS) DO FILESAVE %%a`, DOS will try to run `FILESAVE ON` (i.e. without the slash preceding ON).

The two %%a's in the FOR loop syntax are referred to as dummy parameters. A dummy parameter is sort of a place-holder in the FOR statement. The dummy parameter is replaced by each item in the set for every iteration through the loop. In FOUR.BAT, I chose to use the letter 'a' (%%a) as the dummy parameter. Actually, you can use any letter in the alphabet after the two percent signs. Perhaps the most important rule to remember is that both dummy parameters in the FOR loop must use the same letter. For example, `FOR %%a IN (ON STATUS) DO FILESAVE /%%z` is not a valid FOR loop. In fact, this erroneous FOR loop causes DOS to try and execute FILESAVE twice with a /%z parameter.

Conditional Execution (IF and GOTO)

One of the minor annoyances with DOS' COPY command is that it lets you overwrite files without warning. The command `COPY MYMEMO.DOC YOURMEMO.DOC` copies the file MYMEMO.DOC to YOURMEMO.DOC. If a file named YOURMEMO.DOC existed before executing COPY, it is overwritten by MYMEMO.DOC, and probably gone forever! You can use a batch file like the one shown in Listing 4.5 to copy individual files and reduce the chance of overwriting important data.

Listing 4.5   C.BAT—An Individual File Copy Utility

```
ECHO OFF
REM This batch file helps you avoid accidentally
REM overwriting important files when using the
REM COPY command.
IF NOT EXIST %2 GOTO end
ECHO WARNING...%2 ALREADY EXISTS!!!
ECHO PRESS CNTRL-C TO ABORT THIS COPY...
ECHO PRESS ANY OTHER KEY TO OVERWRITE %2...
PAUSE
:end
ECHO ON
COPY %1 %2
```

86

I have named the batch file in Listing 4.5 C.BAT as an abbreviation for DOS' COPY command. Rather than using DOS' copy command to copy MYMEMO.DOC to YOURMEMO.DOC, I can use C.BAT with the following parameters: `C MYMEMO.DOC YOURMEMO.DOC`. If C.BAT determines that YOURMEMO.DOC already exists, the batch file suspends execution (via `PAUSE`) and lets you abort the copy by pressing the CTRL-C key combination. You can press any other key to let MYMEMO.DOC overwrite YOURMEMO.DOC. C.BAT uses a couple of special commands to perform this intelligent copy process: IF and GOTO.

The IF command in Listing 4.5 `IF NOT EXIST %2 GOTO end` is read "if the file specified by the second command line parameter (%2) does not exist, go to the 'end' label." In all the previous batch files, we have seen that DOS executes one command after another without skipping any in between. The IF...GOTO construction allows us to branch around one or more statements within a batch file. This branching feature illustrates yet another commonality between programming and batch file languages.

Why is it so important to allow branching within a batch file? One of two different situations may arise when running C.BAT: either the destination file already exists or it does not. C.BAT must act differently depending upon the existence of the destination file.

If the destination file does not exist, we want to copy the source file to the destination file with no further intervention by the user. In this case, the GOTO clause of the IF statement causes control to jump to the next statement after the "end" label. A label is an identifier which is preceded by a colon (:) and appears on a line by itself. The ECHO ON statement is the first line executed after this branch (since ECHO ON is the first statement after the ":end" identifier). Then, the file is copied via the COPY %1 %2 statement.

If the destination file does exist, we want to display a message and suspend batch file execution until the user decides whether the file should be overwritten. In this case, the GOTO clause of the IF statement is not executed. Since the condition of the IF statement is not true, the next line in the batch file is executed. More specifically, the three ECHO statements are executed followed by the PAUSE command. At this point the user can press CTRL-C to abort the batch file or any other key to overwrite the destination file. If a key other than CTRL-C is pressed, the ECHO ON and COPY %1 %2 statements are executed. (Notice that the ":end" identifier line is treated like a REMark and is skipped.)

87

> **Note:** This is a very simple example of the IF and GOTO commands. For a more detailed explanation of IF and GOTO, refer to *The Waite Group's Using PC DOS*.

Interactive Batch Files

You have seen how PAUSE can be used to suspend batch file execution until the user presses a key. The previous C.BAT example took PAUSE one step further: it offered a point where the user could press CTRL-C and gracefully abort batch file execution. PAUSE is the only mechanism DOS provides for user interaction with batch files. What if you want to write a menuing batch file which lets you select from a list of applications to run like the one in Figure 4.2?

```
┌─────────────────────────────────────────────────┐
│  ──────── Please make your menu selection: ───── │
│                                                  │
│              1 - WordPerfect 5.1                 │
│              2 - Norton Integrator               │
│              3 - DOS Shell                        │
│              4 - PFS:First Choice                 │
│              5 - Carbon Copy Plus                 │
│              6 - QUIT                             │
│                                                  │
│          Press 1, 2, 3, 4, 5, or 6...            │
└─────────────────────────────────────────────────┘
```

88

Figure 4.2   This sample application menu selection screen was created using a batch file.

It would not be too difficult to write a batch file to display the text shown in Figure 4.2. Further, you could use PAUSE to wait for the user to make a selection. But since there is no way to know what key the user pressed, how would you know which application to start? The answer is simple: use Norton's Batch Enhancer (BE) utility.

BE: Batch Enhancer

The Batch Enhancer utility is different from the other Norton Utilities we have discussed so far. As its name implies, BE can enhance dull and dreary batch files, thus making them more aesthetically pleasing. For my money, however, BE's most important attribute is its ability to handle user entries and permit a batch file to process menu selections. The MENU.BAT listing shown in Listing 4.6 shows how BE can be used in an interactive menuing batch file.

Listing 4.6   The MENU.BAT Batch File

```
ECHO OFF
REM Display application menu
:menu
BE CLS
BE SA WHITE ON MAGENTA
BE WINDOW 1 1 23 78 BRIGHT WHITE ON BLUE ZOOM
BE WINDOW 6 6 18 74 BRIGHT CYAN ON GREEN SHADOW
BE ROWCOL 6 24 " Please make your menu selection: "
BRIGHT WHITE
BE ROWCOL 8 32 "1 - WordPerfect 5.1" BRIGHT YELLOW
BE ROWCOL 9 32 "2 - NORTON Program" BRIGHT YELLOW
BE ROWCOL 10 32 "3 - DOS Shell" BRIGHT YELLOW
BE ROWCOL 11 32 "4 - PFS:First Choice" BRIGHT YELLOW
BE ROWCOL 12 32 "5 - Carbon Copy Plus" BRIGHT YELLOW
BE ROWCOL 13 32 "6 - QUIT" BRIGHT YELLOW
BE ROWCOL 15 24
REM Request input from the user
BE ASK "Press 1, 2, 3, 4, 5, or 6..." 123456 BRIGHT
WHITE
REM Process the user's entry
IF ERRORLEVEL 6 GOTO quit
IF ERRORLEVEL 5 GOTO ccplus
IF ERRORLEVEL 4 GOTO first
IF ERRORLEVEL 3 GOTO shell
IF ERRORLEVEL 2 GOTO norton
REM NOTE: No GOTO for WordPerfect is required since
it is
REM      started by default with the next executable
REM      statement.
REM WordPerfect 5.1 selection
:wp51
CD C:\wp51
WP
GOTO menu
REM NORTON Program selection
:norton
CD C:\NU
NORTON
GOTO menu
REM DOS Shell selection
:shell
REM Inform user how to leave the DOS shell
BE CLS
BE BOX 5 15 19 65 DOUBLE CYAN
```

continued

Listing 4.6 *(continued)*

```
BE ROWCOL 8 25 "YOU HAVE SELECTED TO EXECUTE THE"
BRIGHT WHITE
BE ROWCOL 9 25 "DOS SHELL. THE DOS SHELL ALLOWS"
BRIGHT WHITE
BE ROWCOL 10 25 "YOU TO RUN ANY DOS COMMAND OR"
BRIGHT WHITE
BE ROWCOL 11 25 "PROGRAM. WHEN YOU WANT TO RETURN"
BRIGHT WHITE
BE ROWCOL 12 25 "TO THE APPLICATION MENU, TYPE"
BRIGHT WHITE
BE ROWCOL 13 25 "'EXIT' AND PRESS ENTER." BRIGHT
WHITE
BE ROWCOL 16 25 "THIS MESSAGE WILL SELF-DESTRUCT"
BRIGHT RED
BE ROWCOL 17 33 "IN 5 SECONDS!!" BRIGHT RED
BE BEEP
REM Delay 5 seconds (90 / 18 = 5 secs.)
BE DELAY 90
BE CLS
C:\COMMAND.COM
GOTO menu
REM PFS:First Choice selection
:first
CD C:\CHOICE
FIRST
GOTO menu
REM Carbon Copy Plus selection
:ccplus
CD C:\CCPLUS
CC
GOTO menu
:quit
BE SA NORMAL
BE CLS
ECHO ON
```

When MENU.BAT is executed, it displays the menu selection screen shown in Figure 4.2. You may have noticed the various BE statements throughout MENU.BAT. For example, the fourth line in MENU.BAT is: BE CLS, which illustrates the general syntax for the BE utility. In short, the BE utility name is always followed by a subcommand and, optionally, subcommand parameters. In the BE CLS statement (Listing 4.6), CLS is referred to as the subcommand. Let's look closer at MENU.BAT and discuss each of the BE subcommands it uses.

The CLS Subcommand

CLS is a BE subcommand which clears the screen and moves the cursor to the home position (the home position is the top left corner of the screen). I use CLS in MENU.BAT to provide a fresh, blank screen to display my application menu. The DOS CLS command is functionally identical to BE's CLS subcommand.

The SA Subcommand

> ▶ **Note:** You need to install the DOS device driver ANSI.SYS before you can use the SA subcommand. If you don't know what a device driver is, don't worry—the procedure is quite painless! First, check your DOS directory and make sure a file called ANSI.SYS exists. (Since my DOS directory is called DOS, the remainder of this explanation uses the C:\DOS directory. If your ANSI.SYS file resides elsewhere, substitute that location for my C:\DOS specification.)
>
> Next, see if a file named CONFIG.SYS exists in the root directory of your C: drive. (If your PC does not have a hard disk, look in the root directory of your DOS diskette.) If CONFIG.SYS does not exist, use your text editor to create a CONFIG.SYS file in the root directory with `DEVICE=C:\DOS\ANSI.SYS` in it. Or, if your PC does not have a hard disk, use `DEVICE= A:\DOS\ANSI.SYS` instead. If CONFIG.SYS does exist, examine it with TYPE or your text editor to see if a `DEVICE=ANSI.SYS` line exists. If no such line exists, add it.
>
> Finally, press the CTRL-ALT-DEL key combination to reboot your PC. When your PC reboots, the ANSI.SYS driver is installed and you can use the SA subcommand.

The SA subcommand, which is an abbreviation for Screen Attributes, allows you to set the foreground and background colors on your PC's display. The first example of SA in MENU.BAT sets the foreground color (text) to WHITE and the background color to MAGENTA. The syntax for this usage of SA is `BE SA` *forecolor* `ON` *backcolor* where "forecolor" and "backcolor" are the foreground and background colors respectively. There are eight foreground/ background colors available with SA:

Black	Magenta
Green	Yellow
White	Cyan
Blue	Red

Any combination of these colors may be used for either the foreground or background in SA. Be careful not to set the foreground and background colors to the same value or you will wind up with "invisible" text on your screen.

The foreground color may be modified by either of the two intensity values BRIGHT or BLINKING. For example, the statement `BE SA BRIGHT WHITE ON BLUE` changes the foreground color to BRIGHT WHITE and the background color to BLUE.

As you can see, the SA subcommand lets you customize your screen using your favorite foreground/background colors. You can use the other form of the SA subcommand when you want to return the screen to the default colors. The syntax for this other SA form is `BE SA main-setting` where "main-setting" is either NORMAL, REVERSE, or UNDERLINE.

The second-to-last statement in MENU.BAT: `BE SA NORMAL` resets the foreground and background colors to their default values (for example, on my EGA monitor, the default values are WHITE on BLACK). Also, NORMAL turns off the REVERSE and UNDERLINE main-setting switches if they are on. You can experiment with different foreground/background colors and main-setting values to see what combination you prefer.

The WINDOW Subcommand

The next two lines in MENU.BAT:

```
BE WINDOW 1 1 23 78 BRIGHT WHITE ON BLUE ZOOM
BE WINDOW 6 6 18 74 BRIGHT CYAN ON GREEN SHADOW
```

use the WINDOW subcommand to place two windows on the screen. The syntax for the WINDOW subcommand is: `BE WINDOW top left bottom right attributes` where "top," "left," "bottom," and "right" are the window coordinates and "attributes" specifies characteristics about the window. Valid attributes include any of the colors listed on the previous page and the special window options SHADOW and ZOOM.

Window coordinates are specified by row and column where the top left corner of the screen is row 0 column 0. Column values increase from left to right across the screen and row values increase from top to bottom.

Window colors are specified with the format `BE   WINDOW` *border-color* `ON` *fill-color* where border-color is the color BE will use to draw the window border and fill-color is the color BE will use to fill the window.

When BE draws a window with the SHADOW option, it places a see-through shadow along the bottom and right sides of the window to create the illusion of a 3-dimensional object. Windows drawn with the other special option, ZOOM, appear to explode onto the screen.

With this knowledge, We can now analyze the statement

```
BE WINDOW 1 1 23 78 BRIGHT WHITE ON BLUE ZOOM
```

which draws a window from row 1 column 1 to row 23 column 78. This BLUE window is drawn with a BRIGHT WHITE border. Finally, the ZOOM option is used to create the exploding visual effect.

93

The ROWCOL Subcommand

The next several statements in MENU.BAT use the ROWCOL subcommand to place colored text on the screen. The syntax for ROWCOL is:

```
BE ROWCOL row column text color
```

where "row" and "column" specify where the "text" should be located and "color" is any one of the colors listed on the previous page. These colors may also be modified by the intensity values BRIGHT or BLINKING. So the statement:

```
BE ROWCOL 6 24 " Please make your menu selection: " BRIGHT WHITE
```

places the BRIGHT WHITE text " Please make your menu selection: on the 6th row starting in the 24th column. Several ROWCOL statements are used together to create the application menu shown in Figure 4.2. The last ROWCOL command used for the menu is `BE ROWCOL 15 24`, which places the cursor on row 15 column 24 but does not display any text. This cursor placement is important for the next statement in MENU.BAT which uses the ASK subcommand.

The ASK Subcommand

The ASK subcommand is the key to interactive batch files with the BE utility. The syntax for ASK is:

```
BE ASK text keys color
```

where "text" is the prompt to display in "color" and "keys" are the valid keys which the user may press. For example, the statement:

```
BE ASK "Press 1, 2, 3, 4, 5, or 6..." 123456 BRIGHT
WHITE
```

displays the BRIGHT WHITE prompt "Press 1, 2, 3, 4, 5, or 6..." and waits for the user to press one of the numeric keys 1 through 6 (123456). BE sounds an error tone if you try to press a key not listed in the "keys" list. When a valid key is pressed, BE places a value in a special location called ERRORLEVEL.

The ERRORLEVEL Variable

ERRORLEVEL is a variable whose value may be set by either DOS or an executable program, such as Norton's BE utility. Once a program like BE sets ERRORLEVEL, a batch file may perform conditional operations based upon ERRORLEVEL's value. BE sets ERRORLEVEL to:

  1 — if the first key in the "keys" list was pressed,
  2 — if the second key in the "keys" list was pressed, and so on.

The five IF statements:

```
IF ERRORLEVEL 6 GOTO quit
IF ERRORLEVEL 5 GOTO ccplus
IF ERRORLEVEL 4 GOTO first
IF ERRORLEVEL 3 GOTO shell
IF ERRORLEVEL 2 GOTO norton
```

branch to different parts of MENU.BAT depending upon the value of ERRORLEVEL. Because of a quirk with the ERRORLEVEL feature, you must always list the "IF ERRORLEVEL...GOTO..." statements in descending order of ERRORLEVEL value. Also note that there is no IF statement to check for an ERRORLEVEL value of 1.

Since the batch file commands for menu selection #1 (WordPerfect 5.1) appear immediately after the last IF statement, there is no need to perform a GOTO—DOS automatically executes

/D# /F# /R# /W#

the next sequential batch file statement if ERRORLEVEL is not 2 when the `IF ERRORLEVEL 2 GOTO norton` statement is executed.

Each block of application statements in MENU.BAT is fairly straightforward. In general, a CD is performed to switch to the application's directory, the application is executed, and the menu is redisplayed. The only exception to this general flow is the DOS Shell menu selection, which uses a few more BE subcommands.

The BOX Subcommand

When option #3 (DOS Shell) is selected in MENU.BAT, the screen is cleared and a box is displayed with the BOX subcommand whose syntax is:

```
BE BOX top left bottom right attributes
```

where "top," "left," "bottom," and "right" are the box coordinates and "attributes" specifies characteristics about the box. Valid attributes include any of the colors listed on page 92 and the special box border options SINGLE and DOUBLE. By default, boxes are drawn with a SINGLE line border.

For example, the statement:

```
BE BOX 5 15 19 65 DOUBLE CYAN
```

draws a DOUBLE-line border CYAN box from row 5 column 15 to row 19 column 65. Several ROWCOL statements are then used to display information about the DOS Shell option.

The BEEP Subcommand

The BEEP subcommand is also used within the batch file logic for the DOS Shell selection. The statement BE BEEP plays a tone through your PC's internal speaker. If you are musically inclined, you can use BEEP to play a simple song or just a few random notes. The syntax for BEEP is:

```
BE BEEP /D# /F# /R# /W#
```

and each option is defined as shown in Table 4.2.

Table 4.2   BEEP Subcommand Options

Option	Meaning
/D#	Duration or length of tone to play in 18ths of second (for example, /D9 equals 9/18ths or 1/2 second)
/F#	Frequency of the tone in cycles per second (for example, /F262 represents a frequency of 262 cycles per second (Hz) or a musical note "C")
/R#	Number of times to repeat the tone (for example, /R4 repeats the tone 4 times)
/W#	How long to pause, in 18ths of a second, after playing the specified tone (for example, /W18 equals a pause of 1 second)

The DELAY Subcommand

The DELAY command offers an easy-to-use method of freezing a screen for a period of time without waiting for the user to press a key to continue. The syntax for DELAY is:

```
BE DELAY time
```

where time is expressed in 18ths of a second. So, the statement in Listing 4.6:

```
BE DELAY 90
```

causes the MENU.BAT batch file to suspend execution for 90/18 or 5 seconds.

What You Have Learned

In this chapter you learned some of the fundamental concepts behind DOS batch files. Specifically, you learned:

▶ A batch file is an ASCII text file which contains one or more DOS commands.

▶ Batch files represent a special type of executable file and they support command-line parameters (for example, %1, %2, etc.) Batch files also offer looping and conditional constructs similar to the ones supported by programming languages.

▶ Besides PAUSE, DOS batch files offer no useful means for accepting user input. Further, PAUSE does not allow the batch file programmer to execute certain blocks of statements based upon a specific key depression.

▶ The Batch Enhancer (BE) utility can enhance dull and dreary batch files, thus making them more aesthetically pleasing. Through the use of subcommands, BE can add color, sound, and windows and manage user interaction within batch files.

▶ The ASK subcommand is the key to interactive batch files with the BE utility. ASK allows the batch file programmer to execute specific blocks of batch file statements based on user keyboard

97

Managing Your Disks with the Utilities

In This Chapter

▶ *Working with directories and tree structures*

▶ *Using NCD: Norton Change Directory to simplify directory operations*

▶ *Recovering a deleted directory*

▶ *Finding your way through the forest*

This important chapter discusses a few of the Norton Utilities which help you manage your disks. The disk-based utilities covered in this chapter will help you with everything from working with directories and subdirectories to locating text strings.

We'll begin with an explanation of the DOS directory tree structure. Then we'll talk about the Norton Change Directory (NCD) utility, which offers a visual alternative to several of the DOS directory commands. Finally, we'll cover two important features of the FILEFIND utility which help you to locate files and text strings on your disks.

Directories and Tree Structures

Modern hard disk drives are capable of storing hundreds of megabytes of data. DOS allows you to break a disk down into smaller, more manageable areas known as directories and subdirectories. As you may already know, a disk is similar to a filing cabinet because they both are used to store data. We can take that analogy one step further and say that a disk directory is comparable to a folder within the filing cabinet. A subdirectory is merely a directory within a directory, or, a folder within a folder.

A special director called the *root directory* exists on all disks (for example, C:\). All other directories on a disk are either a direct or indirect descendent of the root directory. For example, in the pathname C:\TEMP, TEMP is a first-level directory from the root C:\. In the pathname C:\TEMP\WORK, WORK is a subdirectory from the first-level directory C:\TEMP. Figure 5.1 shows the relationship between the root directory and other directories/subdirectories.

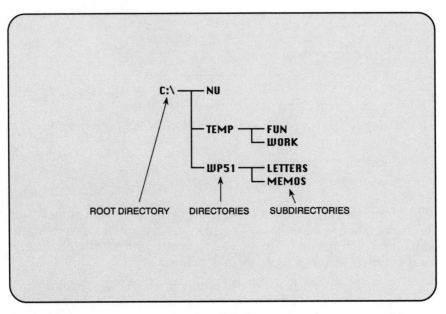

Figure 5.1   Directories on a disk form a tree structure, with multiple branches and levels.

In Figure 5.1, there are 3 directories off the root: TEMP, NU, and WP51. Further, the TEMP and WP51 directories have subdirectories associated with them. Figure 5.1 is a graphical representation of DOS' directory tree structure—each descendent directory is shown as a branch off its parent directory. Unlike a real tree, however, the root of a DOS directory tree is at the *top* of the diagram.

The DOS MD and RD commands are used to make and remove directories, respectively. For example, the TEMP directory shown in Figure 5.1 can be created with the command MD C:\TEMP. And, if the MEMOS directory in Figure 5.1 is empty (i.e. it contains no files or subdirectories), it may be removed with the command `RD C:\WP51\MEMOS`

Once you have created a few directories on your disk, how do you move from one directory to another? The DOS CD command is the basic vehicle for jumping from one directory to another. For example, the command `CD C:\TEMP\WORK` changes the active directory to C:\TEMP\WORK.

▶ **Tip:** Use DOS's PROMPT command to include the active directory in the DOS prompt. The command `PROMPT $P$G` changes the command prompt from C> to C:\> when in the root directory. The advantage of using this type of prompt is more apparent when another directory or subdirectory is active. For example, when the C:\TEMP\WORK directory is active, the DOS prompt becomes C:\TEMP\WORK>.

101

NCD: Norton Change Directory

Although the CD command is adequate for moving about from directory to directory, the Norton Change Directory (NCD) utility offers a fast graphical approach to directory navigation.

 Changing Directories with Norton Change Directory (NCD)

1. At the DOS prompt, type the command `NCD` and press Enter. — This starts the NCD utility and displays a directory tree structure like the one shown in Figure 5.2.

2. Press the right-arrow key to select the destination directory (for example, `WP51`) and press Enter. — The destination directory becomes the active directory and the NCD utility is terminated. □

The screen in Figure 5.2 shows my directory tree structure horizontally. In other words, the root directory is on the left, and the first level of directories appear to the right of the root. In Figure 5.2 the root is the current directory—NCD denotes the current directory with an inverse block around it (see the root (\) in Figure 5.2).

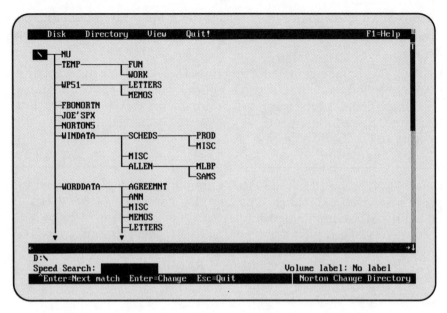

Figure 5.2   The NCD utility provides many useful directory tools.

As shown in the Quick Steps, you can use the arrow keys to move from one directory to another with NCD. In general, the up- and down-arrow keys will move vertically through the tree and the left- and right-arrow keys will move horizontally. The Home and End keys may also be used to jump to the top (root) and bottom (lowest directory/subdirectory) of the tree, respectively. The PgUp and PgDn keys are handy for quickly moving up and down through the tree a screenful at a time.

Although the selection block moves from one directory to another when the arrow keys are pressed, the active directory is not changed until you press Enter (as shown in step #2 of the Quick Steps). You can press Esc at any time within NCD to quit the utility and return to DOS without changing directories.

NCD Speed Search

A Speed Search box appears in the bottom left portion of the NCD screen in Figure 5.2. The Speed Search feature allows you to quickly jump from one directory to another without having to search for your destination with the arrow keys. For example, to move the highlight to the TEMP\FUN directory in Figure 5.2, I can press just the F key and the selection block moves to FUN (Figure 5.3).

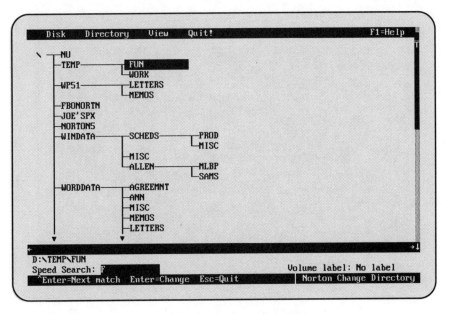

Figure 5.3   Using Speed Search with NCD

Now I can press Enter to make TEMP\FUN the active directory. The Norton Speed Search feature is very simple to use: just keep typing the letters of the name you wish to locate until a match is found. Depending on how you name your directories, Speed Search needs from one to eight keystrokes to locate the desired directory.

NCD Function Keys

The NCD utility isn't just a visual replacement for DOS' CD command; NCD offers several other features as well, which are accessible through the Disk, Directory, and View menus. I find it easier to use these other features via function keys rather than the pull-down menus, though. NCD supports eight function keys: F1, F2, F3, and F6 through F10.

F1—Help

Pressing the F1 key provides helpful information about the NCD utility (Figure 5.4).

F2—Rescan

The first time you run NCD, it scans your disk to create a list of the directories/subdirectories. This information is stored in a file called

Figure 5.4   Pressing F1 accesses the Help screen.

TREEINFO.NCD in the root directory. Each subsequent time you run NCD, it uses the TREEINFO.NCD file to generate the directory tree on your monitor. Unfortunately, DOS directory commands do not keep TREEINFO.NCD up to date. So if you create or remove directories with MD or RD after the TREEINFO.NCD file is created, NCD may report erroneous directory information. If you suspect the TREEINFO.NCD file is out of sync with your disk's directory structure, press F2 to rescan the disk and update TREEINFO.NCD.

F3—Select Drive

Press F3 to switch from one disk drive to another within NCD. When you press F3, the screen in Figure 5.5 is displayed, which lists all the valid drive selections.

Use the up- or down-arrow keys to move the selection block to the desired drive, and press Enter. Or, just type the drive letter (for example, C) and NCD immediately switches to that drive.

F6—Rename

The F6 key gives you the ability to rename a directory or subdirectory. Move the selection block to the directory/subdirectory you wish to rename, and press F6 (Figure 5.6).

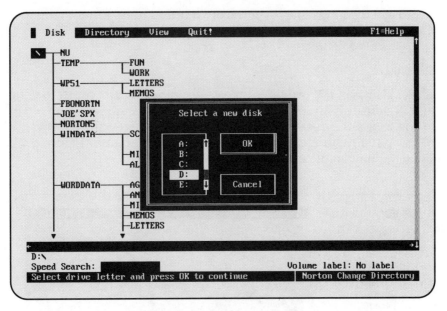

Figure 5.5   The NCD drive selection box lets you change the active drive.

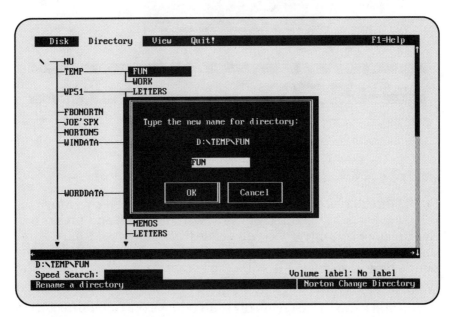

Figure 5.6   Pressing F6 lets you rename a directory.

Type the new name over the old one and press Enter to rename the directory/subdirectory.

F7—MkDir

The MkDir key, F7, provides an easy way to add directories to your disk. To create a directory off the root, first move the selection block to the root and press F7. The screen displays an empty directory block, where you can enter the new directory name (Figure 5.7). Type the new name and press Enter.

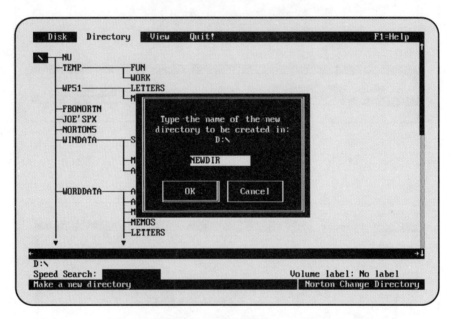

Figure 5.7   Using MkDir (F7) to Create a New Directory

F8—Delete

Empty directories can be deleted in NCD with the F8 key. Move the selection block to the directory you wish to delete, and press F8. If the directory is empty, NCD will delete it and remove it from the tree display. Like DOS' RD command, it is impossible to remove a non-empty directory in NCD—NCD displays an error message if you try to delete a directory which contains files.

If you use NCD to create (F7) and remove (F8) your directories, you won't need to rescan the disk with F2. NCD automatically updates the TREEINFO.NCD file when you use F7 or F8 to create or remove directories.

F9—Set Line Display

If you are using an EGA or VGA monitor, you can use the F9 key to change the number of lines shown on your display. Press F9, then use the up- or down-arrow key to select the number of lines to display and press Enter.

F10—Quit

Press F10 when you want to exit the NCD utility without changing directories. You can also press Esc to accomplish the same thing.

Volume Label Maintenance

DOS allows you to assign a special name, or volume label, to each disk you use. For example, you could assign the volume label MY C DISK to your C: disk or MY FLOPPY to a floppy disk. The DOS LABEL command lets you specify a volume label of up to 11 characters. Norton's NCD utility lets you specify volume labels up to 12 characters long, and provides volume label maintenance help. The active disk's volume label is displayed at the bottom right corner of the NCD screen (Figure 5.2). Press Alt-V to display the Volume Label dialog box shown in Figure 5.8.

107

Figure 5.8   Pressing Alt-V shows the Volume Label dialog box.

When the dialog box in Figure 5.8 is displayed you can either:

▶ change the label by typing over the existing one and pressing Enter, or

▶ press the Delete button to delete the volume label.

After you make your selection, the dialog box in Figure 5.8 is closed and the new volume label is shown at the bottom of the NCD screen.

Recovering a Deleted Directory

We discussed Norton's UNERASE utility in Chapter 3, which allows you to recover accidentally-deleted files. As you may already know, DOS has a built-in safeguard which prevents you from accidentally deleting a directory which contains files. However, you could write a batch file which automates the process of first deleting a directory of files and then removing the directory. Regardless of how you lose a directory full of files, to recover those files you must first recover their directory.

 Recovering Deleted Directories with UNERASE

1. Use the NCD utility to move to the parent of the deleted directory.

   For example, if you are trying to recover C:\TEMP, you should use NCD to make the root directory C:\ active.

2. Type the command UNERASE and press Enter.

   This starts the UNERASE utility and displays the initial UNERASE screen shown in Figure 5.9.

3. Press the up- or down-arrow key to highlight the directory you wish to recover (for example, ?EMP), press the right arrow key to highlight UNERASE, and press U.

   The first character dialog box is displayed.

4. Type the first character of the deleted directory's name (for example, T).

   This recovers the deleted directory and displays the screen in Figure 5.10. ☐

Figure 5.9   The initial UNERASE screen lets you choose the directory or file to recover.

Figure 5.10   When a directory or file has been successfully unerased, the file's first letter appears instead of a question mark.

In Chapter 3's discussion of the UNERASE utility, we saw that a deleted file's name (except for the first character) remains intact in a special table maintained by DOS. The same rule is true for deleted directories; that is why you must supply UNERASE with the first character of the directory you wish to recover.

After recovering a deleted directory, you might think that you would have automatically recovered everything in the directory as well. In reality however, you have only restored the directory name, *not* its contents. You must then use UNERASE to resurrect the recovered directory's subdirectories/files.

For example, let's assume I have a TEMP directory which contains several files and two subdirectories: WORK and FUN. Let's further assume that the WORK and FUN directories contain several files too. If I accidentally delete the contents of all three directories (TEMP, WORK, and FUN) and the directories themselves, I must use UNERASE twice to recover all the deleted directories.

The first UNERASE that I perform will recover the TEMP directory. I must use UNERASE to recover the WORK and FUN subdirectories within TEMP. Once all three directories are recovered I must use UNERASE to recover all the files in TEMP, WORK, and FUN. After I have successfully UNERASEd the directory (Figure 5.10), I can select the recovered directory and press Enter to see what files in that directory can be UNERASED (Figure 5.11).

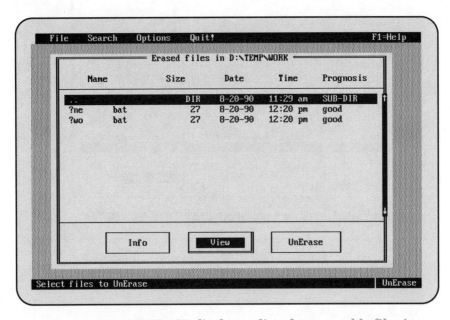

Figure 5.11   UNERASE displays a list of recoverable files in UNERASEd Directory.

I can then use the steps outlined in Chapter 3 to recover all the deleted files shown in Figure 5.11. Or, the Quick Steps outlined earlier in this chapter can be used to recover subdirectories from the recently-recovered directory.

Finding Your Way Through the Forest

After you have created many directories and subdirectories, it is very easy to become lost in the "disk forest." Even if you practice the best disk management techniques, it is possible to forget where you placed a file or two! Fortunately, the FILEFIND utility discussed in Chapter 3 includes two powerful features which let you locate files and text strings. Let's take a look at the file location feature first to see how you can use it to quickly locate a file on your disk.

111

FILEFIND Revisited

If you misplace a file on your hard disk, you could use DOS' DIR command to locate it. However, since the DIR command cannot report on more than one directory/subdirectory at a time, you would have to execute one DIR command for each directory/subdirectory on your disk. For example, if I am looking for the file MYSTUFF.DOC and my disk contains the following six directories:

```
D:\TEMP
D:\TEMP\WORK
D:\TEMP\GAMES
D:\MEMOS
D:\MEMOS\FUN
D:\MEMOS\SERIOUS
```

I may have to execute up to six DIR commands (for example, `DIR D:\TEMP\*.*`, `DIR D:\TEMP\WORK\*.*`, `DIR D:\TEMP\GAMES\*.*`, etc.) to locate the missing file. You may not think that six commands is too much work when you are looking for a misplaced file, but what if your disk has 100 directories? 1000 directories? Norton's FILEFIND utility lets you search for a misplaced file on one or more disks with only one command—regardless of how many directories your disks contain.

Q Searching for a File with FILEFIND

1. Type the command FILEFIND followed by the name of the file you wish to locate (for example, FILEFIND MYSTUFF.DOC).

   This starts the FILEFIND utility and searches for the specified file.

2. Press Enter.

□

The screen in Figure 5.12 shows the result of searching for MYSTUFF.DOC on my hard disk. As you can see in Figure 5.12, FILEFIND has determined that MYSTUFF.DOC is located in my MEMOS\SERIOUS subdirectory.

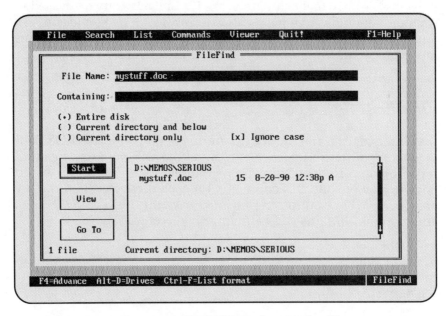

Figure 5.12   I can use FILEFIND to locate the file MYSTUFF.DOC no matter where it is on my disk.

The FILEFIND utility searches through all directories and subdirectories on the currently active drive. You can use the wildcard character * with a colon (i.e. *:) to force FILEFIND to search for the specified file on all drives. For example, the command FILEFIND *:MYSTUIFF.DOC instructs FILEFIND to look for MYSTUFF.DOC on all hard and floppy drives. This feature is especially handy if your hard disk is split into more than one logical partition and you wish to search the entire physical disk (for example, C:, D:, E:, etc.). Don't

worry about not having a disk in your floppy drive when using the
*: feature. If FILEFIND does not find a disk in a floppy drive when
*: is used, it simply continues with the next drive.

FILEFIND supports the DOS wildcard characters * and ? for full
or partial file name specifications. So if you cannot recall the full
name of a misplaced file, you can still use FILEFIND to locate it (for
example, `FILEFIND MY*.DOC` or `FILEFIND CHAPT?.BK`).

Searching for Text with FILEFIND

The FILEFIND utility does a fine job of locating misplaced files. Even
if you know only part of the misplaced file's name, you can use
FILEFIND to locate it. But what if you are looking for a file that
contains information about a trip you recently took to California?
Was the file named TRIP.RPT or CALIFOR.TRP? You have no idea
what name you gave the trip report file, but you *do* know the file
contains the string "trip report." FILEFIND can look inside each file
on the disk, and tell you which files contain your specific text string.

113

Q Searching for a Text String with FILEFIND

1. Type `FILEFIND` and press Enter.

   This starts the FILEFIND utility and displays the screen shown in Figure 5.13.

2. Press Tab, enter the text string you wish to locate (for example, `trip report`), and press Enter.

   This initiates a search for the text string "trip report" and displays a search completion message when finished.

3. Press Enter to acknowledge the search completion message.

   This displays a list of files containing the specified text string (Figure 5.14).

4. Use the up- and down-arrow keys to highlight a file shown in the list, and press Enter.

   This displays the viewer screen, which shows the contents of the selected file and highlights the search text.

5. Press F6 to see if there are any other occurrences of the specified text string in the file being viewed.

   This highlights the next occurrence of the specified text string, or displays a message if there are no more occurrences in the file. □

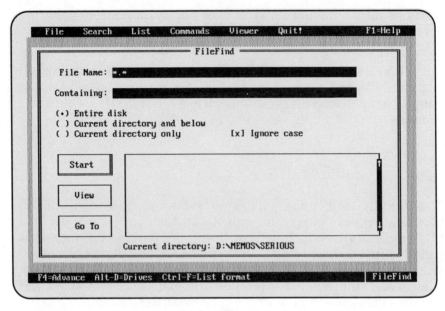

Figure 5.13   Initial FILEFIND Screen

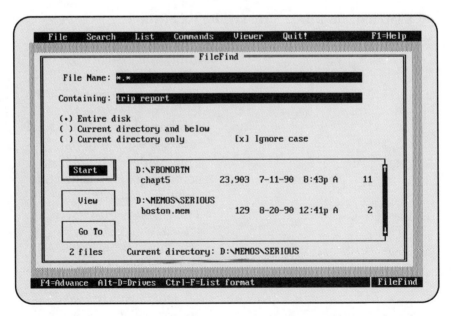

Figure 5.14   List of Files Containing Specified Text String

Press Esc when the viewer screen is displayed if you want to return to the list. You can then highlight a different file and press Enter to view it.

The list screen in Figure 5.14 shows file name, size, date, time, and attributes for all files containing the specified text string. The number of occurrences of the specified text string is also indicated after the file attributes. For example, in Figure 5.14 we can see that the string "trip report" occurs twice in the file BOSTON.MEM and 11 times in the file CHAPT5.

By default, FILEFIND is not case sensitive, so the steps above would find the string "Trip Report," "TRIP REPORT," or even "TrIp RePoRt." Although I almost never use it, FILEFIND does offer a case sensitivity option, /CS. If we had used the /CS option in the Quick Steps example, FILEFIND would only locate files containing the lower-case string "trip report."

The text search feature of FILEFIND is a fast and powerful tool which I use daily in my activities as a computer programmer. The Quick Steps described above show how to run FILEFIND interactively. Once you are comfortable with FILEFIND, you may want to specify all parameters on the command line to save time.

The command `FILEFIND C:\*.* "trip report" /S` provides the same results as the Quick Steps above. The /S option tells FILEFIND to search through all subdirectories. Notice that the text string *trip report* is enclosed in quotes here. When running FILEFIND from the command line, you must place the text string in quotes if it contains spaces. Without the quotes (i.e. `FILEFIND C:\*.* trip report /S`), FILEFIND searches for the string *trip* and ignores *report*.

What You Have Learned

In this chapter you learned about directories and tree structures. More specifically, you learned:

▶ A special directory called the root directory exists on all disks (for example, C:\). All other directories on a disk are either a direct or indirect descendent of the root directory.

▶ Although the CD command is adequate for moving about from directory to directory, the Norton Change Directory (NCD) utility offers a fast graphical approach to directory navigation.

▶ NCD offers a Speed Search feature so you can quickly jump from one directory to another without having to search for your destination with the arrow keys.

115

▶ DOS allows you to assign a special name or, volume label, to each disk you use. Norton's NCD utility lets you specify volume labels up to 12 characters long and offers a mechanism for volume label maintenance.

▶ Norton's UNERASE utility lets you recover deleted directories. Once a directory has been recovered, you can then use UNERASE again to recover deleted files/subdirectories within that directory.

▶ Norton's FILEFIND utility lets you search for a misplaced file on one or more disks with only one command, regardless of how many directories your disks contain.

▶ FILEFIND's text search feature can show you what files contain a specific text string.

116

Maintaining Your Hard Disk Drive

In This Chapter

▶ *Understanding disk structures*
▶ *Preserving important disk information*
▶ *Recovering data from an accidentally-formatted disk*
▶ *Wiping files from a disk*
▶ *Diagnosing and correcting disk problems*

This second chapter on disk utilities shows you how to avoid accidental data loss and explains the physical layout of DOS disks. First you will learn about the fundamental components and structure of DOS disks and how to interpret the disk information reported by Norton's SYSINFO utility. Then we will cover disk formatting and erasure utilities—and how to recover data from accidentally formatted disks. Chapter 6 concludes with coverage of Norton's Disk Doctor II (NDD) utility, which allows you to diagnose and correct disk problems.

Understanding Disk Structures

As the saying goes, "you don't have to know how the engine works before you can drive a car." The same rule holds true for PC users—you don't have to understand the internal workings of a computer to use a PC. A bit of technical insight certainly doesn't hurt, though—in fact, a basic knowledge of PC inner workings is almost mandatory before you can interpret and appreciate the information reported by the more advanced tools in the Norton Utilities.

In order to work with some of Norton's disk utilities, you must first understand the structure of a DOS disk. You have already been introduced to a few of the terms I will use in this discussion, so let's quickly review those first.

Bits, Bytes, Sectors and Clusters

You may recall from Chapter 2 that a binary digit, or *bit*, was defined as the smallest piece of data a computer can store. The discussion in Chapter 2 continued by defining a *byte* as a collection of 8 bits. A bit is very simple, and can only have a value of zero or one. As many as 256 different values can be indicated by combinations of ones and zeros in an eight-bit byte.

The computer industry has created a standard for assigning specific eight-bit values for a slew of characters, including all the ones that appear on your PC's keyboard. This standard is called the *ASCII character set*. (ASCII is an acronym for American Standard Code for Information Interchange.)

If a group of bits is called a byte, what do you call a group of bytes? How about a sector? A *sector* consists of 512 bytes. In order to quickly and easily address an entire disk's data area, DOS works with even larger, more manageable chunks of data called *clusters*.

The number of sectors in a cluster differ among disk types. For example, on my PC's hard disk each cluster is made up of 4 sectors, but on a high-density 5-1/4" floppy disk there is only one sector per cluster. It's not too important to understand why different disk types have different numbers of sectors per cluster. However, you should understand that 8 bits constitute a byte, 512 bytes make up a sector, and a cluster contains one or more sectors (depending on the disk type).

Tracks and Cylinders

Now that you know what sectors and clusters are, let's try to visualize them on a disk. The illustration in Figure 6.1 shows the circular disk platter inside a 5-1/4" disk.

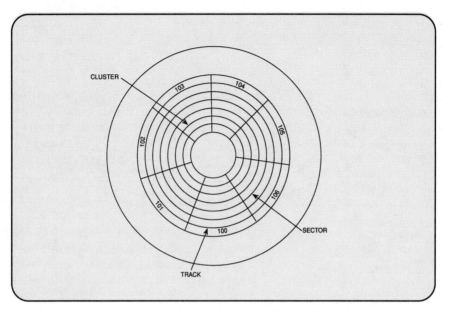

Figure 6.1   Groups of sectors form tracks around the surface of a disk.

As you can see in Figure 6.1, the sectors and clusters are arranged in a circular format; this format resembles the layout of the grooves in a record album. In Figure 6.1, sectors 100 through 106 form a circle on the disk surface. This circle of sectors is called a *track*. These days, virtually all floppy disks are double-sided, so we can say that there are tracks on both sides of the disk platter.

Now let's expand the discussion to include hard disks. The illustration in Figure 6.2 shows the surface of a hard disk.

Hard disks typically contain more than one platter. The hard disk in Figure 6.2 consists of 3 platters. The platters in a hard disk are stacked fairly close together, and each platter contains tracks, clusters and sectors just like floppy disks. In Figure 6.3, we've added an imaginary cylindrical object that appears to cut through the three platters in the hard disk.

The cylindrical object passes through six tracks on the hard disk in Figure 6.3. (Remember, each platter has two sides!) The collection of vertically-stacked tracks intersected by the object in Figure 6.3 is known as a *cylinder*.

Figure 6.2   Hard disks contain several disk platters.

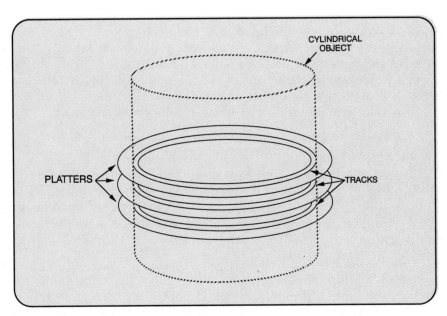

Figure 6.3   Vertically-stacked tracks form cylinders.

Disk Areas

The terms and concepts discussed so far in this chapter apply to all regions of a DOS disk—that is, the entire disk is made up of bits, bytes, sectors, etc. There are special regions or areas on a DOS disk where certain pieces of information must reside. These areas are known as the *system area* and the *data area*. Three components make up the system area: the boot record, the root directory, the file allocation table (or, FAT, for short).

Boot Record

The boot record resides in the *boot sector*, which is the first sector of the first track on the first side of a bootable DOS disk. The boot sector exists on all DOS disks regardless of whether the disk is bootable or not. (When you FORMAT a DOS disk, you can make it bootable by using the /S option, which causes the system files to be copied to the newly-formatted disk.) The information contained in the boot record of a bootable disk instructs DOS on how to bring itself up "by the bootstraps" and prepare for your commands.

121

Root Directory

The root directory area contains information about all the files and directories that reside in the root directory (for example, C:\). Each file and directory in the root has an entry in this area that contains information such as name, size, and date/time of creation. One of the most important items in a directory entry is a number which indicates the file or directory's offset in the file allocation table.

File Allocation Table (FAT)

The file allocation table, or FAT, indicates the status of all the clusters on a DOS disk. The information contained in the FAT is so important that DOS actually maintains two copies of the FAT on a disk, just in case something happens to the first copy. Unlike directories, the FAT is organized by clusters rather than by files. There is one entry in the FAT for each cluster on the disk. The illustration in Figure 6.4 shows the relationship between the root directory area and the FAT.

As you can see in Figure 6.4, the contents of the file LETTER.DOC

Figure 6.4   Relationship between Directory Area and FAT

122

starts in cluster #6. Looking at the 6th offset of the FAT in Figure 6.4, we can see that LETTER.DOC continues into cluster #7. The 7th offset of the FAT tells us that cluster #13 is the next cluster in the sequence for LETTER.DOC. Skipping down to the 13th offset of the FAT, we see that the next portion of LETTER.DOC resides in cluster #15. Finally, the 15th offset of the FAT contains the special value 'FFFF' which indicates the end of the file. So LETTER.DOC occupies 4 clusters on the disk: clusters #6, #7, #13, and #15. Figure 6.4 also shows a directory entry for a file named MEMO.DOC which occupies 2 clusters: #18 and #19.

The FAT in Figure 6.4 illustrates an important point about how DOS allocates clusters for a file. Although it is possible for a file to occupy sequential clusters (for example, MEMO.DOC, which uses clusters #18 and #19), quite often DOS may wind up utilizing non-sequential, or non-contiguous, clusters for a file (for example, LETTER.DOC, which uses clusters #6, #7, #13, and #15). A file which is stored in non-contiguous clusters is called a *fragmented file*. File fragmentation is a leading cause of disk inefficiency because it takes DOS longer to manipulate a file whose data is scattered across the disk. In Chapter 7 you'll see how to use Norton's SPEEDISK utility to determine if your disk contains a high percentage of fragmented files. SPEEDISK also lets you de-fragment your disk by re-writing all the files in contiguous clusters.

Data Area

The last area of a DOS disk is known as the data area. The data area is where all the data for your files and subdirectories is located. All sectors which are not part of the boot record, root directory, or FAT are part of the data area.

Now that you know some of the details behind DOS disk structures, let's revisit the SYSINFO utility and discuss the disk information it reports.

Obtaining Disk Information

Chapter 2's discussion of SYSINFO explained four of the five areas reported by this informative utility. The menu for SYSINFO's fifth area, Disks, offers 3 useful selections: Disk Summary, Disk Characteristics, and Partition Tables.

Q Looking at Disk Information with SYSINFO

1. Type the command `SYSINFO` and press Enter.

   This runs the SYSINFO utility and displays the System Summary screen.

2. Hold down the Alt key and press D; then press Enter.

   This activates the Disks menu, selects the Disk Summary option, and displays the Disk Summary screen.

3. Press Enter.

   This displays the Disk Characteristics screen.

4. Press Enter.

   This displays the Partition Tables screen. ☐

Disk Summary

The Disk Summary screen shown in Figure 6.5 shows four pieces of information, or fields, for each drive defined on your PC: Drive, Type, Size, and Default Directory. The first three fields are fairly self-explanatory; they show the drive's one-letter ID (for example, A:), the drive type (for example, 5-1/4"), and the drive's capacity (for ex-

123

ample, `1.2M`). The Default Directory field indicates the drive's default (active) directory. For example, if I change to the WORK directory of my C: drive using `CD C:\WORK`, WORK becomes the default directory for C:. Even if I move to my D: drive, WORK is still C:'s default directory.

Figure 6.5   The Disk Summary screen shows information about all disk drives on your PC.

Disk Characteristics

The Disk Characteristics screen shown in Figure 6.6 has two main areas: Logical Characteristics and Physical Characteristics.

As you can see in the Logical Characteristics portion of Figure 6.6, my C: drive has 512 bytes per cluster and each cluster contains 4 sectors. Further, there are 16,319 clusters on my C: drive. Using these figures, we can determine exactly how many bytes can be stored on C:. The formula for total capacity is:

Total. Capacity =
# of Bytes/Sector x # of Sectors/Cluster x # Clusters

Now let's insert the values for my C: drive to determine its total capacity:

Figure 6.6   The Disk Characteristics screen reports both logical and physical disk information.

> Total Capacity =
> 512 Bytes/Cluster x 4 Sectors/Cluster x 16,319 Clusters
> Total Capacity = 33,421,312 Bytes

The value shown in the Size area of Figure 6.6, 33 megabytes, is an approximation of the exact capacity we calculated.

The rest of the information shown in Figure 6.6 is not very fascinating unless you are interested in more low-level details about a disk. The Logical Characteristics portion also contains information about a disk's system and data areas, including the starting sector and number of sectors occupied by the FAT, root directory, and data area. The Physical Characteristics section reports a few other disk-related tidbits including the number of sides, tracks, and sectors per track.

Partition Tables

The Partition tables screen (Figure 6.7) shows detailed information about each of the partitions defined on your hard disk. You learned in Chapter 2 that hard disks are partitioned using the FDISK command. When you partition a hard disk with DOS' FDISK command, you are telling DOS how to configure the disk as one or more logical drives. Although you may only have one physical hard disk in your PC, you can have DOS treat it as several logical disks (for example, C:, D:, etc.). Each partition on your hard disk is shown as a line in the Partition Tables screen. The Partition Tables screen reports three important pieces of information: whether or not the partition is bootable (Boot), the partition's starting/ending side/track/sector, and the total number of sectors used by the partition.

Figure 6.7 **Starting and ending partition positions are indicated on the Partition Tables screen.**

126

The three disk-related screens in SYSINFO report several interesting facts about your PC's disk configuration. Now let's see how to use another Norton utility to safely and quickly format floppy or hard disks.

Formatting Disks

One of the first rules you learn when working with PCs is that all disks, whether hard or floppy, must be formatted (using DOS'

FORMAT command) before you can save files on them. DOS' FORMAT command is fairly simple to use. For example, to format the disk in drive A: you use the command FORMAT A:

Like most DOS commands, FORMAT offers a wide variety of options, and sometimes the meaning of these options is not completely obvious. As mentioned before, the /S option causes FORMAT to place the special system files on the formatted disk to make it bootable. Perhaps "B" (for "bootable") would have been a better choice for that feature, but the /B option is used for a totally different purpose! Fortunately for us, the Norton Utilities include a tool which offers a safe and friendly approach to disk formatting.

SFORMAT: The Safe Format Alternative

The SFORMAT utility provides an easy-to-use alternative to DOS' FORMAT command. Although SFORMAT supports many of FORMAT's command-line options, you don't need to remember them because SFORMAT allows you to interactively select formatting options on-screen.

127

Q Formatting a Floppy Disk with SFORMAT

1. Type the command SFORMAT and a disk drive identifier (for example, SFORMAT A:) and press Enter.

   This starts the SFORMAT utility and displays the initial SFORMAT screen shown in Figure 6.8.

2. Press Enter to accept the default SFORMAT settings shown in Figure 6.8.

   If files/directories currently exist on the specified disk, a warning message is displayed; otherwise SFORMAT begins formatting the specified disk.

3. If the warning message is displayed, press Enter to continue. Otherwise, wait until a completion message is displayed.

4. Press Esc twice.

   The screen in Figure 6.8 is displayed the first time Esc is pressed. The SFORMAT utility is terminated the second time Esc is pressed. ☐

```
 Configure                                                    F1=Help




                        ══ Safe Format ═══

      ┌ Drive ┐  ┌ Size ┐  ┌ System Files ─────┐  ┌ Format Mode ┐
      │  A:   │  │ 180K │  │ (•) Don't put on disk │  │ (•) Safe    │
      │  B:   │  │ 320K │  │ ( ) Put on disk     │  │ ( ) Quick   │
      │       │  │ 360K │  │ ( ) Leave space     │  │ ( ) DOS     │
      │       │  │ 1.2M │  └─────────────────────┘  └─────────────┘


          Volume Label: ▐████████▌       [x] Save IMAGE Info


              ┌ Begin format ┐          ┌   Quit   ┐
              └──────────────┘          └──────────┘




 Press ENTER to format or F10 to access the menu          Safe Format
```

Figure 6.8   SFORMAT offers several disk formatting options.

> ▶ **Note:** In Chapter 1 you read how the Norton Utilities' INSTALL program will optionally replace DOS' FOR-MAT command with Norton's SFORMAT Utility. If you instructed INSTALL to make this replacement, you can invoke the SFORMAT utility (in step #1) using either the FORMAT or SFORMAT command.

SFORMAT Options

The SFORMAT utility offers several formatting options. The current status of each of these options is shown on the screen in Figure 6.8. Use Tab to position the cursor in one of the six option areas of Figure 6.8: Drive, Size, System Files, Format Mode, Volume Label, and Save IMAGE Info.

The Drive portion of Figure 6.8 lists all the disk drives SFORMAT can access. Use the up- and down-arrow keys to highlight a drive to format. The Drive list might only show floppy disk drives, since SFORMAT can be configured to prevent formatting of hard disks. If you wish to allow SFORMAT to format hard disks, select the Hard Disks... option of the Configure menu and the screen in Figure 6.9 is displayed.

Figure 6.9   SFORMAT contains a hard disk safety feature, which can be bypassed via the Hard Disk Formatting dialog box.

Press the space bar to place an x next to the Allow Hard Disk Formatting option (shown in Figure 6.9) and press Enter. The initial SFORMAT screen (Figure 6.8) is re-displayed and the Drive portion includes a list of all formattable hard disks. Select the Save Settings option from the Configuration menu if you want to save the hard disk formatting option for future SFORMAT use.

In Chapter 2, you read about the difference between double- and high-density floppy disks. If your PC is equipped with a high-density disk drive, you have the option of formatting either high-, low-, or double-density diskettes. However, keep in mind the warning in Chapter 2: It is not a good idea to format double-density diskettes in a high-density drive.

The SFORMAT utility has the intelligence to know whether the specified drive is either 3-1/2" or 5-1/4". As a result, only valid disk format sizes for the specified drive are displayed in Figure 6.8. After pressing Tab, use the up- or down-arrow keys to select a different format size.

The System Files portion of the screen in Figure 6.8 lets you specify whether or not the system files should be copied to the formatted disk. The system files include all the files which make a disk bootable. You have three options for this selection. You can create

▶ a bootable disk,

▶ a non-bootable disk with room reserved for the system files, or

▶ a non-bootable disk with no room reserved for the system files.

There is an advantage to creating a non-bootable disk with room reserved for the system files—you have the option of easily making the disk bootable in the future (via DOS' SYS command) without having to reformat it. Use the up- and down-arrow keys and press space bar to select a different System Files option.

SFORMAT offers three different methods of formatting a disk: Safe mode, Quick mode, and DOS mode. Use the up- and down-arrow keys and press space bar to select a different Format Mode option.

Safe mode is safe because it does not affect a disk's data areas: it just resets the system area and performs some tests. This allows Norton's UNFORMAT utility (discussed later in this chapter) to easily recover all files from an accidentally-formatted disk. Safe mode also happens to be faster than DOS' FORMAT command. Use Safe mode when working with disks which have not previously been formatted.

When Quick mode is selected, SFORMAT simply clears the disk's file allocation table (FAT) and root directory—no tests are performed. Use Quick mode whenever you are working with a previously-formatted disk. Quick mode cannot be used on disks which have not previously been formatted.

If DOS mode is selected, SFORMAT emulates DOS' own FORMAT algorithm. This means that any files/subdirectories on the disk will be wiped out and unrecoverable after the format. Use this destructive format option with extreme caution!

The Volume Label option lets you attach a name (up to 11 characters) to a newly-formatted disk. This volume label is displayed every time you use DIR to list the disk's contents. Type in the desired volume label using any of the alphanumeric or symbol keys.

If you select the Save IMAGE Info option, SFORMAT will automatically run another utility, IMAGE. IMAGE saves a copy of the disk's system information in a special hidden file called IMAGE.DAT that another Norton Utility (UNFORMAT) can use to

130

recover files if you ever accidentally reformat the disk. (We will talk more about IMAGE and UNFORMAT later in this chapter.) Press space bar to select this valuable file recovery feature.

If you do select any of the special options described above, be sure to use the `Save Settings` option of the Configure menu to preserve your choices for the next time you use SFORMAT.

Preserving Important Disk Information

In Chapter 3 you learned how to use UNERASE to quickly recover accidentally-deleted files. You also learned that you can increase the chances of a successful file recovery by using UNERASE as soon as possible after an accidental deletion. In reality, however, that's not always possible—you may need to recover a file you accidentally deleted yesterday or last week. In addition, recovery of badly-fragmented files can be very difficult if not impossible, even with a powerful tool like UNERASE. To keep the odds of file recovery in your favor, I suggest regular use of Norton's IMAGE utility.

131

Maintaining a Good "Image"

The Norton Utilities tool IMAGE can be used to assist UNERASE and UNFORMAT (discussed later) in data recovery. The IMAGE utility saves a copy of a disk's system area (boot record, FAT, and root directory) in a hidden file called IMAGE.DAT. You may recall that SFORMAT can optionally create an IMAGE.DAT when you format a disk. The IMAGE utility gives you the ability to create/update the IMAGE.DAT file to make sure it reflects the most up-to-date system area information.

 Using IMAGE to Guard Against Data Loss

1. Type the command IMAGE and a disk drive identifier (for example, `IMAGE C:`).

2. Press Enter.

This starts the IMAGE utility. IMAGE runs by itself, and displays the screen shown in Figure 6.10 when it is finished. □

```
D:\NORTON5>image
Image, Norton Utilities 5.0, Copyright 1990 by Peter Norton

Finished updating IMAGE for drive D:

D:\NORTON5>
```

Figure 6.10   IMAGE Screen

I highly recommend you use IMAGE regularly to keep an updated IMAGE.DAT file on each partition of your PC's hard disk. The easiest way to do this is to include the IMAGE command in your AUTOEXEC.BAT file, which executes every time you boot your computer.

You can specify multiple disk drives on IMAGE's command line to update the IMAGE.DAT files for more than one disk partition. For example, the command IMAGE C: D: will update the IMAGE.DAT files on both the C: and D: drives. If IMAGE finds an IMAGE.DAT file on the specified disk, it first renames IMAGE.DAT to IMAGE.BAK and then creates a new IMAGE.DAT file. If you include IMAGE in your AUTOEXEC.BAT file, your hard disks will always contain two generations of system area information which can be used by UNERASE and UNFORMAT.

Recovering Data from an Accidentally Formatted Disk

It's a lot easier to accidentally delete a file than it is to accidentally format a disk. But since both scenarios are possible, the Norton Utilities include two important tools for data recovery: UNERASE for resurrecting deleted files, and UNFORMAT for rescuing data from an accidentally-formatted disk. We explored UNERASE in Chapter 3, and you will read more about it in Chapter 7. Now, let's see how to recover files with the powerful UNFORMAT utility.

> ▶ **Tip:** If you want to recover files from an accidentally-formatted hard disk and you haven't installed the Norton Utilities, *do not* install the utilities now! The Norton installation program copies all the utilities to your hard disk and may overwrite the files you wish to recover. Instead, insert the Norton Utilities Disk 2 into your A: (or B:) drive and substitute A:UNFORMAT (or B:UNFORMAT) for UNFORMAT in the Quick Steps which follow.

UNFORMATting a Disk

133

1. Type the command UNFORMAT and a disk drive identifier (for example, UNFORMAT A:) and press Enter.

   This starts the UNFORMAT utility and displays the IMAGE dialog box shown in Figure 6.11.

2. Press Enter to accept the default IMAGE selection.

   A summary of the selected disk's contents is then displayed.

3. Press Enter to acknowledge the contents summary message and continue the UNFORMAT process.

   This initiates the UNFORMAT process. A completion message is displayed when the process is complete.

If the disk you wish to UNFORMAT contains an up-to-date IMAGE.DAT file, the chances of a complete recovery are excellent. But don't worry if your formatted disk does not contain an IMAGE.DAT file—it is still possible that UNFORMAT will recover everything that was on the disk. Unfortunately, some versions of DOS' FORMAT command will overwrite all the data on a disk during the format process. If you were unfortunate enough to have accidentally formatted a disk with this sort of destructive FORMAT, even UNFORMAT won't be able to recover your files (remember, SFORMAT's DOS Mode performs a destructive format).

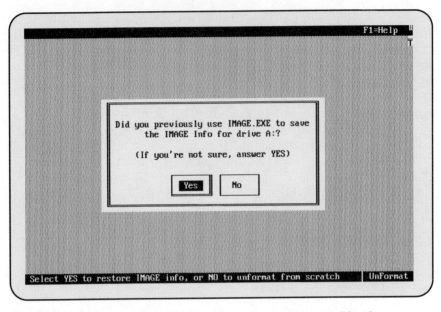

*Figure 6.11   UNFORMAT will utilize an IMAGE file if one
exists on the formatted disk.*

Analyzing an UNFORMATted Disk

If you had the foresight to always use a non-destructive format such
as the Quick or Safe modes of Norton's SFORMAT utility, you
should have no trouble with a full recovery after an accidental
format. It is also very important to make certain that all of your disks
contain an up-to-date IMAGE.DAT file. (Refer to the SFORMAT and
IMAGE utilities for IMAGE.DAT maintenance.)

Perhaps the most important rule to remember for data recovery
is to employ the services of a recovery tool like UNERASE or
UNFORMAT as soon as possible after the accidental deletion or
format occurs. The longer you wait before using UNERASE or
UNFORMAT, the greater the chances are of overwriting precious
data clusters. If the disk you wish to UNFORMAT was non-destruc-
tively formatted and contains an up-to-date IMAGE.DAT file,
UNFORMAT should be able to recover all your files with no
additional intervention on your part. When the UNFORMAT process is complete, you should carefully inspect the contents of the
disk and make certain the files and subdirectories are correct. If you
determine that some files or subdirectories are missing after an
UNFORMAT, you may need to use the UNERASE command to
complete the recovery process.

If UNFORMAT is unable to locate an IMAGE.DAT file but is able to recover files and subdirectories, you'll have to do some additional housekeeping when UNFORMAT finishes. Without the IMAGE.DAT file, UNFORMAT does not know the names of a disk's subdirectories. Therefore, UNFORMAT names the subdirectories DIR.0, DIR.1, DIR.2, etc. You'll need to use the NCD utility to rename these generically-named subdirectories.

Without the IMAGE.DAT file, UNFORMAT also has no idea what was contained in the disk's system area (boot record, FAT, and root directory). This means that UNFORMAT cannot recover the files that previously existed in the accidentally-formatted disk's root directory. You'll have to manually recover root directory files with the UNERASE utility (refer to the Manually UNERASEing Files section of Chapter 7).

> ▶ **Tip:** Refer to the DISKTOOL utility discussed in Chapter 7 if the UNFORMATted disk used to be bootable and you want to restore this feature.

135

Wiping Files from a Disk

In Chapter 3 you learned how to use the WIPEINFO utility to wipe a file from a disk so that its data cannot be recovered. WIPEINFO also lets you wipe an entire disk. Why would you want to wipe an entire disk? During the course of regular PC use, you are creating, copying, and deleting files which may contain sensitive data. As a result, some of this sensitive information may remain in unused clusters (because the DEL command doesn't remove a file's data from the disk). When the disk wipe feature is selected, WIPEINFO overwrites every part of the specified disk, including the unused clusters.

> ⊘ **Caution:** This utility should be used with extreme caution because it overwrites a file's data clusters and makes recovery with UNERASE impossible.

Wiping a Disk with WIPEINFO

1. Type the command WIPEINFO and press Enter.

   This starts the WIPEINFO utility and displays the WIPEINFO screen shown in Figure 6.12.

2. Press the right-arrow key, and

   then press Enter.

   This selects the Drives button in Figure 6.12 and displays the Wipe Drives screen shown in Figure 6.13.

3. Use the right- and left-arrow keys and press space bar to select the drive(s) to wipe.

4. Press Enter.

   A warning screen is displayed reminding you that you are about to destroy the contents of the disk in the specified drive.   □

136

Figure 6.12   The WIPEINFO utility lets you wipe individual files or entire disks.

5. Press Enter to continue the disk wipe process.

   WIPEINFO begins wiping the specified disk. A completion message is displayed when the wipe process is finished.

Figure 6.13   The Wipe Drives screen lets you select which drive(s) you wish to wipe.

6. Press Enter to acknowledge the wipe completion message.

The WIPEINFO screen in Figure 6.13 is redisplayed.   □

Depending upon whether you reconfigured WIPEINFO in Chapter 3 or not, WIPEINFO overwrites each byte in every cluster of the disk one or more times. You can also specify what value WIPEINFO should use when overwriting data on a disk. Refer to the WIPEINFO Configuration section in Chapter 3 for a full discussion of wiping options.

Diagnosing and Correcting Disk Problems

As an experienced PC user, I've had a few encounters with unreliable hard/floppy disks. Unreliable disks can cause a variety of problems, including corrupt and disappearing files. Although the failure rate for disks is very low, even the slightest disk failure can cause great distress!

Consider this scenario: Let's say you've been working on a report for your boss for several days. The report is quite a few pages long and includes a slew of important tables and figures which have taken hours to create. Just as you are about to print the final copy of the report, your PC informs you that the file is "unreadable," or worse yet, it can't even find the file! One of the best steps you can take to avoid and correct disk problems like this is to use Norton's Disk Doctor II (NDD) utility.

Testing a Disk with Norton Disk Doctor II (NDD)

1. Type the command NDD and press Enter.

   This starts the NDD utility and displays the operation screen shown in Figure 6.14.

2. Press Enter to select the Diagnose Disk option.

   This displays the Select Drives to Diagnose dialog box.

3. Use the up- and down-arrow keys to highlight the drive you wish to diagnose, and press Enter.

   NDD analyzes several areas of the specified disk; the Surface Test screen shown in Figure 6.15 is displayed when these tests are completed.

Figure 6.14   Select the desired NDD operation from the Norton Disk Doctor II operation screen.

138

Figure 6.15   The Surface Test screen offers several options for additional NDD disk tests.

Figure 6.16   The NDD completion screen reports the results of all tests performed.

4. Press Enter to accept the default settings shown in Figure 6.15 and begin the surface test.

NDD tests every sector of the specified disk and displays screen in Figure 6.16 when the test is complete.

5. Press Enter.

A report of the NDD session is created which can be viewed on the screen, printed out, or saved to a file.

□

NDD performs a variety of tests in step #3 of the preceding Quick Steps. During these tests, NDD examines the disk's partition table, boot record, file allocation table (FAT), directory structure and file structure. When these tests are complete, NDD examines the disk's FAT in search of *lost clusters*. A lost cluster is a cluster which does not belong to any file but is shown as being in use in the FAT.

The surface test in step #4 is the last test performed by the Norton Disk Doctor. Depending upon the options selected and the size of the disk being analyzed, the surface test can take anywhere from a few minutes to several hours to complete. When the default options are used, NDD tests each sector of the selected disk once and reports any problems it encounters.

Surface Test Configuration

The screen in Figure 6.15 shows all the options available for the surface test operation. These options can be changed each time you run NDD or you can modify and save your settings using the Options button in Figure 6.14. The Disk Doctor Options screen shown in Figure 6.17 is displayed when the Options button is selected.

Press Enter to select the Surface Test button in Figure 6.17 and the Surface Test Options screen (Figure 6.18) is displayed.

The Surface Test Options screen in Figure 6.18 closely resembles the Surface Test screen in Figure 6.15. Both offer four surface test settings: Test, Passes, Test Type, and Repair Setting. Use the Tab key to quickly jump from one setting area to the next. Then use the up- and down-arrow keys and the space bar to select new surface test settings.

The Test option in Figure 6.18 lets you choose between a Disk test and a File test. When the Disk test option is selected NDD tests every sector of the selected disk, including those sectors not currently used by any files/directories (such as unused sectors). Use the File test option if you want NDD to skip unused sectors and only test those sectors currently used by a file/directory.

Figure 6.17   You can customize NDD with the Disk Doctor Options screen.

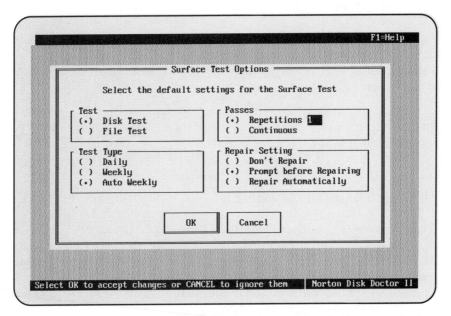

Figure 6.18   The Surface Test Options screen looks very similar to the Surface Test screen (Figure 6.15).

Use the Passes option to alter the number of times NDD runs the surface test. The default value is 1 but you can specify up to 999 repetitions. When the Continuous option is selected, NDD performs the surface test over and over again until you abort it by pressing Esc or the left mouse button.

The Test Type option in Figure 6.18 lets you select either a Daily, Weekly, or Auto Weekly test setting. The Daily test is less sophisticated and time-consuming than the Weekly test, but the Weekly test can uncover certain disk problems which may go undetected by the Daily test. The Auto Weekly test is a combination of the Daily and Weekly tests. When Auto Weekly is selected, NDD performs a Weekly test on Friday and a Daily test every other day of the week.

The last surface test configuration option lets you specify whether or not NDD should repair any disk problems it encounters. You may choose to:

142

▶ prevent NDD from making any repairs,

▶ have NDD prompt you before making repairs, or

▶ let NDD automatically make all repairs without asking for your approval.

NDD repairs disk problems by moving data from questionable clusters to more reliable locations on the disk. Further, NDD marks the questionable clusters as "bad" to prevent DOS from using them in the future.

Once you're satisfied with the surface test settings, press Enter, then select the Save Settings button on the Disk Doctor Options screen (Figure 6.17).

Other Disk Doctor Options

As you can see in the Disk Doctor Options screen (Figure 6.17), NDD offers two other configuration options: Custom Message and Tests to Skip. Use the Custom Message option if you want to display a special message when NDD encounters an error in its test process. The Set Custom Message screen shown in Figure 6.19 is displayed when you select the Custom Message button.

Press the space bar to select the Prompt with Custom Message option in Figure 6.19, then press Tab to move the cursor to the message box. Type the desired custom error message in the message box (for example, NDD has discovered a problem with your disk...please call 555-1234 to report this problem!). Use

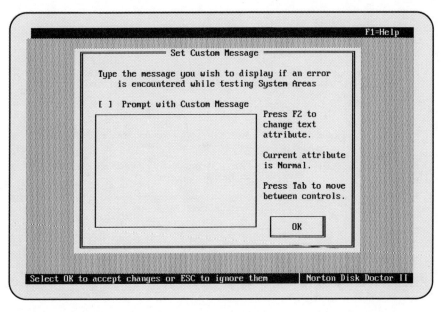

Figure 6.19   Use the Set Custom Message screen to create a special message which will be displayed when NDD encounters an error.

the F2 key to select a special attribute for the error message text. Sample text attributes include underline, bold, and reverse video. When you are satisfied with your custom error message, press Tab to highlight the OK button and then press Enter to return to the Disk Doctor Options screen (Figure 6.17). Finally, select the Save Settings button to save your custom error message.

Use the Tests to Skip option shown in Figure 6.17 when you want to prevent NDD from running certain tests on your PC. The Tests to Skip screen shown in Figure 6.20 is displayed when this option is selected.

NDD may run into problems during its test process if your computer is not a "true 100% IBM-compatible" PC. Certain compatibility problems may cause NDD to misbehave and lock up your PC. If your PC is having a problem running certain NDD tests, select the Skip option for those tests and re-run NDD. Be sure to save your Tests to Skip settings by using the Save Settings button on the screen in Figure 6.17.

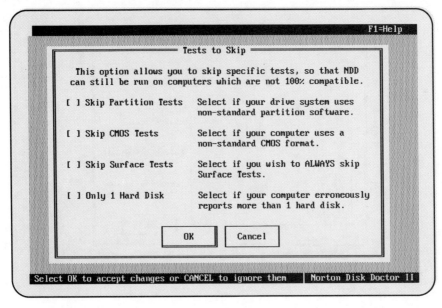

Figure 6.20 *You can define which tests NDD should skip using the Tests to Skip screen.*

Undoing NDD Repairs

Although NDD does a fine job of repairing most files, it is not infallible; that's why it's a good habit to always check its work. You should always create a report whenever you let NDD make repairs to a disk (refer to step #5 in the NDD Quick Steps). Read through the NDD report to see what files or areas of the disk were repaired. Then check the repaired files to ensure that they truly have been "fixed."

For example, NDD recently repaired a file of mine called MEMO.DOC. I know that MEMO.DOC is a WordPerfect file, so I used WordPerfect to load the MEMO.DOC file and check out the repairs. Fortunately, the repairs made by NDD appeared to fix the problems I had been having with MEMO.DOC. But what if my "fixed" file was in worse shape than it was in before NDD made its repairs? It occasionally happens; that's why NDD offers an undo feature.

It only takes a few moments to undo disk repairs made during the last NDD session—this is because NDD saves disk repair information in a special file called NDDUNDO.DAT. NDD can use this undo data file to restore a disk to the same condition it was in before the disk repairs were made. Select the Undo Changes button on the NDD Operation Screen (Figure 6.14), and follow the directions displayed to undo the disk repairs from the last NDD session.

What You Have Learned

In this chapter you learned about disk structures and several of the disk-related Norton Utilities. More specifically, you learned:

▶ 8 bits constitute a byte, 512 bytes make up a sector, and a cluster contains one or more sectors (depending on the disk type).

▶ There are special regions or areas on a DOS disk where certain pieces of information must reside. These areas are known as the system area and the data area.

▶ The SFORMAT utility provides an easy-to-use alternative to DOS' unfriendly FORMAT command.

▶ The IMAGE utility saves a copy of a disk's system area (boot record, FAT, and root directory) in a hidden file called IMAGE.DAT. The UNERASE and UNFORMAT utilities use IMAGE.DAT to assist in quick and easy file recovery.

▶ The WIPEINFO utility can destroy the contents of an entire disk, including the data held in unused clusters.

▶ The Norton Disk Doctor II (NDD) utility can diagnose and correct many common disk problems.

145

Advanced Disk Management

In This Chapter

▶ *Viruses and disk protection*
▶ *Miscellaneous disk tools*
▶ *Protecting sensitive files*
▶ *Using the disk editor*
▶ *Manually UNERASEing files*
▶ *Optimizing disk performance*

This chapter explains the mysteries behind some of the more advanced disk-related tools in the Norton Utilities. The tools covered in this final chapter on the Utilities offer a wide range of disk management power.

Chapter 7 begins with coverage of the DISKMON utility, which lets you monitor all disk activity on your system—a valuable tool for preventing computer "viruses" from wreaking havoc. The chapter continues with coverage of several other utilities which let you do everything from encoding sensitive files to editing any segment of a disk. The last portion of Chapter 7 shows how to use the Norton Utilities to optimize your hard disk's performance.

Viruses and Disk Protection

A computer virus is a program which can cause irreversible damage to the data on your hard disk. Viruses are the computer equivalent of bacterial warfare, usually created by mischievous computer whiz types. Viruses can find their way to your PC in a variety of ways; as a result, it's usually very difficult to determine exactly how and when a computer got "infected." To complicate matters, most viruses operate "behind the scenes" and can completely obliterate your hard disk before you even know what's happened!

Monitoring Disk Activity

148

Norton's DISKMON utility is a TSR (terminate-and-stay-resident program) that lets you monitor all disk activity on your system and can prevent computer viruses from destroying the contents of your hard disk. DISKMON also offers a disk park feature which protects your hard disk from damage when moving your PC from one location to another.

Q Preventing Unauthorized Disk Write Activity

1. Type the command DISKMON and press Enter.

   This runs the DISKMON utility and displays the Disk Monitor screen shown in Figure 7.1.

2. Press Enter.

   This selects the Disk Protect button and displays the Disk Protect screen shown in Figure 7.2.

3. Select the Entire Disk option, then highlight the On button and press Enter.

   This redisplays the Disk Monitor screen and shows the updated status of the Disk Protect feature.

4. Press Esc.

   The DOS prompt returns and DISKMON is activated as a TSR. □

Figure 7.1 *The Disk Monitor screen offers access to three useful disk utilities.*

Figure 7.2 *Use Norton's Disk Protect feature to prevent unauthorized disk access.*

When DISKMON is installed with the Entire Disk option, you will be notified before data is written to any disk on your PC (including both hard and floppy drives). The Disk Monitor dialog box shown in Figure 7.3 is displayed before each disk write operation.

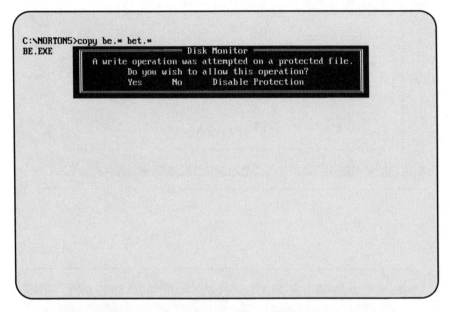

C:\NORTON5>copy be.* bet.*
BE.EXE

```
================== Disk Monitor ==================
A write operation was attempted on a protected file.
        Do you wish to allow this operation?
        Yes      No      Disable Protection
```

Figure 7.3   The Disk Monitor dialog box pops up whenever an application tries to write to a protected.disk.

Press Y to permit or N to prohibit the write operation when the dialog box in Figure 7.3 is displayed. The Disk Monitor dialog box may pop up several times during one file copy or save operation. Press D to temporarily disable the disk monitor feature when the Disk Monitor dialog box is displayed. You can also disable the disk monitor directly from the DOS prompt by executing the command DISKMON /PROTECT- To reactivate the disk monitor execute the command DISKMON /PROTECT+ at the DOS prompt.

Disk Monitor Options

The Disk Protect screen shown in Figure 7.2 offers several disk monitor options. If you're not concerned with entire disk protection, you can elect to protect just the system areas (boot record, FAT, and root directory) or files. In addition, you can use the Files and Exceptions selectors in Figure 7.2 to specify exactly which files you do and do not want protected. For example, let's say you want to monitor all Microsoft Excel spreadsheet data files except for those whose filenames start with TEMP. You could specify `*.XLS` in the Files column and `TEMP*.XLS` in the Exceptions column of the Disk Protect screen.

Depending on the Disk Protect level selected, certain disk operations may cause the Disk Monitor dialog box (Figure 7.3) to pop up several times for write acknowledgement. The disk format process is a good example of an operation which can cause an enormous number of acknowledgement requests. The Allow Floppy Format option listed in the Disk Protect screen lets you format floppy disks without being bothered by the Disk Monitor dialog box. You should consider activating this option if you need to format floppy disks fairly often.

Disk Light

In addition to the Disk Protect feature discussed above, the DISKMON utility lets you monitor all disk activity (disk reads and writes) in a more simplistic fashion. When DISKMON's Disk Light feature is activated, the TSR displays the ID of the drive where disk read/write activity is occurring. The active disk drive ID (for example, C:) is displayed in the top right corner of the screen. Use the /LIGHT+ and /LIGHT- options to turn the Disk Light feature on and off from the DOS command line (i.e. `DISKMON /LIGHT-` disables the Disk Light feature).

> ▶ **Note:** The Disk Protect and Disk Light features will only display messages while your monitor is in text mode. If you are running a graphics mode application (like Microsoft Windows), DISKMON cannot display Disk Protect/Light messages.

Parking Your Hard Disk

Before you move your PC from one position to another, it is *very important* to prepare your hard disk for the relocation process. Hard disk drives are very sensitive devices and can easily be damaged while in transit. Use DISKMON's Disk Park feature to ensure your hard disk's safety before moving your PC. Select the `Disk Park` button on the Disk Monitor screen (Figure 7.1) and the Disk Park dialog box shown in Figure 7.4 is displayed.

Figure 7.4   Park your hard drive to prevent damage during transportation of your PC.

As the dialog box in Figure 7.4 notes, DISKMON has parked your hard disk and you should immediately power down your PC. I suggest using DISKMON to park your hard disk every day before you turn off your PC; you never know when you may need to move your system. You can also use DISKMON's /PARK option to park your disk directly from the DOS prompt (for example, `DISKMON /PARK`).

Miscellaneous Disk Tools

In earlier versions of the Norton Utilities (before release 5.0), the Norton Disk Doctor (NDD) included a feature called Common Solutions. The Common Solutions available through NDD let you perform three useful disk operations: make a disk bootable, recover from DOS' RECOVER command, and revive a defective diskette.

In version 5.0 of the Norton Utilities, the three operations which used to be part of NDD's Common Solutions are now available in a separate utility called DISKTOOL. The DISKTOOL utility also offers a couple of other valuable disk tools which let you mark bad clusters and save/restore important hard disk configuration information.

Using DISKTOOL to Make a Disk Bootable

The DISKTOOL utility can make a formatted disk bootable regardless of whether space was allocated for system files when the disk was originally formatted. (Refer to the SFORMAT Options section of Chapter 6 for a discussion of placing system files on a disk during the format process.)

 Making a Disk Bootable

153

1. Type the command DISKTOOL and press Enter.

   This runs the DISKTOOL utility and displays the Disk Tools information screen.

2. Read the information presented on the Disk Tools screen, then press Enter.

   The Disk Tools selection screen shown in Figure 7.5 is displayed.

3. Highlight the Make a Disk Bootable selection in the Procedures box and press Enter.

   This displays a disk drive selection dialog box.

4. Highlight the drive ID of the disk you wish to make bootable (for example, A:) and press Enter.

   If you select a floppy disk drive in this step, DISKTOOL will ask you to insert a disk in the drive and press Enter. DISKTOOL then begins the process of making the selected disk bootable. □

In order for a disk to be considered bootable, it must contain a couple of special hidden system files and DOS' command interpreter, COMMAND.COM. The Quick Steps outlined above place COMMAND.COM and the hidden system files on the specified disk. DOS' SYS command is also capable of copying the special hidden system files to a formatted disk. However, SYS *only* copies the hidden files and does *not* copy COMMAND.COM. You have to manually copy COMMAND.COM after running SYS to make a disk bootable. It's very easy to forget to copy COMMAND.COM to a disk after running SYS, so use DISKTOOL instead of SYS whenever you need to make a disk bootable.

```
                                                              F1=Help

                        ╔═══════ Disk Tools ═══════╗

             ┌──────── Procedures ────────┐  ┌──────── Description ────────┐
             │ Make a Disk Bootable       │  │ This procedure will make a  │
             │ Recover from DOS's Recover │  │ hard or floppy disk bootable.│
             │ Revive a Defective Diskette│  │                             │
             │ Mark a Cluster             │  │ Use this procedure instead of│
             │ Create Rescue Diskette     │  │ DOS's SYS command, which has │
             │ Restore Rescue Diskette    │  │ many limitations that this  │
             │                            │  │ procedure can overcome.     │
             │                            │  │                             │
             └────────────────────────────┘  └─────────────────────────────┘

                    ┌─────────────┐    ┌─────────────┐
                    │   Proceed   │    │    Quit     │
                    └─────────────┘    └─────────────┘

   Select PROCEED to execute, or QUIT to exit program        │ Disk Tools
```

Figure 7.5   The DISKTOOL utility offers several selections for disk operations.

Backtracking after a Disk RECOVERy

If you've ever used DOS' RECOVER command to rescue files from a defective disk you're probably familiar with the mess it can create. When you ask RECOVER to recover a disk (for example, RECOVER A:) it gathers all the files and directories on the disk, places them in the root directory, and gives them meaningless names like file0001.rec, file0002.rec, etc. When RECOVER is finished, it's up to you to inspect each of the filexxxx.rec files and determine its real name and whether it represents a file or a directory! Use DISKTOOL instead of RECOVER, or to undo the mess created by RECOVER and return a disk to a more acceptable condition.

Q Undoing a Disk RECOVERy

1. Type the command DISKTOOL and press Enter.

   This runs the DISKTOOL utility and displays the Disk Tools information screen.

2. Read the information presented on the Disk Tools screen, then press Enter.

   The Disk Tools selection screen shown in Figure 7.5 is displayed.

3. Highlight the `Recover from DOS' Recover` selection in the Procedures box and press Enter.

This displays a RECOVERy information screen.

4. Read the information presented in the RECOVERy information screen, and press Enter.

This displays a disk drive selection dialog box.

5. Highlight the drive ID of the disk you wish to un-RECOVER (for example, `A:`) and press Enter.

If you select a floppy disk drive in this step, DISKTOOL will ask you to insert a disk in the drive and press Enter. DISKTOOL then displays a couple of warnings before actually performing the unRECOVER; highlight the `Yes` button for each message and press Enter to continue the unRECOVER operation. □

155

DISKTOOL does the best it can to return a disk to its pre-RECOVER condition, but it cannot recreate the names of the files and directories in the root directory—RECOVER zaps them permanently. Therefore, DISKTOOL is forced to use generic names for root directory entries when it undoes the RECOVER operation. When you inspect the contents of a disk after undoing a RECOVER, you'll notice that DISKTOOL uses generic names for root directory entries. For example, the files in the root directory are named file0001, file0002, etc. and the directories are named DIR00000, DIR00001, etc. You must rename these root directory entries to reflect their original names. The non-root directory entries (subdirectories and files in directories/subdirectories) on an unRECOVERed disk should appear as they did before the RECOVER operation.

Reviving a Defective Diskette

The third item in the Procedures box of the Disk Tools selection screen (Figure 7.5), Revive a Defective Diskette, lets you reformat a questionable disk without destroying the disk's contents. You should use this selection if you cannot read files from a disk and you want to preserve the data it contains. To revive data from a defective diskette, select the `Revive a Defective Diskette` option and follow the simple directions provided by the DISKTOOL utility.

Marking Clusters

In Chapter 6 you learned that the Norton Disk Doctor II (NDD) can diagnose and correct many common disk problems. When NDD finds a questionable cluster, it can move that cluster's data to a new location and mark the bad cluster so DOS doesn't try to use it in the future. The DISKTOOL utility also lets you mark bad clusters so DOS doesn't try to use them for data storage. To mark a bad cluster with DISKTOOL, select the Mark a Cluster option from the Procedures box of the Disk Tools selection screen (Figure 7.5) and follow the directions that are displayed.

It's usually best to let an intelligent utility like NDD take care of marking bad clusters. DISKTOOL lets you randomly designate certain clusters as "bad" without performing any test on them. Marking "good" clusters as "bad" is not dangerous since DISKTOOL, like NDD, moves the data in the bad cluster to a different location. However, DISKTOOL also lets you mark **bad** clusters as **good**—which can be very dangerous! There's usually a good reason why "bad" clusters have been marked as such, and you should probably avoid re-marking a bad cluster as good.

156

Using a Rescue Diskette

The last two features in the DISKTOOL utility can be used to preserve and restore valuable system information. The DISKTOOL utility lets you create a "rescue diskette" containing the following system parameters: partition tables, boot records, and CMOS values. If your PC ever loses track of any of this system information, you can use the DISKTOOL utility to restore the values from the rescue diskette.

Q Creating a Rescue Diskette

1. Type the command DISKTOOL and press Enter.

   This runs the DISKTOOL utility and displays the Disk Tools information screen.

2. Read the information presented on the Disk Tools screen, then press Enter.

   The Disk Tools selection screen shown in Figure 7.5 is displayed.

3. Highlight the Create Rescue Diskette selection in the Procedures box and press Enter.

   This displays the Create Rescue Diskette information screen.

4. Press Enter.	This displays a disk drive selection dialog box.
5. Highlight the drive ID of the rescue diskette location (for example, A:) and press Enter.	The DISKTOOL utility saves your PC's system information on the rescue diskette. □

Use the last DISKTOOL selection, Restore Rescue Diskette, as a last resort when you cannot access partitions on your hard disk and the Norton Disk Doctor II (NDD) utility cannot revive the disk.

Protecting Sensitive Files

The DOS ATTRIB command and Norton's FILEFIND utility can both be used to turn on the hidden file attribute for any personal/sensitive files you want to protect on your PC; this is a good way to keep confidential files private since hidden files do not appear in directory listings. However, if someone is clever enough, they can use ATTRIB or the Norton Utilities to un-hide your hidden files and expose your secrets.

157

Encrypting Files

To more effectively protect your private files, you should use Norton's DISKREET utility, which encrypts, or encodes, files so nobody else can interpret them.

 Encrypting a File with DISKREET

1. Type the command DISKREET and press Enter.	This runs the DISKREET utility and displays the Diskreet screen shown in Figure 7.6.
2. Press Enter to select the Files button.	The Files menu is displayed.
3. Press Enter to select the Encrypt... option in the Files menu.	This displays the Encryption File Selection screen shown in Figure 7.7.

4. Use the arrow keys to change the selected directory/drive and highlight the file you wish to encrypt. Then press Enter.

This displays the File Encryption Output screen.

5. Press Enter to accept the default encrypted file name.

The encryption password request screen is displayed.

6. Enter a secret password for the encrypted file (minimum of 6 characters) and press Enter.

The password re-entry screen is displayed.

7. Type the secret password again for verification and press Enter.

DISKREET encrypts the selected file and displays a message when the process is complete. □

158

Figure 7.6   Use DISKREET to protect personal files.

Be careful when selecting an encryption password for step #6 above. You'll need to specify this password later when you try to decode, or decrypt, the file. Don't use simple passwords like your name, address, phone number, etc. because they are obvious choices for others who may try to decrypt your files. On the other hand, don't use passwords which might easily be forgotten, because there's no way to reveal an encrypted file's password—if you forget the password you may never be able to decrypt the file.

Figure 7.7   Use the Encryption File Selection screen to specify which file(s) you wish to encrypt.

Encryption Options

Select the `File options...` entry in the Files menu to display the File Encryption Options screen shown in Figure 7.8.

The DISKREET utility offers two methods of file encryption. The default DISKREET encryption method uses a proprietary encoding technique, and the other method uses the Data Encryption Standard (DES) technique, which has been approved by the U.S. Government as a highly secure encryption standard. Use the arrow keys and space bar to select the desired encryption method.

The other four options shown in Figure 7.8 let you specify:

▶ whether the original file should be deleted after encryption,

▶ whether the encrypted file's read-only and hidden attributes should be set, and

▶ whether the same password should be used for encryption throughout the DISKREET session.

The password retention option is a handy feature if you want to encrypt several files with the same password. When this option is turned on, you only have to enter the encryption password once

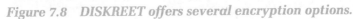

Figure 7.8   DISKREET offers several encryption options.

during the DISKREET session. Use the up- and down-arrow keys and the space bar to select the desired DISKREET options, then highlight the Save button and press Enter to preserve the settings.

Decrypting Files

The DISKREET file decryption process is very similar to the encryption process. Pull down the Files menu and select the Decrypt... option to display the Decryption File Selection screen shown in Figure 7.9.

Use the arrow keys to change the selected directory/drive and highlight the file you wish to decrypt. Then press Enter, and the password request screen is displayed. Enter the password you used to encrypt the file and press Enter. If the correct password is entered, DISKREET will decrypt the specified file and display a message when the process is complete.

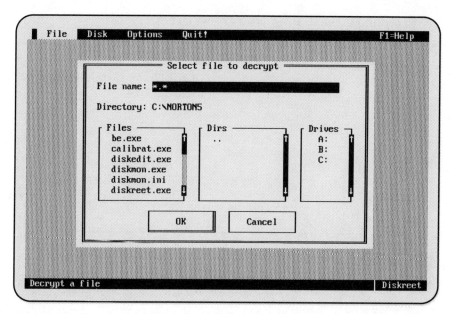

Figure 7.9   Use the Decryption File Selection screen to specify which files you wish to decrypt.

Using the Disk Editor

There are many tools you can use to view the contents of files on your disks. DOS' TYPE command offers one of the easiest ways to view, or dump, a file. To display the contents of a file called LETTER.DOC, use the command TYPE LETTER.DOC. TYPE does a pretty good job as long as the file you specify consists solely of displayable ASCII characters (like AUTOEXEC.BAT and CONFIG.SYS). If you try to use TYPE to view the contents of an executable file (for example, TYPE NORTON.EXE), however, you'll wind up with a bunch of gobbledygook on your screen and your PC may even beep a few times!

As you can see, we need something more powerful than TYPE if our goal is to view the contents of any file on a disk. To complicate matters further, what if you want to browse through other non-file areas of a disk such as the boot record, FAT, or unused clusters? Better yet, what if you're interested not only in viewing but also modifying or editing the contents of any area of a disk? The Norton Utilities include a disk editor (DISKEDIT), which lets you perform a wide variety of tasks including viewing/editing virtually any byte on a disk.

161

Browsing through Files with DISKEDIT

1. Type the command DISKEDIT and press Enter.

   This runs the DISKEDIT utility and displays the DISKEDIT screen shown in Figure 7.10.

2. Use the Object menu to change the active drive/directory if necessary.

3. Highlight the desired file (for example, C:\NORTON5\ READ.ME) and press Enter.

   This displays a hexadecimal/ ASCII view of the selected file (Figure 7.11). □

```
  Object   Edit   Link   View   Info   Tools   Quit                F1=Help
 Name    .Ext     Size      Date      Time    Cluster Arc R/O Sys Hid Dir Vol
 Cluster 5,594, Sector 22,805
 .                      0   7-24-90   5:23 pm   5594                  Dir
 ..                     0   7-24-90   5:23 pm      0                  Dir
 DISKREET EXE     156918   7-17-90   5:00 pm   1492
 DISKREET SYS      52886   7-17-90   5:00 pm  14241
 PCSHADOW SYS        848   7-17-90   5:00 pm  14267
 NORTON   OVL      87068   8-15-90   8:49 am  14268
 FILESAVE EXE      86248   7-17-90   5:00 pm  14311
 READ     ME       23552   7-17-90   5:00 pm  14354
 NDD      EXE     187344   7-17-90   5:00 pm  14366   Arc
 UNERASE  EXE     171447   7-17-90   5:00 pm  14458   Arc
 FILEFIX  EXE     137082   7-17-90   5:00 pm  14542   Arc
 UNFORMAT EXE      74084   7-17-90   5:00 pm  14609   Arc
 CALIBRAT EXE     124566   7-17-90   5:00 pm  14646   Arc
 IMAGE    EXE      11894   7-17-90   5:00 pm  14707   Arc
 DISKEDIT EXE     216730   7-17-90   5:00 pm  14713   Arc
 DISKTOOL EXE     122712   7-17-90   5:00 pm  14819   Arc
 Cluster 5,594, Sector 22,806
 BE       EXE      24304   7-17-90   5:00 pm  14879
 SFORMAT  EXE      91256   7-17-90   5:00 pm  14891
   Sub-Directory                                  Cluster 5,594 ▲
   C:\NORTON5                                     Offset 0, hex 0 ▼
   Press ALT or F10 to select menus              │ Disk Editor
```

Figure 7.10 This DISKEDIT Listing screen shows a listing of the active directory.

A Note on Hexadecimal Notation

Most of the information shown in Figure 7.11 may not be meaningful to you if you're unfamiliar with hexadecimal notation. The hexadecimal or, hex, numbering system is very similar to the decimal number system we use every day. In the decimal number system values are written using some combination of the 10 digits 0 through 9 (e.g. 1, 490, 27662, etc.). These same 10 digits are also used by the hex number system along with 6 additional values, A through F.

```
  Object   Edit   Link   View   Info   Tools   Quit              F1=Help
Cluster 14,354, Sector 57,845
00000000:  0D 0A 20 20 20 20 20 20 - 20 20 20 20 20 20 20 20   ♪☺
00000010:  20 20 57 65 6C 63 6F 6D - 65 20 74 6F 20 74 68 65     Welcome to the
00000020:  20 4E 6F 72 74 6F 6E 20 - 55 74 69 6C 69 74 69 65    Norton Utilitie
00000030:  73 20 56 65 72 73 69 6F - 6E 20 35 2E 30 21 0D 0A   s Version 5.0!♪☺
00000040:  20 20 20 20 20 20 20 20 - 20 20 20 20 20 20 2D 2D                 --
00000050:  2D 2D 2D 2D 2D 2D 2D 2D - 2D 2D 2D 2D 2D 2D 2D 2D   ----------------
00000060:  2D 2D 2D 2D 2D 2D 2D 2D - 2D 2D 2D 2D 2D 2D 2D 2D   ----------------
00000070:  2D 2D 2D 2D 2D 2D 2D 2D - 2D 2D 2D 2D 2D 2D 0D 0A   ------------♪☺
00000080:  0D 0A 20 20 20 20 20 20 - 20 54 68 69 73 20 66 69   ♪☺        This fi
00000090:  6C 65 20 63 6F 6E 74 61 - 69 6E 73 20 69 6E 66 6F   le contains info
000000A0:  72 6D 61 74 69 6F 6E 20 - 77 68 69 63 68 20 64 6F   rmation which do
000000B0:  65 73 6E 27 74 20 61 70 - 70 65 61 72 20 69 6E 20   esn't appear in
000000C0:  74 68 65 20 6D 61 6E 75 - 61 6C 2E 0D 0A 0D 0A 20   the manual.♪☺♪☺
000000D0:  20 20 20 20 20 20 20 20 - 20 20 20 20 20 20 20 49                  I
000000E0:  66 20 79 6F 75 20 77 6F - 75 6C 64 20 6C 69 6B 65   f you would like
000000F0:  20 74 6F 20 70 72 69 6E - 74 20 74 68 69 73 20 66    to print this f
00000100:  69 6C 65 2C 20 74 79 70 - 65 3A 0D 0A 0D 0A 20 20   ile, type:♪☺♪☺
00000110:  20 20 20 20 20 20 20 20 - 20 20 20 20 20 20 20 20
00000120:  20 20 20 20 20 20 20 20 - 20 20 43 4F 50 59 20 52             COPY R
00000130:  45 41 44 2E 4D 45 20 50 - 52 4E 3A 0D 0A 0D 0A 20   EAD.ME PRN:♪☺♪☺
  File                                              Cluster 14,354 ▲
  C:\NORTON5\read.me                                 Offset 0, hex 0 ▼
Press ALT or F10 to select menus                     │  Disk Editor
```

Figure 7.11   Here, DISKEDIT shows a hexadecimal/ASCII view of the file READ.ME.

Valid hex numbers include: 4A, 11, and 3FC. It is customary to prefix a hex number with a dollar sign ($) to avoid ambiguity with decimal numbers. So our list of valid hex numbers may also be written as: $4A, $11, and $3FC.

You don't have to understand hex to use DISKEDIT! In fact, you don't even have to know how to convert between hex and decimal—DISKEDIT includes a built-in hex-to-decimal conversion utility. Select the Hex converter... option from the DISKEDIT Tools menu and the Converter dialog box is displayed. The Converter can convert from hex to decimal or vice versa and it shows the ASCII character value of the number specified. In Figure 7.12 the Converter shows that the hex value $4D is equal to the decimal value 77 which is the ASCII value of the M character.

Working with the Hexadecimal/ASCII View

Each row of information in Figure 7.11 shows the hexadecimal and ASCII values of 16 bytes in the selected file. The column of numbers along the left side of Figure 7.11 shows the offset (in hex) of the first byte in each row. The offset is a position indicator which is relative

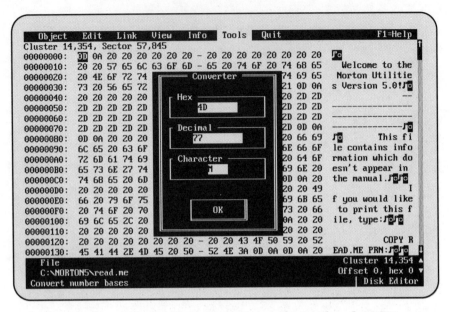

Figure 7.12   The hex converter shows decimal and ASCII translations of hex values.

to the beginning of the selected file. For example, the first byte in the file is at offset 0, the second byte is at offset 1, the third byte is at offset 2, etc.

The row of hex values starting at offset 00000010 is:

```
20 20 57 65 6C 63 6F 6D - 65 20 74 6F 20 74 68 65
```

Note: The dash between 6D and 65 shows the midpoint of the line of 16 bytes and is not part of the data itself.) If you use the Converter to translate each of these values you would learn that a hex 20 is a space, hex 57 is W, hex 65 is e, hex 6C is l, hex 63 is c, etc. This same information is shown on the right side of the row in Figure 7.11; the ASCII translation for the 16 bytes in offset row 00000010 is **Welcome to the**:

```
20 20 57 65 6C 63 6F 6D - 65 20 74 6F 20 74 68 65
      W  e  l  c  o  m      e     t  o     t  h  e
```

You can use any of the arrow keys to move the cursor from one row or byte to another. When you're viewing a file with DISKEDIT there are two highlight blocks which are used in conjunction with the blinking cursor. The highlight blocks work together to easily show the selected byte's location in both the hex and ASCII portions of the line. You can move the blinking cursor from the hex highlight box to the ASCII highlight box, or vice versa, by pressing Tab.

You can modify any of the values in the selected file if DISKEDIT is not restricted to read-only mode. (Note: Read-only mode may be turned on or off by using the `Configuration...` selection in the Tools menu. You should probably leave DISKEDIT in read-only mode until you become more familiar with how the utility works.) DISKEDIT accepts byte modifications in either hex or ASCII depending on the location of the blinking cursor; simply type the new hex/ASCII value(s) over the existing value(s). Press Enter when you are finished entering changes and DISKEDIT displays a dialog box indicating which cluster was modified. You then have the opportunity to write or discard your changes and return to the DISKEDIT Directory Listing screen (Figure 7.10).

Selecting Other Views and Objects

The hex/ASCII view shown in Figure 7.11 is useful when you're looking for a detailed view of the selected file. DISKEDIT offers several other views depending on the type of data you're working with. The READ.ME file we viewed earlier is a text file which is somewhat difficult to read using the hex/ASCII view. READ.ME is shown in a more readable format if you select the `As Text` option in the View menu (Figure 7.13).

DISKEDIT has enough intelligence to select the appropriate view depending on the type of object being displayed. For example, the `As Directory` option is used to display the directory listing in Figure 7.10.

As we saw earlier, DISKEDIT's Object menu lets you change the active drive/directory. The Object menu also provides several other selections including an option to display either the primary or secondary copy of the active drive's FAT. The screen in Figure 7.14 is displayed when the `1st Copy of FAT` option is selected from the Object menu.

When DISKEDIT displays a FAT it shows the information in a FAT-view format. You can use the arrow keys to highlight different clusters in the FAT-view. Each value shown in the FAT-view screen indicates the status of a particular cluster. It's very easy to trace through the chain of clusters used in a file, especially since DISKEDIT highlights the chain in a special color (or places double greater-than signs (>>) next to each cluster in the chain on a monochrome monitor). If you're curious to find out what file the highlighted chain

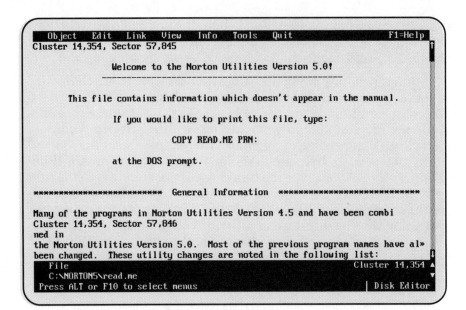

Figure 7.13   The Text View selection shows READ.ME in a
much more readable format.

Figure 7.14   You can browse through the FAT with DISKEDIT.

of clusters represents press Enter and the directory screen is displayed—the file represented by the chain of clusters on the FAT screen is automatically highlighted on the directory screen. As you saw earlier, you can press Enter again to view the contents of that file.

DISKEDIT is perhaps the most powerful and flexible Norton utility—it's so powerful, in fact, that in the hands of a novice user it can be quite lethal! Accidental modification of the wrong byte in a file, FAT, directory, etc. may cause major headaches for you and anyone else who uses your PC. So be careful when using DISKEDIT. As a precaution, you may want to consider leaving the DISKEDIT utility in read-only mode (see the Configuration... selection in the Tools menu). Now let's see how to use the advanced features of UNERASE to manually recover accidentally-deleted files.

Manually UNERASEing Files

In Chapter 3 you learned how to use Norton's UNERASE utility to resurrect accidentally-deleted files. The unerase process can be very quick and simple if there has been little disk activity since the accidental deletion. Every time you COPY a file, save a file from a word processor, etc. you run the risk of overwriting the unprotected data of a deleted file. Therefore, the chances of recovering an accidentally-deleted file are best if you run UNERASE immediately after the deletion.

The UNERASE utility reports a recovery prognosis for each deleted file it finds on your disk (Figure 7.15).

UNERASE usually has no problem automatically recovering deleted files with an "excellent" or "good" prognosis. If you're trying to recover a file with an "average" or "poor" prognosis, however, you'll probably need to help UNERASE with the recovery process. Regardless of the prognosis listed, you should first try the automatic method to recover the deleted file. If UNERASE displays a message like the one shown in Figure 7.16, you'll have to try and manually recover any of the file's data which may still reside on the disk.

Select the Manual unerase... option from the UNERASE File menu to begin the manual recovery process. UNERASE then asks you to supply the first character of the name of the file to be recovered. After you type the file name's first character the Manual UNERASE screen in Figure 7.17 is displayed.

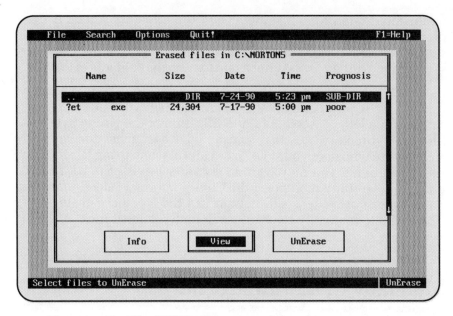

Figure 7.15   The UNERASE screen shown here reports a poor recovery prognosis for the ?et.exe file.

Figure 7.16   UNERASE displays a failure message if automatic recovery is unsuccessful.

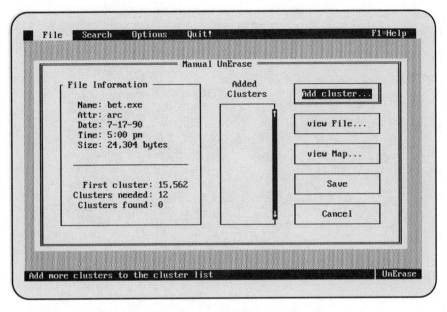

*Figure 7.17   Use the Manual UNERASE feature to recover
files which cannot be automatically unerased.*

The panel on the left side of the Manual UNERASE screen
shows the file information UNERASE was able to locate including
the file's name, attributes, time/date stamp, and size. The File
Information panel also reports cluster information as you manually
rebuild the deleted file.

The right side of the Manual UNERASE screen contains several
operation buttons you can select during the manual recovery process. Select the `Add cluster...` button to start rebuilding the file
and the screen in Figure 7.18 is displayed.

Even though UNERASE may not be able to automatically
recover a deleted file, it can still offer some useful information about
which clusters the file occupied. The first time you try to manually
unerase a file, you should select the `All clusters` button in Figure
7.18; when you select this button, UNERASE uses all available
information to try and piece together the clusters from the deleted
file. The Manual UNERASE screen (Figure 7.17) is redisplayed after
UNERASE gathers all the likely clusters for the file. Select the `View
file...` button in Figure 7.17 to have a look at the clusters
UNERASE has gathered.

Depending on what the View file... selection displays, you may
want to either save the file with the recommended clusters or try
another manual recovery approach. If you want to save the recovered file, press Esc to return to the Manual UNERASE screen and

Figure 7.18   UNERASE offers several ways to add clusters to a file as you recover it.

select the Save button. If the data contained in the recommended clusters doesn't even resemble the previous contents of the deleted file, you can try another, less automated, mode of manual recovery. Press Esc a couple of times to return to the initial UNERASE screen (Figure 7.15), then follow the directions provided earlier to reach the Add Clusters screen (Figure 7.18). Rather than letting UNERASE guess at the entire chain of clusters for the deleted file, you can select the Next probable or Data search buttons to manually build the cluster chain—the Data search feature is particularly useful when trying to recover text files because you can search the entire disk for a specific string of characters. As you manually add each cluster to the chain, be sure to use the View file... button to monitor the contents of the rebuilt file.

UNERASE is a powerful tool, but it's not without limitations. If some of the clusters from a deleted file have been overwritten, you cannot completely recover the file with UNERASE— however, you can still use UNERASE to manually recover as many clusters as possible. Now let's take a look at three important utilities which can improve the efficiency and speed of your hard disk.

Optimizing Disk Performance

There are several tricks you can use to make your PC operate at its peak performance level. I use the Norton Control Center utility (NCC, discussed in Chapter 2) to set my keyboard rate at the fastest setting—this step alone can create the illusion of a much faster PC! The Norton Utilities include three other tools which you can use to optimize your hard disk's performance. When used properly, these disk optimization tools can significantly increase the performance of even the slowest hard disk.

Using SPEEDISK

A badly fragmented disk is one of the most common causes of sluggish PC performance. The fragmentation that results from the everyday process of copying and deleting files can cause even the fastest hard disk to appear slow as molasses! Use Norton's SPEEDISK utility regularly to keep your hard disk defragmented and efficient.

171

 Defragmenting Your Disk

1. Type the command SPEEDISK and press Enter.

   This runs the SPEEDISK utility and displays a drive selection dialog box.

2. Use the up- and down-arrow keys to highlight the drive you wish to optimize, and press Enter.

   SPEEDISK analyzes the selected disk and displays the recommended optimization method (Figure 7.19).

3. Press Enter to accept the recommended method and begin disk optimization.

   SPEEDISK optimizes the specified disk and displays a message when the process is complete. □

SPEEDISK offers five different methods of optimization, ranging from a full optimization to a file sort which simply rearranges the order of files on the disk. After you specify which disk to optimize, SPEEDISK analyzes the disk and determines which optimization method should be used. You can accept SPEEDISK's recommended optimization method, or you can select a different method. Select the Optimization Method... option from the Optimize menu to see the list of optimization methods offered (Figure 7.20).

Figure 7.19   SPEEDISK recommends an "Unfragment Files Only" optimization method.

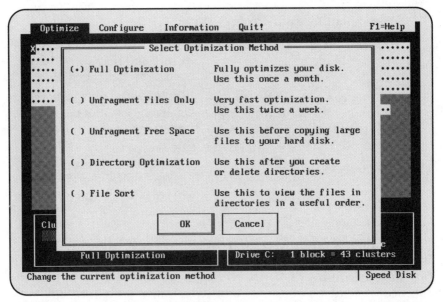

Figure 7.20   SPEEDISK offers several optimization methods.

Of the five optimization methods offered, the Full Optimization and Unfragment Files Only methods are perhaps the most valuable. SPEEDISK defragments files and moves all unused clusters to one contiguous area on the disk when the Full Optimization method is used. Full Optimization is the most time-consuming method offered by SPEEDISK but it also organizes the disk in the most efficient manner possible.

In contrast, the Unfragment Files Only method is less time-consuming than Full Optimization but it doesn't create the most efficient disk possible. As its name implies, the Unfragment Files Only method concentrates on unfragmenting files on the specified disk. However, there's no guarantee that every single file will be unfragmented when the optimization process is complete. Further, a disk optimized with the Unfragment Files Only method will probably still contain "holes" of non-contiguous unused clusters.

Use the Full Optimization method monthly and the Unfragment Files Only method weekly to maintain a highly efficient and organized disk.

173

Using a Disk Cache

Disk read/write operations are very slow compared to the time required to manipulate data in RAM. A disk cache utility maintains frequently-accessed disk data in a RAM buffer to help expedite disk read/write operations.

Before a time-consuming disk read operation is performed, the disk cache checks its RAM buffer to see if it contains the requested data. If the requested data is found in the RAM buffer the cache can provide it to DOS without having to perform a timely disk read operation. Similarly, the cache utility may buffer several disk write operations and perform them together in a more efficient manner.

The Norton Utilities include two disk caching programs: NCACHE-F for a fast cache, and NCACHE-S for a small cache. Besides being faster than NCACHE-S, NCACHE-F also uses more memory for its larger RAM buffer.

> ▶ **Note:** The Norton Utilities INSTALL program includes an option to automatically install either the fast or small disk cache utility. You can use the instructions below to manually install one of the cache utilities if you skipped this step in the INSTALL process.

To utilize one of the Norton caching programs you must use a text editor to add the following line to your CONFIG.SYS file:

`DEVICE=C:\path\NCACHE-x.EXE`

where `path` is the pathname where the Norton Utilities can be found (e.g. NORTON5) and `x` is either `F` or `S`, depending on the cache you wish to use. After you add the NCACHE statement to your CONFIG.SYS file you must reboot to activate the cache utility.

The statement above creates a cache for all disks on your PC, including floppy disks. If your PC has a hard disk you probably utilize the hard disk much more often than you utilize your floppy drives. Therefore, you probably don't need to maintain a cache for your floppy drives. Use the -A option to deactivate caching for a specific drive. For example, the CONFIG.SYS statement:

`DEVICE=C:\NORTON5\NCACHE-F.EXE -A A: -A B:`

174

deactivates caching for both the A: and B: drives.

Using CALIBRAT

The CALIBRAT utility is perhaps the most powerful disk optimization tool included in the Norton Utilities. CALIBRAT performs several tests to determine many important characteristics, including your hard disk's *interleave factor*. The interleave factor indicates how sectors are laid out within each track on a disk. The disk in Figure 7.21 has a 1:1 (pronounced "one to one") interleave factor, which means that each sector is adjacent to the next consecutive sector.

The disk in Figure 7.22 has a 2:1 interleave factor, which means that you must skip a sector to get to the next consecutive one.

Similarly, a 3:1 interleave factor means that you must skip two sectors to get to the next consecutive one.

Your hard disk's interleave factor was probably set by the disk's manufacturer or your PC dealer when the disk was installed. Regardless of how your disk's interleave factor was set, a different interleave factor may produce a faster, more efficient hard disk. Use the CALIBRAT (short for "Calibrate") utility to determine and/or modify your hard disk's interleave factor.

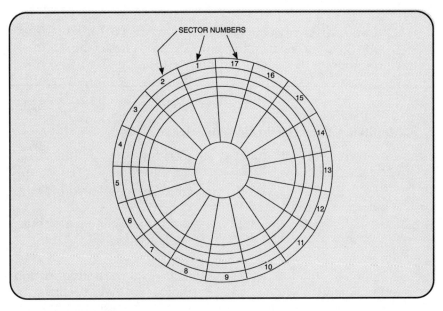

Figure 7.21   CALIBRAT shows that this disk has a 1:1 inter-leave factor.

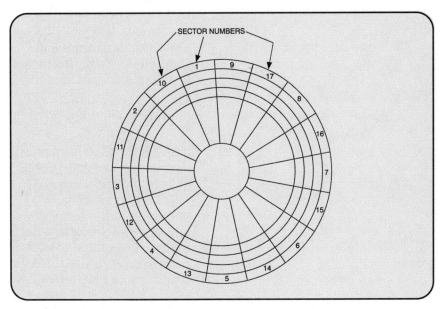

Figure 7.22   This disk has a 2:1 interleave factor.

> ⊘ **Caution:** Always backup your hard disk before modifying the interleave factor with CALIBRAT (see the Norton Backup program discussed in Chapter 11).

Q **Modifying Your Hard Disk's Interleave Factor**

1. Type the command CALIBRAT and press Enter.

   This runs the CALIBRAT utility and display a Calibrate information dialog box.

2. Press Enter to acknowledge the Calibrate information dialog box.

   A drive selection dialog box is displayed.

3. Use the up- and down-arrow keys to highlight the desired disk, and press Enter.

   This displays an information dialog box that explains each of the tests that will be run on the specified disk.

4. Press Enter.

   CALIBRAT performs a series of integrity and performance tests on your hard disk.

5. Keep pressing Enter until the screen in Figure 7.23 is displayed.

   The screen in Figure 7.23 indicates the Current and Optimal interleave factors for the specified disk.

6. Press Enter if the Current and Optimal interleave factors are not identical.

   This displays another test information dialog box.

7. Press Enter.

   CALIBRAT performs a non-destructive format and changes the disk interleave factor to the recommended optimal value. When the format process is complete, follow the on-screen instructions to create a CALIBRAT report and/or exit the utility.

□

Figure 7.23   CALIBRAT reports current and optimal interleave factors.

As indicated in step #7 of the previous Quick Steps, CALIBRAT performs a "non-destructive" format of the specified hard disk when it alters the interleave factor. In other words, none of your disk's data should be lost during this format process. However, I highly recommend that you back up your disk before changing the interleave factor with CALIBRAT—you never know when something may go wrong!

What You Have Learned

In this final chapter on the Norton Utilities, you learned how to use several advanced disk management tools to protect your valuable data and optimize your disk's performance. Specifically, you learned:

▶   The DISKMON utility is a TSR that lets you monitor all disk activity on your system and can prevent computer viruses from destroying the contents of your hard disk.

▶ The DISKTOOL utility also offers a couple of other valuable disk tools which let you mark bad clusters and save/restore important hard disk configuration information.

▶ The DISKREET utility encrypts, or encodes, files so nobody else can interpret them.

▶ The DISKEDIT utility lets you perform a wide variety of tasks including viewing/editing virtually any byte on a disk.

▶ The Norton Utilities include a set of three tools which you can

178

Introducing the Commander

In This Chapter

▶ *What the Commander provides*
▶ *Installing, starting, and using the Commander*
▶ *Configuring the Commander for your use*
▶ *Getting on-screen help*

The Commander is a program that fulfills two important functions. Its major function is to act as a DOS shell—that is, it provides you with a visual interface for DOS. Instead of *typing* path names, file names, and long command lines at the DOS prompt, you simply *select* what you want from a list or pull-down menu, using your keyboard or mouse. In a sense, it "hides" the complicated workings of DOS behind a simple graphical interface, giving you more control over your directories and files. Its second function is to help transfer information between computers and facilitate the exchange of MCI mail. In this chapter, we'll look at some of the basic features of the Commander, how to install it, and how to run it. Once you get this program up and running, you may never want to return to your DOS prompt again!

What the Commander Provides

On a daily basis, you probably perform some sort of disk management activities. You might copy or delete files, rename them, or sort the files in a particular directory. To perform any of these tasks at the DOS prompt, you must remember the structure of your directory tree and enter a path name that leads to the directory that holds your files. Then, you must remember the syntax of the command and the names of the files you want the command to affect. Although that doesn't take a mastermind, it can get cumbersome, especially if you're in a hurry. With the Commander, you use *visual display panels* to help you view and select directories and files, and you select the commands you want to enter from menus.

Figure 8.1 shows how the visual display panels can simplify your disk management activities. The panels in Figure 8.1 have been set up to display a split screen. On the left is a picture of the directory tree for the C drive. On the right are all the files contained in the chosen directory. If you wanted to view this same list of files in DOS, you would have to change drives, enter a path to the TILES directory (cd\pbrush\tiles), and then enter a directory command to list the files (including some switch to keep the directory from scrolling by too quickly). With the Commander, you simply enter the letter of the drive you want to view and then select the directory with the arrow keys. You can scroll through the list as quickly as you like and stop at any file. Selecting files is as simple as pressing the Enter key or clicking a mouse button.

Another advantage of the Commander is that you can view the contents of a file without having to load the file into an application. Using the Commander's file view interpreters, you can view (without changing) the data stored in files created with a variety of word processing, spreadsheet, database, and graphics programs. Table 8.1 provides a list of the formats you can view through the Commander.

180

> ▶ **Tip:** If you don't see one of your application file formats listed in Table 8.1, don't panic. You can often convert your files to an acceptable format before using the Commander to view them. For example, you can save most word processing files in the ASCII format and some spreadsheet programs using the Lotus 1-2-3 format.

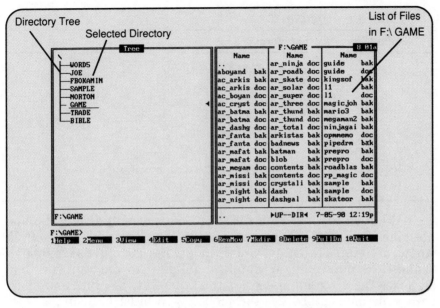

Directory Tree

Selected Directory

List of Files
in F:\ GAME

Figure 8.1   The Commander's simplified interface makes it easy to find and manipulate files.

Table 8.1   File formats available for viewing

Application	Format
Word Processing	WordPerfect (4.2, 5.0)
	Microsoft Word (4.0, 5.0)
	MultiMate (all versions)
	WordStar Pro (all versions)
	WordStar 2000 (all versions)
	Windows Write (all versions)
	Microsoft Works (all versions)
	XyWrite (all versions)
	ASCII text files
Spreadsheets	Lotus 1-2-3 (1.x-3.x)
	Symphony (1.0-2.0)
	Microsoft Excel (1.0-2.2)
	Multiplan (4.0)
	Microsoft Works (all versions)
	Quattro (all versions)
	VP-Planner Plus (all versions)
	Mosaic Twin (all versions)
	Words & Figures (all versions)
Databases	dBASE II, III, III+, IV
	Clipper (all versions)

continued

181

Table 8.1 *continued*

Application	Format
	FoxBASE (all versions)
	Paradox (all versions)
	R:BASE (all versions)
	Microsoft Works (all versions)
	dBXL (all versions)
	Reflex (all versions)
Graphics	Any file with the .pcx format, such as PC Paintbrush files

Although most of your disk management will deal with data files, the Commander helps you with your program files as well. If you want to run a program, you no longer have to enter a command at the DOS prompt. You simply highlight the program file that launches the program and press the Enter key, or point and click with your mouse. (To use the mouse, you must be using a DOS version later than 3.3 or have the required mouse driver—the software that came with your mouse.) In addition, you can use the Commander's "point and shoot" feature to load data files automatically into their applications. Just click on the file name for the data file, and the Commander will run the application and then load the file.

The Commander provides several additional features that you may find useful as well. For example, the Commander Mail feature lets you send and receive documents via MCI Mail, an electronic mail service that's available through MCI Telecommunications Corporation. If you use a laptop computer and need to transfer data between it and your desktop computer, you'll find the Commander Link feature especially useful.

Installing the Commander

To get the most out of the Commander, you should have a hard disk; we'll assume that you do. Installing the Commander is easy. Before you begin, make a backup copy of all the diskettes of the size appropriate for your computer. (The software package includes two 5 1/4" diskettes and one 3 1/2" diskette.) Put the original diskettes in a safe place, and use the backup copies for the installation.

The Commander diskettes include an Installation program. To ensure proper installation, you should use this program to copy the program files to your hard disk. As shown in Figure 8.2, the installation process is menu-driven. Following is a step-by-step summary of the procedure:

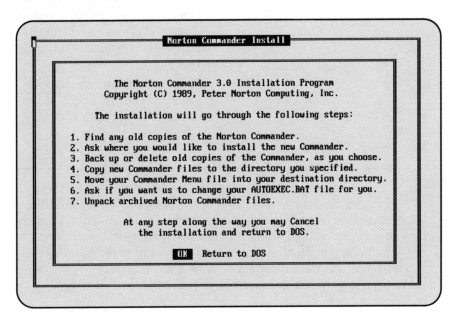

Figure 8.2   The Norton Commander Install menu takes you step-by-step through the installation process.

Installing the Commander

1. Turn on your computer and take any steps needed to reach the DOS prompt.

   For example, `c:>` or a similar prompt must appear on screen.

2. Type the letter of the floppy disk drive you're going to use followed by a colon, and press Enter.

   For example, if you're going to use the A drive, type `a:` and press Enter. The drive letter appears on screen.

3. Insert Disk 1 of the two 5 1/4" diskettes (or the 3 1/2" diskette) into the selected drive.

   For example, if you selected the A: drive in step 2, and `A:>` appears on screen, insert the diskette in the A drive.

4. Type `install` and press Enter.

   This starts the Installation program. Soon you will see the first of a series of questions.

183

5. Answer each question as it pertains to your system.

When asked if you want to put the Commander in your AUTOEXEC.BAT file, answer Yes, unless you have some reason for doing otherwise. If you answer Yes, you'll be able to run the Commander from any drive or directory by typing the required command at the DOS prompt.

6. When you are finished with the installation program, press Ctrl-Alt-Del to reboot your system.

This updates any changes to your AUTOEXEC.BAT file to ensure the program runs correctly.

□

> ▶ **Tip:** You can find out about last-minute updates or corrections to the program by viewing the READ.ME file located on one of the Commander diskettes. This information is probably not contained in the documentation that's included with the package. Print or view this file as soon as possible after installing the Commander. To view the file, start the Commander, select `READ.ME` from the Commander file directory panel, and press F3.

Starting the Commander

You can run the Commander in either of two ways, depending on whether you installed the program on your hard disk or are limited to using only floppy disks:

▶ If you installed the program on a hard disk, run the Commander as a stand-alone program. The Commander will exit RAM when you run another application and reload itself when you quit that application. This keeps the Commander from taking up valuable RAM.

▶ If you have only a floppy disk system, run the Commander as a memory-resident program. The Commander stays in RAM, freeing up your floppy disk drives for other work.

> ▶ **Note:** Although you can run the Commander in memory-resident mode with a hard drive, you're better off keeping it out of RAM. Run the Commander in memory-resident mode only if you have more RAM than you need or if you have to keep a floppy drive open. Besides, it doesn't take long for the Commander to quit and reload itself—you gain little by keeping it in RAM.

If you chose to modify your AUTOEXEC.BAT file, you can load the Commander as a stand-alone program by typing `nc` at any DOS prompt and pressing Enter. (If you did not choose to modify AUTOEXEC.BAT, you need to change to the directory that holds your Commander files before typing the command.)

If you want to run the Commander as a memory-resident program (one that stays in RAM), type

```
ncmain
```

185

at the DOS prompt and press Enter. (Again, if you chose not to modify the AUTOEXEC.BAT file, change to the Commander directory before entering the command.) Since this option keeps the Commander in RAM, less RAM is available for other programs. So why do it? If you have no hard drive, and you don't want to swap disks whenever you need to access the Commander directory files, this option keeps the Commander readily available.

The Commander Interface

Once you've loaded the Commander, you're greeted with the Commander interface, as shown in Figure 8.3. This screen consists of four parts: a panel on the right, a mini status box, a DOS prompt, and a function key bar. If you're wondering why there's no left panel like the one in Figure 8.1, don't worry; you'll learn how to display the second panel a little later.

The panel on the right initially displays the contents of the root directory of the current drive and any subdirectories within it. The names of the subdirectories (if any) are displayed in all uppercase letters. The names of the individual files appear in all lowercase letters. You'll see later how to configure the panel to display other information, such as a directory tree or the dates and times the files were created.

Figure 8.3   The Commander interface screen is the "main menu" or starting point for all operations.

Just below the right panel is the *mini status box*. This box is handy for determining the size of the selected file and the date and time it was created. For example, when you first start the Commander, the mini status box shows this information for the highlighted file in the current directory.

You will also notice that the familiar *DOS prompt* still appears on screen in the lower left corner. You can use the DOS prompt to enter and execute any valid DOS command. You can use the DOS prompt and the Commander in tandem to gain even more control over your files. For example, you can change drives at the DOS prompt by typing the letter of the drive (a: b: c: etc.) and pressing Enter. The files and directories for that drive then appear in the active display panel.

At the bottom of the screen is the *function key bar*. This bar lets you access many of the Commander operations by pressing the function key associated with that operation or by clicking on it with the mouse. As shown in Figure 8.4, you can activate a pull-down *menu bar* at the top of the screen by choosing the PullDn option on the function key bar. Either click on this option with the mouse or press F9. To pull down one of the menus, either click on it with the mouse, type the first letter of the menu name, or highlight the menu name with the left or right arrow key and press Enter.

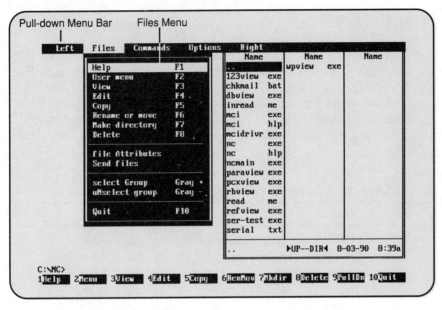

Figure 8.4   *The pull-down menu bar is shown here with the Files menu open.*

Selecting Items

The Commander makes it easy to move through a list of files and directories using either the mouse or the keyboard. Since all the file and directory names of the current directory are displayed in a panel, you can simply use the cursor keys or the mouse to scroll through the contents of that directory. Keep in mind that the panel remains visible even if you execute a DOS or Commander operation.

To change directories, simply select any of the directory names (the names in all uppercase letters) using the keyboard or mouse. If you're using the keyboard, press the cursor control keys (up, down, left, and right arrow keys, PgUp, PgDn, Home, and End) to highlight the name of the directory, and then press Enter to activate it. To return to the parent directory, select the [. .] symbol. If you're using a mouse, move the mouse pointer to the directory you want to activate and double-click the mouse button.

Once you activate a directory, the contents of the directory are displayed in a panel and are ready for further Commander operations. By selecting files in this way, you reduce the chances that you'll mistype a directory or file name.

Using the Keyboard

You've already seen that you can use the keyboard to perform any Commander operation. You can enter commands by pressing the appropriate function key, activate the pull-down menu bar, and use the cursor movement and Enter keys to select directories and files. For additional operations, the Commander offers several special keys you can press in combination with the function keys, as shown in Table 8.2.

Table 8.2 Special Keys and Operations

Key	Operation
Alt	Pressing Alt in combination with a function key executes several commands that are listed in the pull-down menus. Instead of having to work your way through a list of menus, you can enter one of these "hot-key" combinations.
Ctrl	The Ctrl key in combination with other keys serves as a toggle. For example, Ctrl-O turns both panels on and off.
Esc	The Esc key is generally used to quit several operations in progress. For example, pressing Esc quits the Edit and View operations, clears the command line at the DOS prompt, and cancels and closes any dialog and alert boxes.
Shift	Pressing Shift in combination with a function key produces a more general version of the same operation without the shifted command.

188

Using a Mouse

If you have a mouse, choosing items on the Commander screen is even easier. However, you need to keep a few rules in mind. To use your mouse more effectively, refer to Table 8.3 for some basic rules.

> ▶ **Note:** Throughout our discussion of the Commander, we assume that you're using a two-button mouse that's configured for right-hand use. To configure the mouse for your left hand, refer to the section on configuring the Commander later in this chapter. If you configure your mouse for your left hand, use the left button when we say to use the right button.

Table 8.3   ***Mouse rules.***

Location	Operation
In Panels	*Point*—Click left button to move highlight bar.
	Scroll—Hold down left button and move mouse up or down.
	Load Program—Double-click left button.
	Change Directories—Double-click left button.
	Select or Unselect—Click right button.
	Select or Unselect Group of Files—Hold down right button and drag cursor to highlight group.
In Menus	*Show Menu Bar*—Click either button on top line or click left button on PullDn option.
	Select Menu Item—Click either button.
In Dialog Boxes	*Select Item*—Click left button.
	Select Item and Exit Dialog Box—Click right button.
	Accept Highlighted Action—Click right button outside dialog box.
	Cancel Dialog Box Action—Click left button outside dialog box.
Escaping	*Escape from Alert or Dialog Box*—Click left and right buttons.
	Escape from Dialog Box Only—Click left button.

189

Configuring the Commander for Your System

Now that you know how to move around the screen, you're ready to start setting up the Commander for your own personal use. First, you'll set up the overall appearance and operation of the Commander:

1. Press the F9 key (or click on the PullDn command in the Function key bar) to display the menu bar at the top of the screen.
2. Choose Options from the menu bar, opening the Options menu.

3. Press Enter to choose the `Configuration` command. This opens the Configuration dialog box, as shown in Figure 8.5.

4. Use the up- and down-arrow keys to move between options, and use the space bar to select a given option. The following list explains the various options:

Screen colors: You can configure your system for a black-and-white, color, or laptop display, depending on your system.

Screen blank delay: If you don't touch your keyboard or mouse for a certain amount of time, your screen will go blank and display star bursts. This protects your screen against damage caused by burn-in. Choose the desired delay time or turn it off altogether.

File panel options: If you don't want hidden files to be displayed (for security reasons), unselect the first option. If you want the cursor to move to the next file when you select a file with the Ins key, select the second option.

Tree panel options: If you select the Auto Change Directory option, whenever you highlight a directory in the tree panel, its files are listed in the opposite panel.

Other options: This option box lets you set other useful options. You can choose to display the menu bar at all times, automatically save your configuration changes, reverse your mouse buttons, and reset your mouse more quickly after entering a command (for the mouse port on a COMPAQ or PS/2).

Using the Panels

Now that you have the overall configuration set, you can begin setting up your panels. The setup is easy to perform and easy to change whenever you like, so feel free to stop reading and play with different setups along the way.

If the pull-down menu is not displayed at the top of the screen, choose the `F9 PullDn` command from the function key bar. As you can see, the pull-down menu bar contains five menu options, two of which control the panels: Left and Right. The menus are identical except for the fact the one controls the left panel and the other controls the right one. If you want to turn the left panel on, open the Left menu and press Enter. Only one panel is active at a time. To

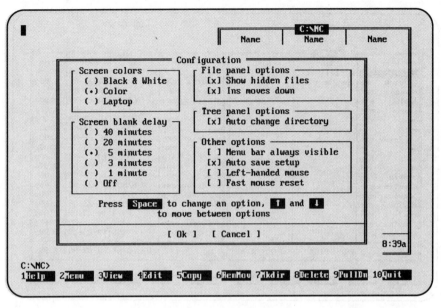

Figure 8.5   The Configuration dialog box allows you to customize the Commander to your specifications.

switch from one to the other, press the Tab key. The title of the active panel appears in reverse video, and the highlight bar appears in its directory listing.

Now, open either the Left or Right menu to see how you can manipulate these panels. The first option on the menu is Brief. Select the option now, and the panel you've just selected will look something like the left one in Figure 8.6. This option displays a list of the subdirectories and file names for the chosen directory—nothing else. Now, reopen the Left or Right menu, and choose the Full option. Your panel should now look something like the panel on the right. This display gives you a little more information about your file, telling you not only the name of the file but also it's size and the date and time it was created.

If you want to know some information about your system and your current drive and directory, choose the Info command from the Left or Right menu or press Ctrl-L. This opens a dialog box that tells you how much RAM is installed in your system, how much is available, the capacity of your drive, how much storage space you have left, and how much storage space your files are taking up. To return to the previous display of the panel, press Ctrl-L.

The next option on the Left or Right menu is Tree. By choosing this option or typing Ctrl-T, you can display a directory tree of the current drive. One of the most common ways to use the two panels

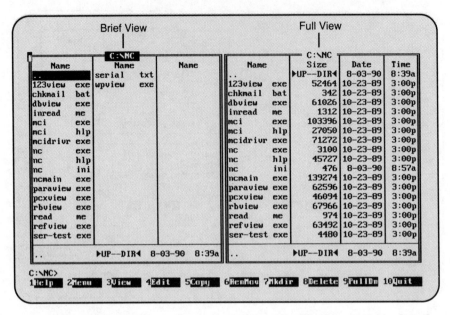

Figure 8.6   *You can choose between two display options: brief and full.*

is to set up the left panel to display a directory tree and the right panel to display a brief or full list of files. (You saw such a setup in Figure 8.2.) That way, you can choose a directory in the left panel and then switch to the right panel (with the Tab key) to work with the files in that directory.

The next option, `quick View`, lets you view (but not alter) the contents of a selected file. Just highlight the file in question (make sure it's one the Commander can handle) and choose the `quick View` option or press Ctrl-Q. The contents of the file appears in the opposite window, helping you decide whether that's really the file you want to work with.

The last option we will deal with in this section is the `On/Off` option. This option simply lets you turn either of the panels on or off. Choose this option or press one of the following hot-key combinations:

Hot Key	Action
Ctrl-P	Turns inactive panel on or off.
Ctrl-O	Turns both panels on or off.
Ctrl-U	Flips panels (left to right and vice versa).
Ctrl-F1	Turns left panel on or off.
Ctrl-F2	Turns right panel on or off.

Changing Drives

You can change the drive that either panel represents at any time. The procedure is simple. Press Alt-F2 or choose the Drive command from the Left or Right menu, depending on which panel you want the change to affect. A dialog box appears, presenting you with a list of available drives. Select the drive you want to activate.

> ▶ **Tip:** Don't forget that you still have your DOS prompt at the bottom of the screen. The easiest way to change drives is to type the drive letter followed by a colon next to this prompt and press Enter.

Sorting Your Files

193

After you activate the drive you want to work in, you may want to change the way the files are sorted in the panel display. Press F9 to activate the pull-down menu bar, and open either the Left or Right menu. The second set of options on this menu lets you select various sorting schemes for your files. Choose Name, and the Commander will sort files and subdirectories alphabetically by name first then by extension. If you choose eXtension, files will be sorted by extension first and then name.

The files in the left panel in Figure 8.7 are sorted by extension. Notice that all files with the .bak extension precede files with the .doc extension. The files in the right panel have been sorted by size, largest to smallest. You can also sort according to the date and time the files were created, or you can leave the files unsorted.

Narrowing Down the List

If your panel is cluttered with a bunch of files you don't want to work with, choose the fiLter option from the Left or Right menu. This command lets you display only the range of files you want to work with. For example, you can display only those files with the .doc extension and filter out all those superfluous .bak files.

When you choose this option, the Commander presents a dialog box, giving you three choices. The ALL option lets you view all the files in the directory. The Executable Files Only option lets you view only program files. This is useful if you want to run applica-

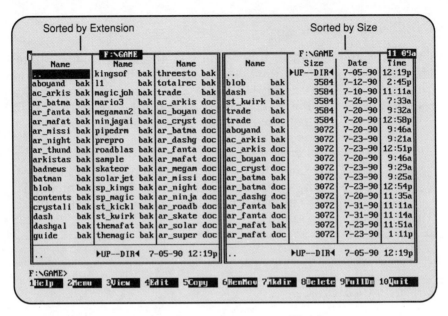

Figure 8.7   You can choose to sort your files by name, extension, time, or size.

tions from the Commander, and you don't want to wade through a bunch of data files. The last choice lets you customize the filter with wild-card entries of your own.

Getting Help

If you ever need help when you're performing an operation in the Commander, press F1 or choose the Help command from the Files menu. This displays a window, as shown in Figure 8.8, that gives you helpful information about whatever task you're performing at this time. You can scroll up or down in the window to read all the information available, or you can choose Previous or Next to view the next item in the window. Choose Cancel to close the Help window and return to the task you were performing.

If the Help window doesn't pertain to what you're trying to do, choose the Index option at the bottom of the screen. This opens the Help index, shown in Figure 8.9. This index provides a comprehensive list of topics that the Commander can help you with. Highlight the item you need help with and press Enter, or double-click on it with the mouse.

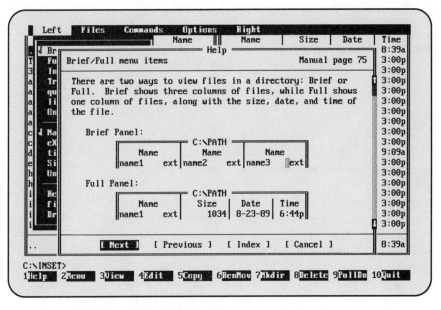

Figure 8.8 *A Help window is available at any time by pressing F1.*

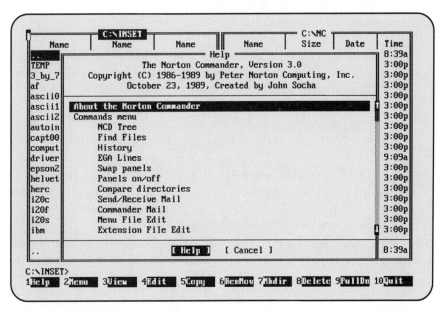

Figure 8.9 *The Help index allows you to locate help screens for any topic quickly.*

In addition to Help windows and the Help index, the Commander displays dialog and alert boxes to help guide you in your tasks. The dialog boxes ask you to enter further information or to confirm your choice. The alert boxes warn you that you may be getting yourself into trouble.

Leaving the Commander

You can leave the Commander in either of two ways. The fastest way is to select the F10 Quit command from the function key bar at the bottom of the screen. A dialog box appears, asking you whether you really want to quit the Commander. If you're sure you want to exit, press Y; if not, press N. The other way to quit is to choose the Quit command from the Files menu. This displays the same dialog box mentioned earlier, and you have to confirm your request.

What You Have Learned

▶ The Commander serves two functions. First, it acts as a visual interface for DOS, giving you more control over your disks, directories, and files. Second, it helps you transfer information between two computers.

▶ The Commander lets you view the contents of data files, run program files, and automatically load a program into an application.

▶ You can load the Commander as a stand-alone program or as a memory-resident program. As a stand-alone program, the Commander exits RAM when you run an application program and reloads when you quit the application.

▶ The Commander's visual interface lets you select directories and file names by pointing at them rather than by typing path names and file names at the DOS prompt. You can also enter commands by choosing them from menus rather than typing them.

▶ You can configure the Commander for however you intend to use it, and you can manipulate the panels to display various views of your directories and files.

Managing Files and Disks with the Commander

In This Chapter

197

- ▶ *Finding, selecting, and copying files*
- ▶ *Renaming, moving, and deleting files*
- ▶ *Viewing and editing files*
- ▶ *Maintaining your directories*
- ▶ *Using the DOS command line*
- ▶ *Running applications from the Commander*

You can see just from looking at the Commander's opening screen that from now on, disk management is going to be a lot easier. Everything you need is right there on screen—all you need to do is make your selections. In this chapter, you'll start using the Commander to perform common disk-maintenance tasks, such as copying, deleting, and moving files. You'll also learn how to use advanced features that let you view and edit files without leaving the Commander, and other features that let you automatically load application programs from within the Commander. You'll also learn to use the Commander for building and manipulating your directory structure.

> **Tip:** You'll notice that several of the heads in this chapter include the name of a function key or keystroke. These *hot keys* give you a short-cut to performing the task. Instead of working your way through a series of menus, just press the specified hot key. Of course, if you can't remember a particular hot key, the menus are always there to help.

Managing Your Files

Most of your work in the Commander will center around file management. You can use the Commander's shell structure to take control of your files—you'll no longer be a slave to the syntax of DOS commands or to the jumbled lists of files that scroll by faster than you can read.

Finding Files (Alt-F7)

Before you can perform any operation on a file or a group of files, you need to find the files you want to work with. In DOS, you had to rely on your memory. Forget where you put the file or what you named it, and you're in for a long search. Mistype the file name, and DOS tells you the file does not exist. Type the right name at the wrong prompt, and you get the same blank stare.

The Commander gives you a lot more help in finding your files. You simply activate one of the drives where you think your file is located and enter a file name (which may include wild cards). The Commander searches all the directories in that drive and displays a list of all the files that match your entry. You can then switch to the directory that contains that file and proceed with whatever task you wish to perform.

The first step in searching for a file is to activate the drive where you think the file is located. You can do this in either of two ways. The quickest way is to type the letter of the drive next to the DOS prompt and press Enter. You can also change drives by choosing the `Drive` command from either the Left or Right menu and supplying the necessary information. Once you've selected the drive you want to search, perform the following quick steps to find your file.

Q Finding Files

1. Press the Tab key to activate the panel you want to search.	The title of the active panel appears in reverse video, and the highlight bar appears within the panel.
2. Select the Find file command from the Commands menu, or press Alt-F7.	The Commander displays the Find File dialog box, shown in Figure 9.1.
3. Type the name of the file you want to search for (wild-card characters are permitted).	For example, if you want to find all files with the .DOC extension, type *.doc. Type something like ch?.doc to find a list of files such as CH1.DOC, CH3.DOC, etc.
4. Press Enter.	The Commander begins its search and displays all the files that match your entry. Figure 9.2 shows such a listing.
5. Move the highlight bar over the file you want.	
6. Press Enter to activate the directory that holds the file.	The Commander automatically activates the panel for that directory and moves the highlight bar to the file you selected. □

199

Selecting and Unselecting Files

One of the most complicated aspects of working with files in DOS is selecting the files you want to work with. Working with an individual file is usually no problem, but when you want a command to affect several files at once, DOS is inflexible. For example, if you want to copy three files—CASH.WK1, CH8.DOC, and FIG0801.PIX—from one directory to another, you have to enter three separate copy commands. With the Commander, however, selecting files is as simple as pressing a single keystroke or clicking with your mouse.

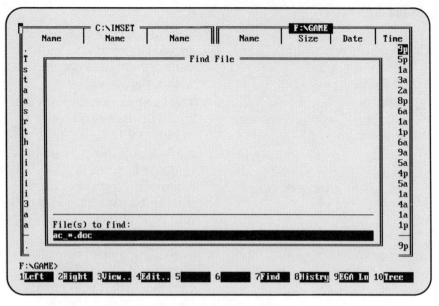

Figure 9.1 *The Find File dialog box lets you search for a file by name.*

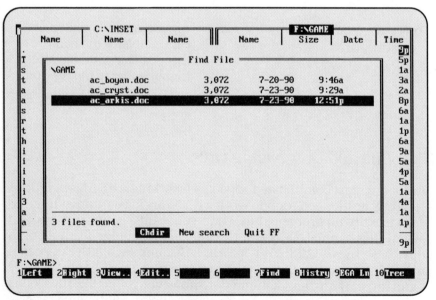

Figure 9.2 *The Commander displays a list of files that match the search entry.*

Individual Files (Ins)

To select an individual file with the keyboard, move the highlight bar over the name of the file you wish to select and press the Ins key. The selected file name turns yellow on a color monitor or appears brighter on a monochrome monitor. You can select as many files as you like. To unselect a file, highlight it again and press the Ins key. Selecting individual files with the mouse is even easier. Point to the file you wish to select, and press the right mouse button.

Groups of Files (Gray +/–)

To be fair to DOS, we must admit that the wild-card entries that DOS permits do help in handling files. What would we do without the * . * entry? The Commander offers this same flexibility, allowing you to select a range of files. But the Commander doesn't stop there. It also offers an Unselect feature. You can select all the files within a given directory, then use the Unselect feature to unselect the group of files you *don't* want to work with. The following quick steps lead you through the file selection process:

201

 Selecting or Unselecting a Group of Files

1. Press the Tab key to activate the panel you want to work with.

   The title of the panel appears in reverse video, and the highlight bar appears.

2. Press the gray + key (the + key on the numeric keypad) to select a group of files, or gray – to unselect a group.

   A dialog box appears as in Figure 9.3, asking you to type an entry for the files you wish to select or unselect. * . * appears in the box, indicating that unless you type an entry, all the files in that directory will be affected.

3. Type your entry.

   You can use the standard DOS wild-card characters. * matches any group of characters. ? matches any single character. For example ch? . doc will select CH1.DOC, CH2.DOC, etc., but not CH10.DOC or CH2.WP5.

4. Press Enter.

If you selected files, those files turn yellow on a color monitor or appear brighter on a monochrome screen. If you unselected files, the file names return to their original appearance. □

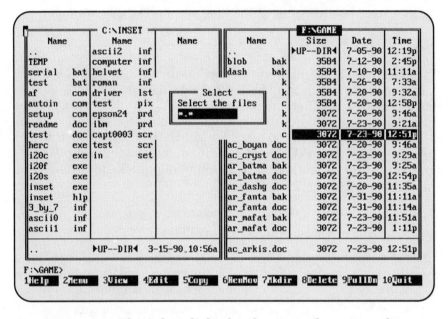

Figure 9.3   The Select dialog box lets you select or unselect groups of files.

⊘ **Caution:** Review the group of files you selected to make sure those are the files you want to affect. If you select the wrong group of files and then enter a command such as Delete, you could get yourself into trouble. The Commander's dialog and alert boxes will force you to be careful, but take your own precautions anyway.

When you select a group of files, the mini status box (at the base of the panel) shows you how many files you selected and how many bytes those files occupy. This is helpful information if you're running out of room on your hard disk. If you're copying files to a floppy disk, however, the Commander will let you start copying the

202

files and will tell you if you need to insert an additional disk to hold the rest of the files. Just make sure you have enough blank, formatted disks on hand.

Copying Files (F5)

Once you've selected the file or group of files you want to copy, copying the files is easy. Choose the Copy command from the Files menu or press F5. The Copy Files dialog box appears, as shown in Figure 9.4. Choose this same command with the Shift key pressed down, and you'll see the dialog box in Figure 9.5. This dialog box lets you supply the source and destination for the files as well.

Figure 9.4   The Copy dialog box lets you specify a destination for the selected file.

As you can see, the dialog box assumes that you wish to copy the files to the directory represented by the inactive panel. You can edit the entry by moving the cursor to the part you want to change, entering the correct information, and deleting the incorrect information. If you want to cancel the original entry altogether, type the name of the drive and directory to which you want to copy the files. For example, if you want to copy the files to D:\SAMPLE\FILES, type d:\sample\files. As soon as you begin to type, the entry that was originally displayed disappears, and the characters you type appear in the box.

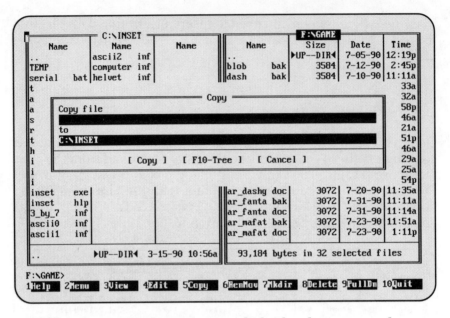

Figure 9.5   The alternate Copy dialog box lets you supply both a source and a destination.

In the bottom of the Copy Files dialog box are three options: Copy, Tree, and Cancel. To begin copying the selected files to the specified drive and directory, press Enter to choose the Copy option. The Tree option lets you choose the copy destination from a directory tree of the active directory. The Cancel option lets you change your mind about copying the files.

If you choose the Copy option, the Commander begins copying the selected files from the source to the destination. A dialog box appears on screen, indicating which file is being copied and how the process is progressing. If you want to abort the copy process at any point, press Ctrl-Break or Esc. If you try to copy a file to a disk or directory that contains a file of the same name, you'll see the alert box shown in Figure 9.6. This box warns you that you are about to overwrite an existing file, giving you a chance to change your mind. If you want to overwrite the file, press Enter. If you want to skip the file and proceed to the next one, choose the Skip option. If you want the Commander to overwrite all files on the target that have the same file names as those in the source, choose All.

Figure 9.6   *The overwrite warning alert box warns that you are about to replace an existing file.*

   Tip: You can use the `Copy` command to print a text file. When the dialog box asks you to name the target for the copy, type `prn`. This tells the Commander to copy the file to the printer.

Renaming Files (F6)

Occasionally, you may have to rename a file or a group of files either to give you a better idea of what those files contain or to allow you to use their current names for other files. Whatever the reason, the Commander makes it easy to rename your files.

Renaming Files

1. Highlight the file you want to rename.

2. Press F6 or choose the `Rename or move` command from the Files menu.

The Rename dialog box appears, as in Figure 9.7, prompting you to enter a new name for the file.

3. Type a new name for the file, following the DOS file name restrictions.

    The file name can be no more than eight characters long. The extension can be up to three characters.

4. Press Enter.

    The dialog box disappears. The file is renamed but kept in the same directory. □

⊘ **Caution:** If you try to use a file name that's already in use in the current directory, the Commander will display an alert box telling you that the name is already being used. You cannot use the same name for two files in the same directory.

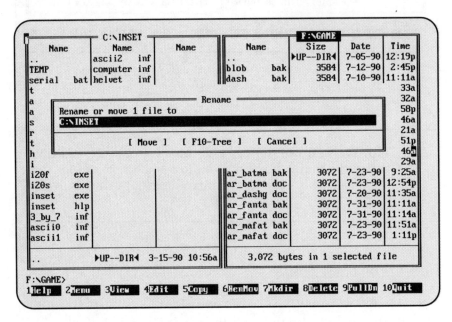

Figure 9.7   The Rename dialog box prompts you to enter a new name for the file.

Moving Files (F6)

Move Files is one of the Commander's most useful features, simply because DOS has no comparable command. If you want to move files in DOS, you have to copy the files from the source to the target and then delete the files from the source. With the Commander, you move the files from the source to the target with a single command that operates a lot like the Copy command.

To begin, select the file or files you want to move. Then, press F6 or choose the `Rename or move` command from the Files menu. The Commander displays the same dialog box as in Figure 9.7. The Commander assumes that you want to move the file to the directory represented by the inactive panel. If that's not the case, type the path name of the directory you want to use for the target. For example, if you want to move the files to D:\SAMPLE\FILES, type `d:\sample\files`. You can also choose the target by selecting the Tree command at the bottom of the dialog box and choosing the directory from a tree display. After you've selected the target, press Enter to move the selected files.

▶ **Tip:** You can rename and move a file at the same time. When the Rename dialog box appears on screen, type the path name of the target directory, including the new file name for the file.

207

Deleting Files (F8)

Deleting files is easy. In fact, it may be too easy, so be careful, especially when using wild-card characters.

 Deleting Files

1. Select the files you want to delete.

   Use the Ins key, the mouse, or the gray + or – keys as explained above.

2. Press F8 or choose `Delete` from the Files menu.

   A dialog box appears, asking for your confirmation.

3. If you're absolutely sure you want to delete the files, press Enter. If you're not sure, select `Cancel`.

   If you selected a single file and pressed enter, the file is deleted. If you tried to delete a group of files, the Commander asks again for confirmation.

4. Press Enter to confirm your request or choose Cancel to cancel it.

If you press Enter, the Commander displays a dialog box that displays the name of each file it deletes. When the dialog box disappears, all the files have been deleted. □

By holding down the Shift key when choosing Delete, you can access the Delete dialog box as shown in Figure 9.8. You can enter a path name to activate any directory, and you can use wild cards to select a range of files. Although that's convenient, it makes this command almost as dangerous as the DOS DELETE command; that is, if you attempt to delete a single file, the Commander won't ask for your confirmation. It will, however, ask you to confirm the deletion of several files. Be careful with wild-cards, or you may need to make use of the Norton Utilities.

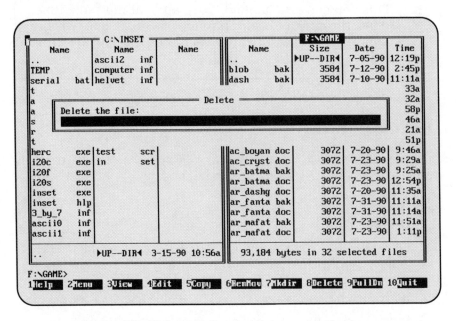

Figure 9.8   The Delete dialog box lets you activate any directory and delete a group of files.

Setting File Attributes

If you share your computer with others, or if you're connected to a modem or network, you may wish to protect some of your files from accidental or intentional mangling. To do so, you can change your files' attributes. Begin by selecting the file or group of files whose archive bit you want to change. Then, choose the file Attributes command from the Files menu (sorry, there's no hot key for this one). The Commander displays the Attributes dialog box, as shown in Figure 9.9.

Figure 9.9   Use the Attributes dialog box to protect your files.

To set an attribute, use the space bar or mouse to place an X in the box next to the attribute. When the attributes are set as desired, choose the Set command at the bottom of the box to set the attributes or the Clear command to clear them. Let's look at the attributes in turn:

Read only: The read only attribute write-protects the file. You can read the file or execute it, but you can't change it.

Archive: The archive attribute shows whether or not the file has been modified since the last time it was backed up. Setting this attribute ensures the file will be backed up.

Hidden: This attribute hides the files so that they don't appear in your directory. If you try to edit the file, the Commander won't let you. To exit the edit process, you must choose Don't Save.

System: This attribute hides and write-protects system files, giving you some protection against viruses and hackers. Don't set this attribute unless you know what you're doing.

209

Viewing a File's Contents (F3)

Many times, you'll need some information or a document, but you're just not sure which file contains the information you're looking for. You could load each file its application to view its contents, but that would take a while. The Commander helps you solve this problem by letting you view the contents of any selected file that's compatible with the Commander. (Refer to Chapter 8 for a list of applications that the Commander supports.)

To view a file, first highlight the name of the file you want to view. Press F3 or choose the View command from the Files menu. The contents of the file appear on screen, as shown in Figure 9.10.

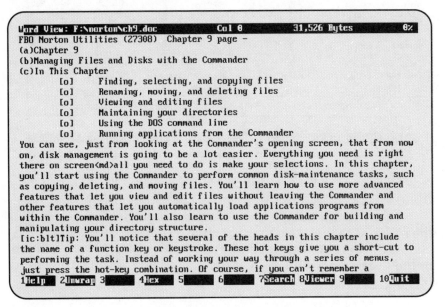

```
Word View: F:\norton\ch9.doc            Col 0            31,526 Bytes            8%
FBO Norton Utilities (27308)  Chapter 9 page -
(a)Chapter 9
(b)Managing Files and Disks with the Commander
(c)In This Chapter
        [o]     Finding, selecting, and copying files
        [o]     Renaming, moving, and deleting files
        [o]     Viewing and editing files
        [o]     Maintaining your directories
        [o]     Using the DOS command line
        [o]     Running applications from the Commander
You can see, just from looking at the Commander's opening screen, that from now
on, disk management is going to be a lot easier. Everything you need is right
there on screen<md>all you need to do is make your selections. In this chapter,
you'll start using the Commander to perform common disk-maintenance tasks, such
as copying, deleting, and moving files. You'll learn how to use more advanced
features that let you view and edit files without leaving the Commander and
other features that let you automatically load applications programs from
within the Commander. You'll also learn to use the Commander for building and
manipulating your directory structure.
[ic:blt]Tip: You'll notice that several of the heads in this chapter include
the name of a function key or keystroke. These hot keys give you a short-cut to
performing the task. Instead of working your way through a series of menus,
just press the hot-key combination. Of course, if you can't remember a
1 Help  2 Unwrap 3       4 Hex  5       6       7 Search 8 Viewer 9       10 Quit
```

Figure 9.10   A word processor view screen showing the contents of a Microsoft Word 5.0 document.

At the top of the screen is a title bar that displays the name of the application (in this case, Word) and the path and file name for the file that's displayed. This line includes additional information that varies depending on the type of file you're viewing. For a database file, the Commander shows you which record you're viewing. For a word-processor document, you see the column number for the left margin, the size of the file, and the percent of the file that's above the top of the screen. At the bottom of the screen is function key bar. This, too, varies depending on the type of file. Refer to Table 9.1 for a list of the function keys and their use.

Table 9.1   The View function keys.

Key	Text	Database	Spreadsheet
F1	None	Gives information about the file	Gives help regarding spreadsheets
F2	Toggles word wrap	Reveals the name of each field or attribute	None
F3	Toggles Unzoom if screen was originally a quick view	Toggles Unzoom screen	Toggles Unzoom screen
F4	Switches view from hex to ASCII format.	Provides spreadsheet view of records. Press F4 again to view highlighted record	None
F5	None	Lets you choose the number of the record you wish to View	Lets you specify the cell number you wish to view
F6	None	None	None
F7	Search for text string. Shift-F7 repeats the search	Search for text string. Shift-F7 repeats the search	Search for label or text string. Shift-F7 repeats the search
F8	Displays a list of viewer options	Displays an index of tables you've created	None
F9	None	None	None
F10	Quit	Quit	Quit

211

Editing Files (F4)

The Edit File feature lets you edit files that are smaller than 25K. To edit a file, first highlight the name of the file. Then, press F4 or choose the `Edit` command from the Files menu. The file is loaded into the Commander's File Editor and appears on screen, as shown in Figure 9.11.

> ► **Tip:** If you know the name of the file you want to edit, and you don't want to mess around highlighting it, or if you want to open a new file, press Shift-F4. A dialog box will appear, letting you enter a name for the file. Type a path name (if necessary) and a file name, and press Enter. If the file exists, it will appear on screen. If the file does not exist, the Commander will ask whether you want to create the file.

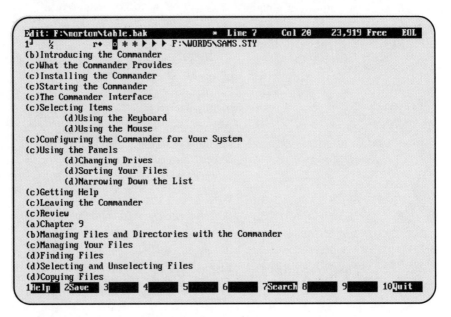

Figure 9.11   A word processor document loaded into the Commander's File Editor.

Let's take a look at this screen. At the top of the screen is a status line that provides some information about the display. On the left is the title of the file editor (**Edit**), followed by the path name and file name of the file that's displayed. When you begin to edit, an asterisk appears in the middle of this line. To the right of the asterisk is the line number and column number, specifying the cursor location. The number on the far right indicates the amount of space available in the editor's buffer. To the right of that number is the ASCII code for the character that's under the cursor.

At the bottom of the screen is the now-familiar function key bar. Notice that many of the function keys are similar to those that appeared in the View screen. The only difference is that now the F2 key is used for saving a file. You can press Shift-F2 to display a dialog box that lets you enter a new name for the file. To exit this screen, press F10 or choose `Quit` from the function key bar. By pressing Shift-F10, you can quit and save the changes to disk.

You can move the cursor around with the standard cursor control keys, as shown in Table 9.2, or use your mouse for even quicker movement. This table also lists some keys you can use to delete text. To insert text, simply type the text you wish to insert using the keyboard. If you prefer to work with a different file editor, choose the `Editor` command from the Options menu. Select the `External` option, and then enter the name of the external editor you wish to use; for example, if you have the Norton Editor and you want to use it instead, enter `ne`.

Table 9.2   The Edit text keys.

Key Combination	Action
↑	Move cursor up one line
↓	Move cursor down one line
←	Move cursor left one character without deleting
→	Move cursor right one character without deleting
Ctrl-←	Move cursor left one word
Ctrl-→	Move cursor right one word
Home	Move cursor to beginning of line
End	Move cursor to end of line
PgUp	Move cursor one page up
PgDn	Move cursor one page down
Ctrl-Home	Move cursor to beginning of file
Ctrl-End	Move cursor to end of file
Backspace	Delete character to left of cursor
Del	Delete character under cursor
Ctrl-Backspace	Delete one word to left
Ctrl-T	Delete one word to right
Ctrl-Y	Delete line
Ctrl-K	Delete from cursor position to end of line
Ctrl-Q	Quote next character

Managing Your Disks and Directories

Gaining control over your files is an important first step in keeping your hard disk organized and uncluttered. But to do a complete job, you need to be able to manipulate your directory structure; that is, you need to be able to create new directories and remove directories that are no longer in use. The Commander gives you all the tools you need to perform these tasks quickly.

In addition, the Commander gives you much more freedom in how you structure your disk. For example, in the past, most books would tell you to make your directory tree very shallow. If you made the tree too deep, you ended up with path statements a mile long. Every time you wanted to access a file, you'd have to enter these ungodly path statements, without making a typo. Now that you can *select* a directory rather than *typing* a path name, you can make your directory tree as deep as necessary, making it possible to work with smaller groups of files.

214

The Norton Commander Directory (NCD) Tree

You've already seen that the Commander displays the structure of your disk in the form of a directory tree. Because of this simplified display, you can attach new directories and lop off empty ones by simply highlighting the directory and entering the appropriate command. You can do this in either the panel display or a special display called the *NCD Tree*, as shown in Figure 9.12. To see this display, press Alt-F10 or choose the NCD Tree command from the Commands menu. The currently active directory is highlighted.

You can move the highlight bar to any directory by using the cursor keys or clicking on the directory with the mouse. If you press the Enter key, and this display disappears, and the directory you highlighted becomes the active directory. You can even search for a directory on the directory tree.

Q Searching for a Directory on the NCD Tree

1. Press Alt-F10 or choose NCD Tree from the Commands menu.	The currently active directory is highlighted.
2. Press the left-arrow key or the mouse to move the cursor to the beginning of the tree.	The root directory is highlighted.

3. Start typing the name of the directory.

As you type, the highlight bar moves to the directory that matches the characters you typed so far until it reaches the directory that matches your latest entry.

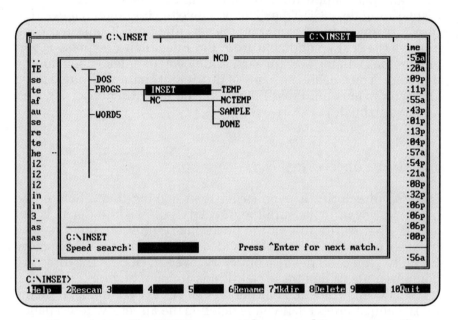

Figure 9.12 *The NCD tree provides a graphic representation of your directory structure.*

215

At the bottom of the screen is a function key bar that offers the following additional commands:

Rescan: Whenever you add or delete a directory, your change may not appear in the directory tree. Choose this command or press F2 to have the Commander update the directory structure to display the changes.

Rename: Choose this command or press F6 to rename a directory. A dialog box will appear asking you to enter the new name.

Mkdir: Move the highlight to the directory for which you want to create a subdirectory. Then, press F7 or choose this command. You'll be asked to enter a name for the subdirectory. Type the name and press Enter. You now have a new subdirectory.

Delete: To delete a directory, make sure the directory you want to delete is not active and is empty; otherwise, the Commander will not delete it. Then, choose this command or press F8.

Quit: Press F10 or choose the `Quit` command to close this window and return to your panels.

Making Directories (F7)

You can create a new directory either in the tree view of the panel display or in the NCD Tree display. Move the highlight bar over the directory under which you want the new directory. Then choose the `Make Directory` command from the Files menu or press F7. In either case, a dialog box appears, asking you to enter a name for the directory. You can enter a name of up to eight characters plus a three character extension. Press Enter, and the new directory is created and highlighted.

Deleting Directories (F8)

Deleting directories is even easier than making them. Before you begin, however, make sure the directory you wish to delete is not active. That is, the title of the panel that represents the directory must not be displayed in reverse video. Also, make sure the directory is empty. You can't delete a directory, even in DOS, if the directory contains a file. When these conditions are met, highlight the directory you want to delete. Then choose the `Delete` command from the Files menu or press F8. If you're deleting the directory from a panel, the Commander displays a dialog box asking you to confirm your choice. Press Enter to delete, or choose `Cancel` if you change your mind. If you're deleting the directory from the NCD Tree, the directory disappears without asking for confirmation.

> **Note:** If you selected the `Auto Change Directory` option in the Configuration dialog box, you cannot delete a directory using the panel tree display. As soon as you highlight the directory, it becomes active, and the Commander prevents you from deleting it. To delete the directory, open the menu for the panel with the tree display and select `Full` or `Brief` to turn off the tree display. You can now delete the directory. Your other option is to turn off the Auto Change Directory option. Choose `Configuration` from the Options menu. Move the cursor to the `Auto Change Directory` option and press the space bar. Move the cursor to the `Ok` button and press Enter. You can now delete a directory from the tree.

Running Applications from the Commander

If you're working in the Commander and you decide you want to exit and begin working in some other application, you can exit the Commander and load your other application with a single command. All you need to do is highlight the name of the file that executes your program, and press Enter. For example, if you wanted to run Microsoft Word, you would highlight the file WORD.EXE in the panel and press Enter.

The Commander offers two additional features that let you load your applications. The first lets you set up a menu that lists all your applications. To run the application, you choose its name from the menu. The second lets you launch an application and load a file into it simply by selecting the data file you want to work with from the panel listing. The following sections tell you how to set up and use these more advanced features.

217

Creating a Menu for Running Your Applications

You may have noticed the F2 Menu command in the function key bar at the bottom of the screen. If you press that key now, you'll see a dialog box that tells you there's no file available for that command. Let's fix that problem by creating the file.

Press F9 and pull down the Commands menu. At the bottom of this menu are two choices: Menu file edit and eXtension file edit. Choose the Menu file edit option. The Commander displays the User Menu dialog box, asking you which menu you want to edit. The Main option lets you edit the Commander's main menu. This menu is accessible from anywhere in the Commander. The Local option lets you create a local menu that's accessible only from within a particular directory. Choose the Main option now to display a screen like the one in Figure 9.13 (yours won't have text at the top). At the bottom of the screen is a help window that provides a brief explanation of the operation.

Now you're ready to begin typing the commands that run your applications. Choose an application you want to run (for example, WordPerfect). Type a single letter to represent a quick-key command for running the application. For example, you may wish to type P for WordPerfect. Type a colon and a space followed by the name of the program you want to run. Your first line should look something like this:

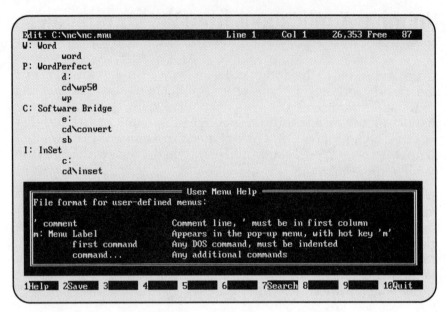

```
Edit: C:\nc\nc.mnu                    Line 1      Col 1      26,353 Free    87
W: Word
        word
P: WordPerfect
        d:
        cd\wp50
        wp
C: Software Bridge
        e:
        cd\convert
        sb
I: InSet
        c:
        cd\inset

═══════════════════════ User Menu Help ═══════════════════════
║File format for user-defined menus:                                ║
║                                                                   ║
║' comment                    Comment line, ' must be in first column║
║m: Menu Label                Appears in the pop-up menu, with hot key 'm'║
║       first command         Any DOS command, must be indented     ║
║       command...            Any additional commands               ║
═══════════════════════════════════════════════════════════════

1Help  2Save  3     4     5     6     7Search 8     9          10Quit
```

Figure 9.13   *The Edit Menu screen is shown here with a Help window.*

P: WordPerfect

Press Enter, and then press the Tab key to indent the second line. (Press the Tab key to indent all subsequent command lines as well.) Type the commands you would normally type at the DOS prompt to run your program. For example, you probably have to access the drive and directory that holds your program files and then type a command to load the program. If you were creating a menu item to run WordPerfect, and your program files were in D:\WP5, your command lines would look like the following:

P: WordPerfect
    d:
    cd\wp5
    wp

Press Enter at the end of the last line. You can create as many of these entries as you need. When you're done typing your entries, press F2 or choose Save to save the file and then F10 Quit to exit the screen. Now, when you choose the F2 Menu command, you'll see a User menu like the one in Figure 9.14. Type the letter that corresponds to the application you want to run, or select the application with the highlight bar. The Commander automatically loads the application.

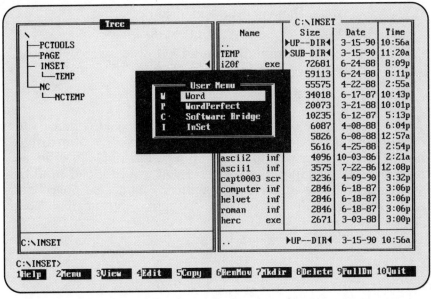

Figure 9.14   The User Menu screen lets you select the application you want to run.

The Point-and-shoot Feature

The point-and-shoot feature lets you run an application and load a file into the application by selecting the file from the panel listing. To be able to do this, however, you must create an *extension file* (NC.EXT) similar to the menu file explained above. To begin, choose the `eXtension file edit` command from the Commands menu. This opens an Edit screen similar to the one in Figure 9.13.

Type the file extension of the files you want to be able to automatically load into a given application. For example, if you want all files with the extension .DOC loaded into Word, type `doc` followed by a colon. Press the space bar, and type the command required to run the application *from any directory*. That is, if you can run Word by typing `word` at any DOS prompt, then type `word`. If, however, you must supply a path to the Word files, then type the complete path followed by the command— for example,

```
f:\word5\word !.!
```

The parameter `!.!` tells the Commander to enter the file name on the command line. The following list provides alternatives to what you can have entered on the command line:

! . !	Enter file name and extension
!	Enter file name without extension
! :	Enter current drive letter followed by colon
! \	Enter path statement
! !	Enter single exclamation point

After typing the command, press Enter. Repeat the process for as many extension files as desired. Press F2 to save the setup to disk. Then, whenever you want to run an application and load a file into that application, simply select the file you want to load from the panel listing. That is, either highlight the file name and press Enter or double-click on the file with the left mouse button. The Commander does the rest.

What You Have Learned

▶ The Find Files feature lets you search an entire disk drive for a file or group of files.

▶ You can select and unselect individual files using the Ins key or groups of files using the gray + or gray – key.

▶ Once you've selected a file or group of files, you can enter any of several commands to copy, delete, rename, or move the files. You can even change file attributes for a file to protect it from external threats.

▶ The F3 View command lets you view the contents of a file without changing the contents.

▶ The Commander's File Editor lets you edit files without exiting the Commander.

▶ The NCD tree (Alt-F10) gives you an overall view of your directory tree. This tree offers several commands that simplify directory maintenance, making it easy to create new directories or delete empty ones.

▶ The Commander's User menu lets you run applications from the Commander by selecting the application from a menu.

▶ The point-and-shoot feature lets you run an application from the Commander and load a file into the application with a single command.

Communicating with the Commander

In This Chapter

▶ *Connecting two computers with Commander Link*
▶ *Copying files from another computer*
▶ *Configuring your system for Commander Mail*
▶ *Sending messages via Commander Mail*
▶ *Checking your mail*

The Commander offers two features that let your computer communicate with other computers. Commander Link creates a communication link between two computers so you can copy files from one computer to another—from laptop to desktop, for example. Instead of having to use floppy disks as an intermediary, you can copy files directly from hard disk to hard disk. Commander Mail allows you to send E-mail, FAXes, and telexes, via modem, using your MCI Mail account. In this chapter, you'll learn how to set up your system and configure the Commander to perform these two important tasks.

Using Commander Link

Like all of the Commander features, Commander Link is easy to run. Once the two computers are connected and are running Commander Link, you simply copy files from one to the other, just as you would copy files from one directory to another. Before you can do that, however, you must connect the two computers with the proper cable and have the Commander installed on both systems.

Connecting the Two Computers

The first step in establishing a link between the computers is to purchase the proper serial null-modem cable (RS-232) for the two computers you intend to connect. Make sure the cable is a null-modem cable (it should be marked). If it's not a null-modem, you'll need to purchase a null-modem adapter. You need a cable to connect the COM1 or COM2 port on one computer to the COM1 or COM2 port on the other. Check the back of your computer to see if the ports are marked. If they are, you're in luck; if not, refer to the documentation that came with your computer or call your dealer. Write down how many pins each has (9 or 25) and whether the port is male (has pins) or female (has receptacles for pins). (The serial ports are usually male, but don't bet on it.) When you've figured out what you need, obtain the required cable and any necessary adapters from your local computer store.

> **Note:** Your printer is probably connected to the parallel port at the back of your computer. If you have a mouse or a modem, it is probably connected to your serial port. If you have only one COM port on your computer, you'll have to disconnect any device that's connected to it before you can proceed.

With both computers turned off (to protect them), connect the COM1 or COM2 ports using the cable. Then, boot each computer. Make sure the Commander is installed on both computers, and start the program on each.

Before you perform the next step, decide which computer you want to use to control the transfer of data. This computer will be your *master*. The other computer will be the *slave*; it will do only what the master computer tells it to do. If you've connected a laptop to your desktop computer, use the desktop as the master and the laptop as the slave. Now, open the Left or Right menu on your master computer and choose the Link command. This opens the dialog box shown in Figure 10.1.

> **Tip:** If your slave computer is on the right, use the Left menu to establish the link. The Right menu will then show a list of files on the slave, organizing the panels to correspond to the location of the computers.

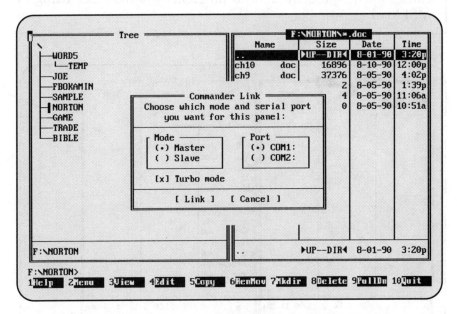

Figure 10.1   Use the Commander Link dialog box to set up the link.

Choose the **Master** option by highlighting it and pressing the space bar or by clicking on it with the mouse. Choose **COM1** or **COM2** in the same way depending on which COM ports you connected. Highlight the **Link** button and press Enter. A dialog box appears, telling you that Commander Link is waiting for you to set up Link on the slave.

Now, move to your slave computer. Open either the Left or Right menu, and select the **Link** command. Select **slave** for this computer, and select the same COM port you specified for the master. Highlight the **Link** button and press Enter. It takes a few seconds for the Commander to establish the link. A dialog box appears, telling you that your slave is now set up to process requests from the master. The right panel on the master computer shows a list of files on the current directory of the slave, as shown in Figure 10.2.

> ▶ **Note:** If you get a message telling you to set up the other computer as the master, and you already did that, you may have a problem with the connection between the serial ports. Activate the directory C:\NC, highlight the file called SERIAL.TXT, and press F3. This file provides a list of possible causes for the problem and for problems you may face using MCI Mail.

224

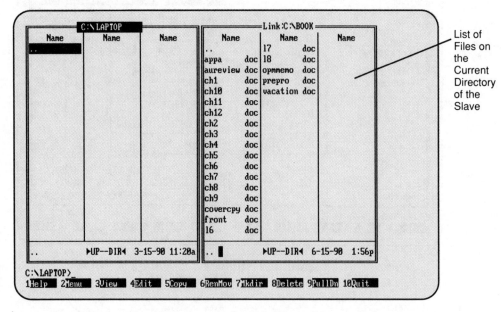

List of Files on the Current Directory of the Slave

Figure 10.2   The Link screen displayed on the master computer.

Transferring Files

Now that the two computers are linked, the rest is easy. You can copy or move files between the two computers or rename or delete files on the slave by entering commands on the master. The following Quick Steps tell you how to copy files from slave to master. You'll be working on the keyboard of the master computer.

Q Copying Files Using Commander Link

1. Press Tab to activate the panel for the slave.

The highlight bar moves to the slave panel.

2. Change to the drive and directory you want to access.

The panel display changes, listing all the files in the active directory.

3. Select the files you want to copy by pressing the gray + key, by pressing Ins, or by clicking with the mouse.

The files are highlighted in the right panel.

4. Press F5 or select the Copy command from the Files menu.

The Copy dialog box appears, telling you the destination of the copied files.

5. If the destination is correct, press Enter. If it's not correct, enter a new drive and directory and press Enter.

Link begins copying the selected files to the specified drive and directory on the master. □

Terminating the Link

225

When you're done performing your tasks with Link, open the Left menu on the master and choose the Link command again. Power down both computers as you normally would, and with both computers off, disconnect the serial null-modem cable. (To protect your system, you should always turn off the power before connecting or disconnecting a cable.)

Using Commander Mail

The most difficult thing about Commander Mail is setting up your system to run it. Once you've established an MCI Mail account and have your system hooked up to a modem, the feature itself is very easy to use. The system lets you transfer data to and from others who are hooked into the same system. Commander Mail also lets you send letters, FAXes, and telexes (paper mail) to those who do not have MCI accounts, or messages to those who use CompuServe or Telemail X.4000.

Basic Requirements

If you don't have an MCI Mail account, call 1-800-444-6245 for information on what you must do. When this is taken care of, you are ready to begin. Make sure your modem is properly connected. The modem must be connected to a power supply and a phone line that works. Many offices have separate phone receptacles that are marked DATA for modem connections. If you have an external modem, connect the modem to the COM1 or COM2 port on the back of your computer. If the port is not marked, refer the manual that came with your computer or call your dealer. If you have an internal modem, connect the phone line to the modem jack at the back of your computer. Once your computer is connected to the modem, you are ready to set up the Commander Mail feature.

Setting Up Commander Mail

The first time you select the `Commander Mail` command from the Command menu, you're greeted by the screen shown in Figure 10.3. Press Enter, and the Commander displays the screen shown in Figure 10.4, requesting information about your account.

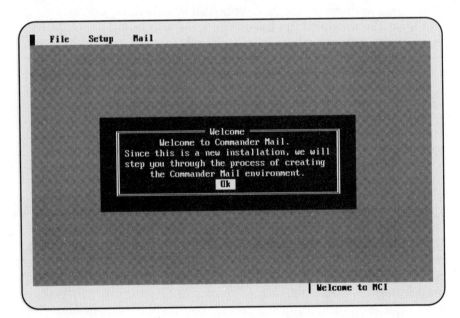

Figure 10.3   The opening Commander Mail screen greets you at startup.

Enter your first initial and your last name, and press Enter. Type a password up to eight characters to prevent unauthorized access to your account. In the MCI ID field, type your seven-digit MCI ID number (this is optional). Move the cursor to the Receive box. If you

Figure 10.4   The Account 1 dialog box prompts you to enter account information.

want to be able to receive messages, move the highlight to Yes and press the space bar. If you only want to send messages, select No. If necessary, use the Tab key to move around the dialog box and change any of the information.

When the information is correct, move the highlight to the Yes button at the bottom of the box and press Enter. Another dialog box appears, asking you whether you want to use the account you set up, add or modify an account, or delete an account altogether. If you're sharing your computer, you may set up Commander Mail for more than one account.

When you're finished setting up all your accounts, select the Ok button at the bottom of the box. Another dialog box appears, showing you the paths to your IN, OUT, and SENT directories. These directories act as mailboxes. Later, you'll put files in the OUT directory to send them, and you'll check your IN directory for incoming mail. If these defaults are acceptable, press Enter. If you want to change the defaults, move the cursor to the path you want to change and type a path to the directory you want to use. When you're done, select the Yes button. This opens the modem dialog box shown in Figure 10.5.

Figure 10.5   Use the Modem dialog box to configure the Commander Mail for your system.

In the Port box, select the COM port that your modem is connected to. Next, find out if you have tone or pulse telephone service. To do this, pick up your phone and dial a few numbers. If you hear tones of varying pitches, you have tone service. If you hear clicks of various lengths, you have rotary or pulse service. Press the Tab key to move the highlight to the Dialing box and select the correct setting. If you want to listen to the modem as it works, move the highlight to the Modem Sound box and press the space bar. Next, move the highlight to the Baud Rate box, and select the baud rate for your modem. (Check the documentation that came with your modem to determine the baud rate.) At the bottom of the dialog box is a Modem initialization string. This information is supplied for you, and you should not have to edit it. If you have problems sending or receiving mail, check the documentation that came with your modem to determine whether you have to edit this string.

When you're done, select the Yes button at the bottom of the box. This opens the Phone Number dialog box. The Phone field contains the national 800 number you can dial to contact MCI. You can change this to a local number. In the Prefix field, enter any number you have to dial to get an outside line. In many offices, for example, you have to dial 9 before dialing your number. Type a comma after the prefix, telling the modem to pause for a dial tone. Select the Yes button to end the setup operation and display the Commander Mail screen.

A dialog box appears asking if you want to make a directory C:\NC\IN. Press Enter three times to create the IN, OUT, and SENT directories. Another dialog box appears, informing you that Commander Mail has created a parameter file. Press Enter, and your In Box appears on-screen. This is the box that contains any messages you may receive. Whenever you run Commander Mail, it displays this screen first, to inform you of any incoming mail.

The Commander Mail Screen

When you press Esc or select ok, the In Box disappears from the screen, leaving the main Commander Mail screen, shown in Figure 10.6. At the top of the screen is a pull-down menu bar listing three available menus:

> File
> Setup
> Mail

Press F9 to activate the menu bar, then select the name of the menu you want to open.

Figure 10.6   Press F9 to activate the menu bar on the main Commander Mail screen.

The File menu offers three options. You can get on-line help by selecting the He l p command or pressing F1. This menu also lets you access MCI customer support. To quit Commander Mail and return to the main Commander screen, select Qui t.

The Setup menu offers several options that let you configure the Commander Mail. The first option, Address Book, is one of the most useful options on this menu. It lets you create an address book to store all the information you need to send messages and mail to your most frequent contacts. If you choose Add, a dialog box appears, asking you to choose the type of mail system you want to use. After making your selection, the Mail Subscriber Address box appears, as in Figure 10.7. This box lets you enter information about your contacts. The remaining options on the Setup menu let you change any of the information you entered to originally set up Commander Mail.

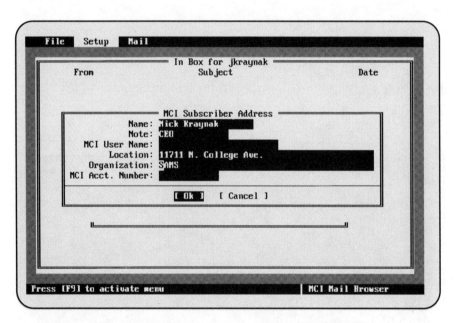

Figure 10.7 Creating an entry for the Address Book.

The third menu, Mail, lists the options you'll use to send and receive messages. You can check your In Box for incoming messages, create new messages, send and receive messages, reply, and lots more. You'll learn more about these options in the following sections.

Creating a Message

Before you can send a message, you have to create one. Press Ctrl-N or select New Message from the Mail menu, displaying the screen shown in Figure 10.8.

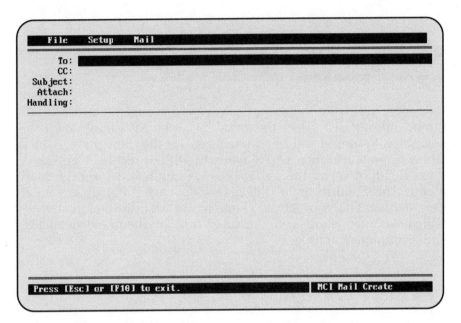

Figure 10.8   Press Ctrl-N to begin creating a message.

With the highlight in the To: or CC: field, press Enter to display the Edit Send List dialog box. This box lets you enter information about the person you wish to contact. At the bottom of this box are the following 5 buttons:

List gives you access to your Address Book. Instead of typing in the required information, you can select a destination from the book.

New lets you bypass the Address Book and create a new entry.

Remove lets you delete a name on the list.

Handling gives you four options that let you specify how you want the mail handled. You can ask for confirmation of receipt or for priority status; you can specify a charging category; or you can alert your contact by phone that the mail has been received.

Ok lets you accept the information entered in the box.

After you've entered the required information about the receiver, move the cursor to the space under the Handling field, and type your message. Press F10 or Esc to leave the screen and open a dialog box asking if you want to save the message. Press Enter to select the Save option. This returns you to the main Commander Mail screen. You can create additional messages or send the messages you just created.

Sending and Receiving Messages

Whenever you want to send or receive information, you must tell Commander Mail to initiate contact between MCI mail and your computer. You send and receive messages at the same time, using a single command. When you're ready to send or receive a message, Press Ctrl-S or select the Send/Receive command from the Mail menu. The Send/Receive dialog box appears, informing you of Commander Mail's progress. Commander Mail automatically establishes contact, sends your messages, receives incoming messages, and terminates the process.

Checking Your In Box

If anybody sent you a message before you established contact with MCI mail, that message should now be in your IN directory. Press Ctrl-B or select In Box from the Mail menu to display the In Box screen, shown in Figure 10.9. This screen lists the messages that are stacking up in your In Box. Perform the following quick steps to check your In Box.

 Checking Your In Box

1. Press Ctrl-B or select In Box from the Mail menu.

   This opens the In Box screen, giving you a list messages that are in your Box.

2. Move the highlight bar to the message you want to read, and press Enter.

   The message appears on screen.

3. Use the cursor keys to read the rest of the message.

4. Use the gray + and gray – keys to read the next message or the previous one.

5. Press Esc.   This takes you back to the list of messages in your In Box.

6. Press Esc.   This takes you back to the main Commander Mail screen.   □

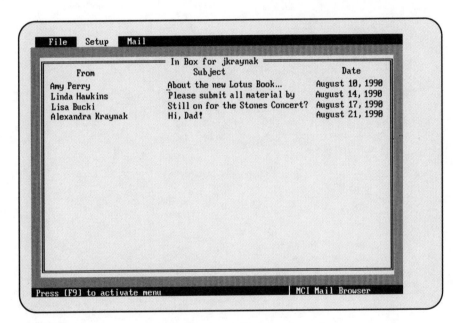

Figure 10.9   Press Ctrl-B to view a list of messages in your In Box.

What You Have Learned

▶ Commander Link lets you transfer files directly from one computer to another.

▶ In order to run Commander Link, you must connect both computers with a serial null-modem cable and install the Commander on both computers.

► The Commander Mail feature lets you send E-mail, FAXes, and telexes, via modem, using your MCI mail account. Before you can use Commander Mail, your computer must be connected to a modem, and you must have an MCI Mail account.

► The Address Book lets you store information about several of your most frequent contacts, so you don't have to reenter the information every time you want to send a message.

234

Using the Norton Backup

In This Chapter

- ▶ *Setting up the Norton Backup*
- ▶ *How to back up your hard disk*
- ▶ *How to restore data from backup diskettes*
- ▶ *Basic and advanced level options*
- ▶ *How to create Setup files for PreSet backup and restore*

An Ounce of Prevention

The Norton Backup, which is a separate program from the Norton Utilities, provides a simple means of protecting your information and the time it took you to create it. The program *"backs up"* (copies) files from your hard disk onto floppy diskettes in a special compressed format. Should you lose your hard disk files, the Norton Backup lets you "decompress" and *restore* them from your backup diskettes onto your hard disk.

How can you lose files from a hard disk? Let me count the ways. Your hard disk can "crash" due to power spikes, system failure, or physical damage. You can inadvertently erase files or directories. You can accidentally reformat your hard disk. You can even lose your hard disk contents to a computer virus.

Regular backup of your hard disk files prevents their total loss in the event of disaster. The frequency with which you back up your hard disk depends on how often you use it and how sensitive or difficult it is to recreate your files. With the Norton Backup, you can easily back up all files on a daily basis. Many users, however, find that a complete monthly backup, with weekly or daily backups of new or changed files only, is adequate for their needs.

The Norton Backup provides options that let you not only set your backup frequency, but also select the files that you want to back up, the degree of compression (which determines whether a backup requires more diskettes or more time), whether you want the accuracy of copied data verified (which also affects speed), and more. The options available to you depend on which of the three Norton Backup levels you use:

Basic Lets you select which files to back up, choose between five types of backup, and select from eight backup options.

Advanced Lets you choose from more backup options and create custom setup files that let you use the Norton Backup at PreSet level.

PreSet Lets you run a backup or restore operation with only a few keystrokes, with options previously set up in the Advanced level.

This chapter explains the Basic level in detail; as a beginner, that is the level you will most likely use. It also explains Advanced options and the PreSet backup and restore, although in less detail.

Getting Started

Before you can perform your first backup, you must install and configure the Norton Backup. Both procedures are easy and quick. Screen prompts guide you through the process of copying files from the Norton Backup diskettes, answering a few questions, and starting tests that set up the program for your particular computer system. In the following sections, you will learn how to install, configure, start, and exit from the Norton Backup, as well as how to use the On-Line Help system.

Keyboard and Mouse Use

As you run the Norton Backup, dialog boxes both provide information and ask for input. You provide some of the input by selecting items on the screen. To select an item using the keyboard, highlight it by pressing the Tab or arrow keys; then press Enter. To turn a checkbox on or off, highlight it and then press the space bar. Use the backspace and Del keys to erase characters that you type.

To select an item using the mouse, position the cursor over the item and click with either button. To select or deselect drives, directories, and files to back up or restore, right-click on your selection.

Installing the Norton Backup

To begin installation, you need the Norton Backup Diskettes (two 5-1/4" or one 3-1/2"). Installation is an eight-step process, as shown on the initial Norton Backup Installation screen in Figure 11.1. The final step begins program configuration, which is explained in the next section. During installation you are asked to make certain decisions:

237

▶ Which floppy drive you are installing the Norton Backup from. This will be A: or B:.

▶ Where the Norton Backup will be installed. This will be your hard drive, usually C:, in a directory called NBACKUP that the program creates. If your hard disk contains more than one drive, you can specify a different drive (for example, D:). You can also give the directory a different name, as long as it is no more than 8 characters long.

▶ Whether or not you want to save or write over an existing version of the Norton Backup, if you already have the program on your hard disk.

▶ Whether or not you want the Norton Backup to revise the PATH command in your AUTOEXEC.BAT file so that you can run the Norton Backup from any directory. This is a good idea, as it saves you the trouble of changing to the NBACKUP directory before running the program.

▶ Whether or not you want the program to change your CONFIG.SYS file to set the BUFFERS parameter at 30. This allows you to run the Norton Backup more efficiently.

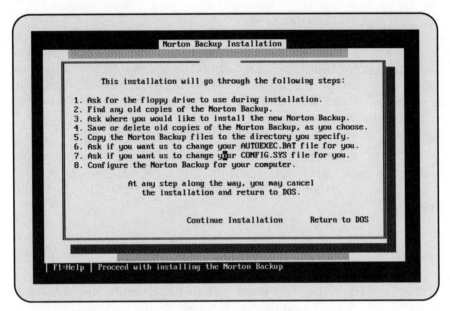

Figure 11.1   The initial Norton Backup Installation screen shows the eight steps you need to follow.

238

At any time during installation, you can stop the process and return to the DOS prompt by selecting `Return to Dos` on the Installation screen. You can also skip certain steps, such as changing the AUTOEXEC.BAT and CONFIG.SYS files or running the program configuration. If you are installing from 5-1/4" diskettes, you will be prompted to insert Diskette 2 during the file copy operation.

 The Norton Backup Installation

1. Insert the Norton Backup Diskette 1 in A: or B:. Change to that drive by typing `A:` or `B:` and pressing Enter.

   The `A>` or `B>` prompt appears.

2. Type `Install` and press Enter.

   The copyright screen appears, followed by the initial Norton Backup Installation screen in Figure 11.1.

3. Select `Continue Installation`.

   A dialog box asks you which drive contains Backup Diskette 1.

4. Select the drive that contains Backup Diskette 1 (A or B).

The program searches for existing Norton Backup files, then asks for the drive and directory on which the program will be installed. C:\ NBACKUP is the default.

5. Type in a new drive and/or directory name if you do not want the default. Skip this step if the default is okay.

The new names replace the default.

6. Select Accept Directory.

If the program already exists on disk, you may be asked if you want to save or write over the old program. Otherwise, the Copy Files dialog box appears.

7. Select COPY to begin copying program files. Repeat this step for Diskette 2 if prompted to do so.

The AUTOEXEC.BAT dialog box appears when all files are copied.

239

8. Select OK on the AUTOEXEC.BAT and CONFIG.SYS dialog boxes.

The Configuration dialog box appears.

9. Select OK at the Configure Now prompt to proceed with program configuration (described in the next section).

□

Configuring the Norton Backup for Your System

The Norton Backup Configuration screen shown in Figure 11.2, appears automatically when you select OK at the Configure Now prompt at the end of installation. You can also reconfigure your system at any time by selecting Configure from the Norton Backup main menu, displayed when you start the program.

The Norton Backup Configuration screen shows several setup parameters for which you will choose options. These include:

Program Level: Basic, Advanced, or PreSet
Mouse: Right- or left-handed and degree of sensitivity
Video Display: Type and resolution of your monitor

Figure 11.2   *The Norton Backup Configuration screen shows setup options. The Program Level: dialog box is selected automatically.*

Floppy Drives:	Drives available on your computer
Configuration Tests:	Diagnostic tests of your computer and the program

The default program level is Basic. Leave this setting at the default until you become more experienced with the Norton Backup. It is easy to change the setting later if you desire.

The **Mouse** settings let you configure the mouse for ease of use. The Mouse Button setting lets you choose between Left-Handed or Right-Handed operation. Instructions in this book are based on the Right-Handed option; the Left-Handed option reverses mouse instructions. The Sensitivity setting determines the distance that the cursor moves across the screen when you move the mouse. It can be set to Low, Medium, or High, with Low producing the least amount of screen movement. Medium is the default.

The **Double Click** setting determines how rapidly one click must follow another to be recognized as a double click. Slow allows a longer interval; the default is Medium. The Acceleration setting determines the acceleration of mouse movement, and can be set to None, Medium, or Fast. The default is None.

The **Video Display** configuration settings are set automatically to match your monitor, but can be changed if necessary. Accept the default settings unless you are sure that they are incorrect. Turn on the Reduced Display Speed option if you have an older CGA monitor that is subject to "snow." Turn off the Expanding Dialog Windows option if you want dialog boxes to pop on the screen rather than appearing more gradually.

The **Floppy Drives** configuration settings are set to match your floppy drives. Check the settings and change them if necessary.

The **Configuration Tests** are conducted automatically and require only that you (1) approve their continuation at various points by selecting OK from a dialog box, and (2) insert floppy diskettes when prompted by the Insert Diskette message within flashing brackets. The diskettes do not need to be formatted, but they do need to match the floppy drive configuration (size and density) set up earlier. When the tests are complete, you are shown the configuration settings; approve them by selecting Accept Settings.

 Caution: The first Configuration Test, the Direct Memory Access (DMA) test, checks your computer's DMA chip to make sure the Norton Backup uses the chip's optimum speed. Some DMA chips may fail the test and cause the computer to "freeze," particularly if you are running a version of the Norton Backup prior to Version 1.1. If this occurs, simply turn your computer off and on again, then restart the program by typing nbackup at the DOS prompt. Select the following options in order on the next three screens: Configure, Configuration Tests, and Confidence Test. You can then complete configuration.

The Norton Backup Configuration

1. From the initial Norton Backup Configuration screen, select the program level you want, then OK.

   The Mouse Configuration dialog box appears.

2. Select Mouse Button, Sensitivity, Double Click, and Acceleration options. Then select OK.

   The Video Configuration dialog box appears.

3. Check the Color Palette and Screen Lines options and change if necessary. Turn check boxes for Reduced Display Speed and Expanding Dialog Windows on or off as desired. Select OK.

The Floppy Drive Configuration dialog box appears.

4. Check that Floppy Drive settings match your floppy drive specifications, and change them if necessary. Select OK when done.

The first Configuration Test screen appears. The program can read your system configuration, so the Floppy Drive settings should normally not need to be changed.

5. Follow the screen prompts to complete all tests. Insert diskettes when flashing brackets and message prompts you to Insert Diskette # 1 and Insert Diskette # 2. You will need to insert the diskettes again during test verification.

The Configuration Tests dialog box appears showing the final system settings determined by the tests.

6. Select Accept Settings.

The Save Configuration dialog box appears.

7. Select Save.

The DEFAULT.SET setup file alert box appears.

8. Select Create.

A dialog box asks you to personalize your copy of the program.

9. Complete the registration by typing in your name and your company name (if appropriate). Then select OK.

The screen shows a dialog box stating that the Norton Backup has been installed.

10. Select OK from the dialog box.

You are returned to the DOS prompt. □

Running the Norton Backup

If you allowed the program to alter your AUTOEXEC.BAT file during installation, you can start the Norton Backup from any directory on your hard disk. For example, you can start the program from any of the following prompts:

```
C:\>
C:\WORD5>
C:\NBACKUP>
```

To start the program, simply type

nbackup

This takes you to the Norton Backup main menu, shown in Figure 11.3. From this menu you can choose one of four boxes: Backup, Restore, Configure, or Quit. Backup and Restore begin immediately upon selecting them, at the level you selected during configuration. Choosing Configure takes you to the main Configuration screen, which allows you to reconfigure the program (to change the program level or any other system settings). Selecting Quit exits the Norton Backup and returns you to the DOS prompt.

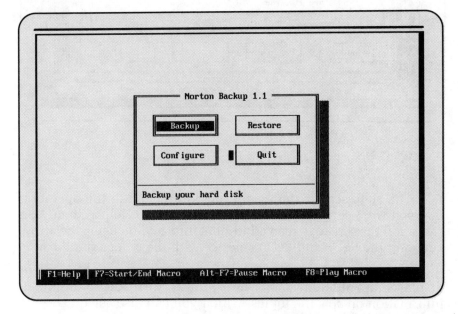

Figure 11.3   Use the Norton Backup main menu to start the backup or restore process, to change configuration options, or to exit the Norton Backup.

Getting Help When You Need It

Although the Norton Backup is easy to use, you may occasionally need help with a particular operation or desire more information on available options. This help is available at any time from within the program through the On-Line Help system. To enter this system, press the F1 key or click with the mouse on the F1=Help command in the lower left corner of the screen. A screen similar to the one shown in Figure 11.4 appears.

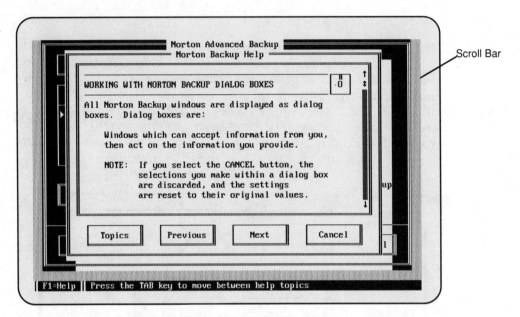

Scroll Bar

Figure 11.4   The Norton Backup Help screen displays information on the last operation you were performing.

The Help screen shows information related to the operation that you were performing when you entered the Help system. You can scroll the screen to read additional information using the arrow keys and the PgUp and PgDn keys, or with the mouse scroll bar.

Some words or phrases on the screen may be highlighted or displayed in a different color. These phrases are linked to additional information on specific topics, which you can also select. Use the Tab key to highlight a linked phrase, then press Enter to display the information—or right-click on the phrase with the mouse.

At the bottom of the screen is a menu of additional Help options:

Topics displays an index of all Help topics. Select a topic from the list to see more detailed information on it.

Previous shows the last Help screen viewed. If you are at the initial Help screen, this option is not available.

Next shows the next available Help screen on the topic selected.

Cancel takes you out of the On-Line Help system and returns you to the screen from which you left.

If an option is not available, the highlight will skip over it when you attempt to select it.

Exiting the Program

When you are finished using the Norton Backup, exit the program by selecting Quit from the main menu (Figure 11.3). This returns you to the DOS prompt from which you started the program.

If you select the Quit After Backup (or Quit After Restore) option at the start of either operation, the program quits automatically when the operation is complete and returns you to the DOS prompt. These options are explained later in the chapter.

245

The Basic Backup

The Basic backup gives you considerable power and a number of options for protecting your hard disk files. While not as fully featured as the Advanced backup, it gives you as much control as you are likely to need in the beginning.

The following sections take you through the initial setup, options, and execution of a Basic backup. The steps described here are essentially the same for the Advanced backup, so they are not repeated in the Advanced backup section. The Quick Steps for the Basic backup take you through the process in an abbreviated form. More detail on each step is provided in the sections that follow.

Q **Running the Basic Backup**

1. Select Backup from the main menu.

   The Norton Basic Backup screen appears, as shown in Figure 11.5.

2. If you want to back up a different drive than the one currently selected, select the new drive(s) in the Backup From: box.

   ALL files appears next to the selected drive.

3. If you want to change the floppy drive that the backup files will be copied to, select the `Backup To:` box. Choose the drive you want in the window that appears; then select `OK`.

The Norton Basic Backup screen reappears with the new floppy drive shown.

4. If you want to specify a different type of backup than the one shown, select the `Backup Type:` box. Choose the desired type in the window that appears; then select `OK`.

The Norton Basic Backup screen reappears with the new backup type shown.

5. Select `Options` to check or change the Basic options.

The Backup Options window appears.

6. Select the desired options. An `X` in the checkbox indicates that the option is selected. When all desired options are checked, select `OK`.

This sets your options, and the Norton Basic Backup screen reappears.

7. If you want to check or change which files are set to be backed up, choose the `Select Files` box. Otherwise, skip to step 9.

The Backup Files screen appears. If you are running Backup for the first time, all files in all directories in the selected drive are marked for backup. Otherwise, the files last selected for backup are marked.

8. Select (or deselect) the directories and files to be backed up. Select `Display` to check and change any file display options. When all files are selected, select `OK`.

The Norton Basic Backup screen reappears.

9. Select `Start Backup`.

The Norton Backup screen appears, and the backup begins.

10. Watch in the lower left `Diskette Progress` box and replace diskettes as prompted.

When the backup is complete, you are returned automatically to the DOS prompt (if the Quit after Backup option is set to On), or a `Backup is complete` prompt is displayed.

11. Select OK at the prompt to complete the backup.

You are returned to the main menu.

□

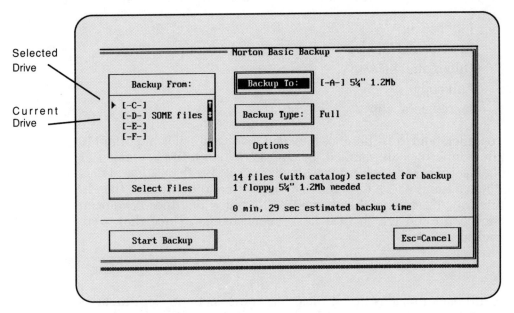

Selected Drive

Current Drive

Figure 11.5   *The Norton Basic Backup screen prompts you for backup information and options.*

Selecting the Backup Drives

You may back up files from one or more hard drives, but the drives must contain files before you can select them. The Backup From: box on the Norton Basic Backup screen shows all drives available on your hard disk. The current drive (whether selected or not) is marked with an arrow. When you choose Select Files, the contents of the current drive is displayed.

The drive that you back up *to* is the target drive onto which you will save the backed up files. Next to the Backup To: box is the default floppy drive selected by the program. If you want to change this drive, select the Backup To: box, then select a different drive from the list displayed.

> ⊘ **Caution:** Although you can specify a hard disk drive to back up to, your resulting backup files will do you little good in the event of a total hard disk disaster. It is better to back up your files onto floppy diskettes.

Selecting the Backup Type

There are five types of backups from which you can choose:

Full backup
Incremental backup
Differential backup
Full copy
Incremental copy

To understand the difference between these types, it is important to know how files are marked, or *flagged*. When a file is created or changed (worked with in any way), it is marked with one type of flag. When a file is backed up, it is marked with another type of flag. In this way, the program is always able to tell which files have been backed up and which files have been changed since they were backed up.

Full Backup

A full backup backs up all files that you select and flags them as backed up. When you first back up your hard disk, you should perform a full backup. After that, you may need to do a full backup only once a week or once a month, depending on how often you use your computer.

Incremental Backup

An incremental backup backs up only selected files that are marked as created or changed since your last full backup. After it backs up these files, it "updates" their backup flags. In subsequent backups, if these files have not been changed, they are not backed up. However, the next time you work with the files, they are again marked as changed and included in your next backup. Use this type of backup if you work with many different files. Use different diskettes for each incremental backup, however, unless you don't mind losing the older versions of the backed up files.

Differential Backup

A differential backup backs up *all* selected files that you have worked with since your last full or incremental backup. Unlike an incremental backup, it does *not* flag the files as backed up, so on your next backup, the files are backed up again, even if they haven't been changed. Use this type of backup if you work with the same few files every day and want a continuously-updated set of backup files.

Full Copy

This type of backup backs up all selected files, regardless of whether they have been changed or not. It does *not* flag the backed up files, so it does not affect full or incremental backups that you have regularly scheduled. Use this type of backup when you want to transfer files from one location to another.

> ⊘ **Caution:** Do not confuse a Full Copy backup with the COPY command in DOS. With COPY, files on the floppy are ready-to-use; with Norton Backup, Full Copy, you must restore the files before you can use them.

249

Incremental Copy

An incremental copy is similar to a full copy, but only backs up selected files that have changed since the last backup of any type, and does not change the backed up flag on any files copied.

Selecting Backup Options

The options that you select in a Basic level backup determine the speed of your backup operation, the number of backup diskettes required, the accuracy of the backup, and other factors, all of which are explained in the following sections. These options, shown in Figure 11.6, can be set to On or Off only. After all options are set to your satisfaction, select ok to return to the Basic Backup screen.

> ▶ **Note:** Although some of the options you set affect the backup time and number of backup diskettes, their effect may not be reflected in the estimated backup time and number of diskettes shown on the Basic Backup screen.

Verify Backup Data (Read and Compare)

This option instructs the program to check the backed up data to make sure there are no errors in it and that it matches the original

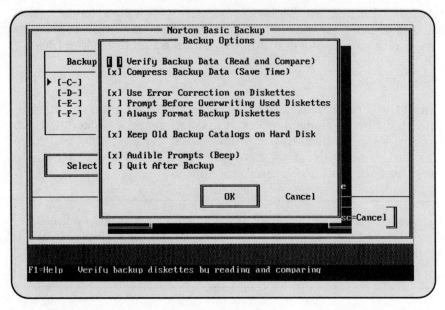

Figure 11.6   An X in the brackets indicates that an option is on.

data. In a Basic backup, only the highest level of verification—Read and Compare—is available. This assures you of an accurate data transfer; it also slows down the backup by as much as 50 percent when turned on.

Compress Backup Data (Save Time)

This option saves the data in a compressed format that requires fewer backup diskettes. There are higher levels of compression available in an Advanced backup, which save even more diskette space, but they slow down the backup process more.

Use Error Correction on Diskettes

The Norton Backup makes available a special error correction system that increases the possibility of recovering data from damaged diskettes. It is best to leave this option on.

Prompt Before Overwriting Used Diskettes

With this option on, the Norton Backup alerts you if your backup diskette already contains files. You can then choose whether or not you want to overwrite (and erase) those files.

Always Format Backup Diskettes

This option instructs the program to format all backup diskettes before writing to them. The format occurs automatically, even if the diskette is already formatted.

Keep Old Backup Catalogs on Hard Disk

A backup catalog provides an index of your backed up files and is necessary for the restore operation. Normally, when you perform a full backup, all interim catalogs since the prior full backup are deleted. With this option on, catalogs from previous backups are saved, so you can restore files from earlier backups. However, these catalogs do occupy space on your hard disk.

Audible Prompts (Beep)

This option adds a beep to prompts during the backup. This is a useful option if you don't want to sit and watch the screen during your entire backup.

251

Quit After Backup

With this option on, the program automatically returns you to the DOS prompt rather than the program main menu when the backup operation is finished.

Selecting Files To Back Up

You can back up all files in all directories on your hard disk, or you can back up only selected files in selected directories. The Select Backup Files screen, shown in Figure 11.7, is where you make your selections. The directories are listed on the left side of the screen; the files in the highlighted directory are listed on the right side of the screen. An arrow to the left of a directory means that all files in it are selected for backup. A smaller double arrow means that some files in the directory are selected for backup. A checkmark next to a file name means that the file is selected for backup.

When you have selected all the files to include in the backup, select OK from the options menu. If you change your mind about your file selections, select Cancel to return to the Norton Basic Backup screen without changing your original file selections.

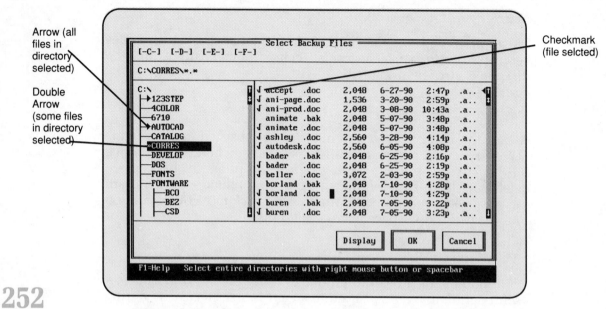

Figure 11.7   The Select Backup Files screen shows the selection status of all directories and of the files in the highlighted directory.

The Display Option

This option lets you choose the way in which files are sorted and displayed on the Select Backup Files screen. It also lets you display information about the size and number of selected files. Choosing this option brings up the Display dialog box, shown in Figure 11.8.

The first display option, *Sort Files By:*, lets you arrange the displayed files by file name, file extension, size, date, or attribute (hidden, archived, etc.). For example, if you arrange files by name, they are sorted alphabetically. If you arrange them by size, they are sorted with the largest files first. Arranging by date sorts files with the most recently created files first.

The *File Filter:* option lets you limit the range of files that are shown in the file list. The default shown in Figure 11.8 is *.*, which means that all files in the directory are displayed. If I changed this default to *.COM, then only files with the COM extension would be displayed. If I changed it to ANSI.*, then only files with the file name ANSI and any extension would be displayed.

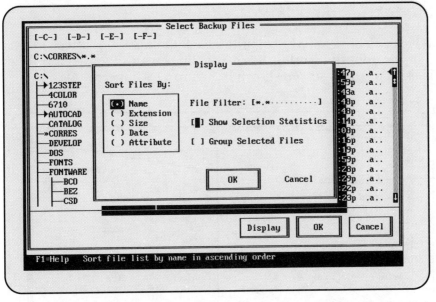

Figure 11.8   The Display dialog box lets you arrange selected files for easier viewing.

> ▶ **Note:** Any files selected before you set a file filter remain selected, even though they are not displayed on the file list.

The *Show Selection Statistics* option, when on, displays information on the total size of all files on your hard disk, total number of files on your hard disk, total size of all selected files, and total number of selected files.

Turning the *Group Selected Files* option on causes all selected files in a directory to be grouped together at the start of the file list, followed by unselected files.

> ▶ **Note:** All of the backup selections you make are stored automatically in a *setup file*. In a Basic backup, this file is named DEFAULT.SET. This file loads automatically and sets the default settings for all backups and restores until you change the settings again. In Advanced backups, you can save setup files under other names.

Starting the Basic Backup

When you are ready to begin the backup operation, select Start Backup from the Norton Basic Backup screen (Figure 11.5). The backup progress screen shown in Figure 11.9 appears.

HIghlight indicates directory being backed up

Checkmark appears as file is backed up

Blinking prompt tells you when to insert diskette

Information shows actual progress of backup

254

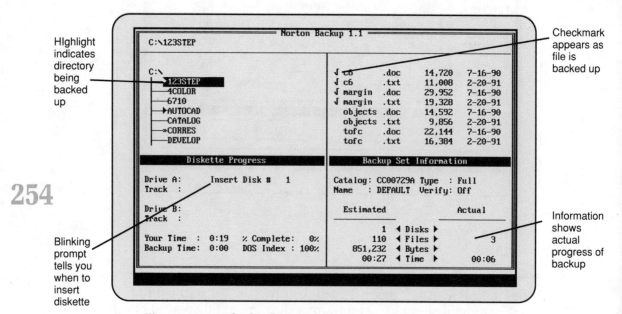

Figure 11.9 *The backup progress screen shows the status of your backup operation.*

Once the backup begins, you simply insert floppy diskettes when prompted by the message in the blinking brackets. If the Always Format Backup Diskettes option is on, the diskettes do not have to be formatted. An estimate of the number of diskettes you will need is shown in the lower right window of the screen. This estimate is based on the last backup you performed. If you have changed the compression option since your last backup, you may need more or fewer diskettes than the estimate shows.

After you insert each diskette, the message changes to a bar that moves across the bracketed area, tracking the actual transfer of data until the diskette is full. If the diskettes you insert are not blank and the Prompt Before Overwrite option is on, you will be asked if you want to overwrite the files on the diskette. Select Overwrite if you want to continue the backup with that diskette. Otherwise, insert a different diskette and select Retry.

> ► **Note:** During backup, the disk drive light on your computer always remains on, even while you are removing and inserting diskettes. This is normal, and not a cause for alarm.

Other information shown on the screen during backup includes:

Your Time	The time it takes you to swap diskettes
Backup Time	The computer's time backing up files
% Complete	How much of the backup is complete (useful for estimating how many more diskettes you may need)
DOS Index	An indicator of the program's efficiency
Catalog	The name under which the backup catalog (index) will be stored. Include this name on each backup diskette label.
Type	The backup type you selected
Name	The setup file name (DEFAULT.SET in a Basic backup)
Verify	Data Verification option selected (on or off)
Disks	Estimated vs. actual number of diskettes used
Files	Estimated vs. actual number of files backed up
Bytes	Estimated vs. actual bytes of data backed up
Time	Estimated vs. actual total backup time

255

After you remove each full backup diskette, label it with the date, backup diskette number, and the catalog name shown on the screen. You can cancel the backup operation at any time by pressing the Esc key. When backup is complete, a dialog box informs you. Select OK from this box to exit the backup progress screen and return to the main menu.

Advanced Backup

An Advanced backup is performed in essentially the same way as a Basic backup. The difference between the two is in the options available. One of these options, Setup File, is discussed in a later section of this chapter because it relates specifically to the PreSet level backup and restore.

To perform an Advanced backup, you must first set the level on the Configuration screen. Select Configure from the main menu. From the Configuration screen, select Program Level, then Advanced. When the Configuration screen reappears, select Save Configuration, then OK. When you return to the main menu, select Backup. The Norton Advanced Backup screen shown in Figure 11.10 appears.

256

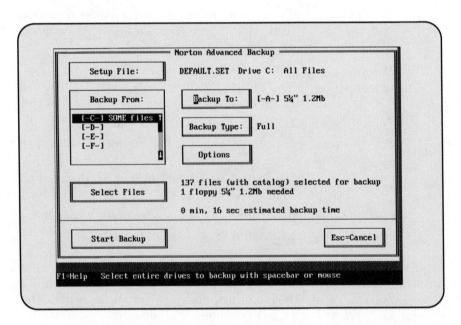

Figure 11.10   The Norton Advanced Backup screen is similar to the Norton Basic Backup screen, but offers the Setup File: box.

Select the drive to backup from, the drive to backup to, and the backup type as described in the Basic backup. The Advanced Backup Options and Select Backup Files screens are described in the following sections.

Advanced Backup Options

Many of the Advanced backup options are similar to the Basic options. However, instead of being limited to turning the option on or off, you have a number of choices for each option. The advanced Backup Options screen, shown in Figure 11.11, contains five options that you can set and five options that you can turn on or off. Four of the five on/off options are the same as the corresponding Basic backup options. They are:

> Always Format Diskettes
> Use Error Correction
> Keep Old Backup Catalogs
> Quit After Backup

The remaining on/off option, Proprietary Diskette Format, sets up the program to use a special diskette format that lets the backup run faster and store more data on each diskette.

257

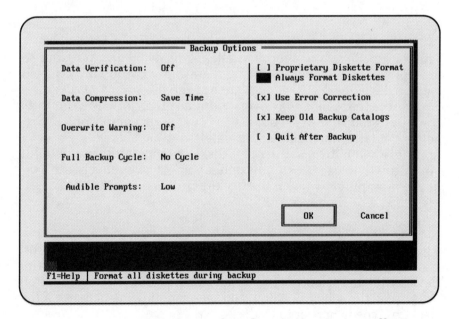

```
╔══════════════════════════════════════════════════════╗
║                    Backup Options                      ║
║                                                        ║
║  Data Verification:    Off      [ ] Proprietary Diskette Format
║                                 ███ Always Format Diskettes
║  Data Compression:     Save Time [x] Use Error Correction
║
║  Overwrite Warning:    Off      [x] Keep Old Backup Catalogs
║
║  Full Backup Cycle:    No Cycle [ ] Quit After Backup
║
║  Audible Prompts:      Low
║
║                                   ┌─────┐
║                                   │  OK │     Cancel
║                                   └─────┘
║
║  F1=Help │ Format all diskettes during backup
╚══════════════════════════════════════════════════════╝
```

Figure 11.11   The Advanced Backup Options screen offers additional backup options.

Data Verification Option

Selecting this option brings up the Data Verification dialog box, containing four choices. o f f results in the fastest backup, but there is no guarantee that the backup data will match the original data. Read Only reads the data on the backup diskette to make sure there were no recording errors. Sample Only reads every eighth track on the backup diskette, checks it for recording errors, and compares it to the original data. Read and Compare reads all data on the backup diskette, checks it for recording errors, and compares it to the original data. This slows down the backup process by the greatest amount, but assures you that your backup is completely accurate.

Data Compression Option

There are four Data Compression choices. The choice you make affects both the speed of the backup (and restore) and the number of backup diskettes required. Off gives you the fastest backup speed, but uses the greatest number of diskettes. Save Time gives some degree of compression and slows down the backup process a little. Save Disks (Low) sets the program for a higher degree of compression; consequently, it uses fewer diskettes and takes more time. Save Disks (High) gives maximum compression, uses the fewest diskettes, and takes the most time.

Overwrite Warning Option

This option lets you choose whether you want the program to prompt you before overwriting (and erasing) existing files on used backup diskettes. Your choices are Off (no prompt), Regular DOS Diskettes (prompts before overwriting any DOS formatted diskette containing data), Norton Backup Diskettes (prompts only if diskettes contain previous backup data), and Any Used Diskette (prompts before overwriting any diskette containing any data). If you regularly reuse backup diskettes, you may want to choose Off, as the prompts slow down the backup process.

Full Backup Cycle Option

This option lets you set up a regular schedule for performing full backups. You set the interval between backups to any number of days, with the default set at 7 days. When you start the Norton Backup on the scheduled day, you see the following message if the Backup Type is not set to Full:

```
The backup schedule indicates that you should do a
full backup today.
```

The backup type is then set automatically to Full.

Audible Prompts Option

This option lets you set the volume of the beep that accompanies backup prompts. The choices are Off (no beep), Low, and High.

Advanced File Selection

File selection in an Advanced level backup is the same as in the Basic level backup, with the addition of three options, shown in Figure 11.12.

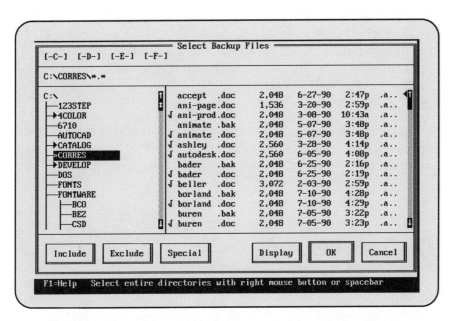

Figure 11.12   The Advanced level Select Backup Files screen offers additional selection options.

The Include, Exclude, and Special options give you alternate ways of selecting files to back up, other than marking them individually on the file list. *Include* lets you specify files to include in the backup. *Exclude* lets you specify files to exclude from the backup. And *Special* lets you further specify files to exclude by date, type, or name. Files excluded on the Special screen are marked on the File Selection screen with a dot instead of a checkmark, and cannot be selected for backup.

For example, assume that you store all files for a particular client in a directory called \CLIENT on your C: drive. Some files are created in Word and have a DOC or BAK extension. Other files are spreadsheet files with a .WK1 extension. You want to back up all files in this directory except the BAK files and two highly sensitive budget files (call them BUDGET1.WK1 and BUDGET2.WK1). The following steps show how you would make this file selection.

1. From the File Selection screen, select `Include`.
2. In the Path box type `C:\CLIENT`. In the File box, type `*.*`. Then select `OK`.
3. From the Select Files screen, select `Exclude`.
4. Type `C:\CLIENT` in the Path box and `*.BAK` in the File box. Select `OK` again.
5. From the Select Files screen, select `Special`.
6. In the Special Selections box, select `Copy Protected Files`. In the next dialog box, type in the two file names that you want to exclude: `C:\CLIENT\BUDGET1.WK1` and `C:\CLIENT\BUDGET2.WK1`).
7. Finally, select `OK` twice.

If you have more than one directory to include or exclude, you can select the `Include` or `Exclude` box, then `Edit Include/Exclude List`, then `Edit`, and type in the drives, directories, and file names on the resulting screen.

The Basic Restore

The Restore operation is the means by which you can retrieve any or all of the files you back up. Hopefully, you will never experience the sort of hard disk disaster that requires restoration of all backed up files. A more likely scenario is that you will accidentally overwrite an important file with a newer version, then discover that you need information from the older file. With Restore, you can easily retrieve that one important file.

The following Quick Steps give you an overview of the Restore operation. Each step, option, and concept is then explained in greater detail in the sections that follow.

Q Running the Basic Level Restore

1. Select `Restore` from the main menu.

The Norton Basic Restore screen appears, as shown in Figure 11.13.

2. Select the drive to Restore From. The default is the floppy drive to which you copied your files during your last backup.

3. Select the Catalog: box from the Norton Basic Restore screen.

The Catalog screen appears.

4. Select the catalog name that matches the backup you wish to restore. Select any other catalog options, and then Load.

The Norton Basic Restore screen returns (Figure 11.13).

5. Select Options to check or change the Basic Restore options.

The Basic Restore Options screen appears, with a checkbox beside each option.

6. Turn options on or off, then select OK.

The Norton Basic Restore screen returns.

7. Select the Select Files box.

The Select Restore Files screen appears.

261

8. Select the directories and files to restore. Select Display to check or change file display options. Select Show Versions to display multiple versions of a file if you have selected a master catalog to restore. When you have marked all files to be restored, select OK.

The Norton Basic Restore screen returns, showing the total number of files selected for the Restore operation.

9. Select Start Restore.

The Restore in Progress screen appears. A prompt indicates which backup diskette to insert.

10. Insert the diskette(s) when prompted.

The program automatically restores your selected backup files and prompts you when the restore process is complete.

11. Select OK.

The program returns you either to the main menu or to the DOS prompt, depending on the setup option you chose.   ☐

Figure 11.13   *The Norton Basic Restore screen assumes that you want to restore files to the drive from which they were backed up.*

Selecting the Drives To Restore To and From

You do not have to choose a drive to restore to; the program knows which drive you last backed up from and automatically restores to that drive. (If you want to restore to a different drive than the one you backed up from, you must perform an Advanced restore.)

Likewise, the program sets the Restore From drive as the drive you last backed up to. You can change the Restore From drive—if, for example, you wish to restore an earlier backup that was made on a different drive than your most recent backup. Select Restore From: on the Basic Restore screen. This gives you a list of all drives on your system. Then select the desired drive and OK.

What Is a Catalog?

A catalog is a list of the files that are included in a particular backup, with information about each file's location on the backup diskette(s). The information contained in a backup catalog is critical to the successful restoration of backed up files. For this reason, a catalog file is created automatically during each backup and stored in two locations: on the hard disk (in the directory containing the Norton Backup) and on the last backup diskette. Thus, if your hard disk is ever erased completely, the backup catalog can still be retrieved from the backup diskettes themselves.

There are two types of catalogs: the *individual* catalog for a particular backup and a *master* catalog. As a rule, you use an individual catalog to restore backup files.

Catalogs for individual backups each have distinctive names, but the names follow a format. Once you learn to read this format, you can tell a lot about a backup from its catalog name alone. Table 11.1 shows the elements in the sample catalog name CC10315A.INC.

Table 11.1 Elements in the Sample Catalog Name CC10315A.INC

Element	Description
C	First drive backed up
C	Last drive backed up
1	Last digit of backup year
03	Backup month
15	Backup day
A	Sequence of backup (A–Z). Indicates first backup of day. B would indicate second backup of day, etc.
INC	Type of backup (.FUL = Full; .INC = Incremental; DIF = Differential; .CPY = Full or Incremental Copy)

The second type of catalog, the master catalog, contains all of the catalogs created with the same setup file since the last full backup. A master catalog name is the same as the name of the setup file used to create it, but has a .CAT extension. So if you use the DEFAULT.SET setup file when you back up, the master catalog created has the name DEFAULT.CAT. If you perform many backups using the same file, the master catalog lets you see all of the individual catalogs for the different backups (and view the files they contain), to determine which catalog you need to use.

Selecting Catalog Files

When you choose the Restore operation, the program checks its own directory for catalog files and selects the most recently created catalog. You can choose a different catalog file by selecting `Catalog` on the Basic Restore screen. This brings up the `Select Catalog` dialog box shown in Figure 11.14.

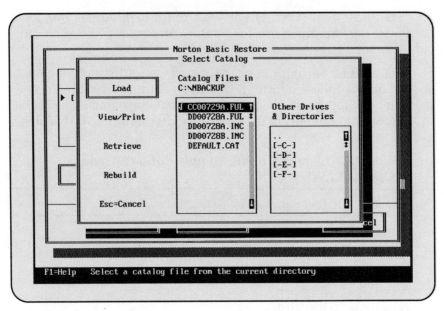

Figure 11.14   The Select Catalog dialog box includes several options.

On the right side of the screen is a list of available drives with the current drive highlighted. In the center of the screen is a list of catalogs available on the highlighted drive. Select a different drive or catalog by highlighting your choice and pressing Enter (or click on your choice with the right mouse button).

The screen also makes available four options. Two of them—**Retrieve** and **Rebuild**—are explained in the next section. **Load** does what its name implies: loads the selected catalog and returns you to the Norton Basic Restore screen. If you change the catalog selection, you must load it before you can proceed with the Restore operation.

View/Print lets you preview the selected catalog, so you can see if it contains the file(s) you want to restore. It also lets you print the contents of a catalog, for a hard copy "index" of your backup. Selecting this option takes you to a screen similar to the Select Backup Files screen. The View Catalog screen, shown in Figure 11.15, shows all directories on the selected drive and all files backed up in the highlighted directory.

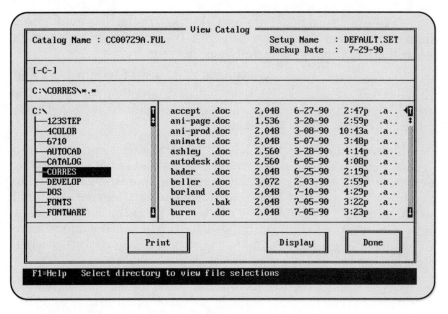

┌─────────────────── View Catalog ───────────────────┐

Catalog Name : CC00729A.FUL   Setup Name : DEFAULT.SET
                                     Backup Date : 7-29-90

[-C-]

C:\CORRES*.*

```
C:\                  ⬆  accept  .doc   2,048   6-27-90   2:47p  .a..  ◀⬆
    ├─123STEP        ⬍  ani-page.doc   1,536   3-20-90   2:59p  .a..  ⬍
    ├─4COLOR            ani-prod.doc   2,048   3-08-90  10:43a  .a..
    ├─6710              animate .doc   2,048   5-07-90   3:48p  .a..
    ├─AUTOCAD           ashley  .doc   2,560   3-28-90   4:14p  .a..
    ├─CATALOG           autodesk.doc   2,560   6-05-90   4:08p  .a..
    ├─CORRES            bader   .doc   2,048   6-25-90   2:19p  .a..
    ├─DEVELOP           beller  .doc   3,072   2-03-90   2:59p  .a..
    ├─DOS               borland .doc   2,048   7-10-90   4:29p  .a..
    ├─FONTS             buren   .bak   2,048   7-05-90   3:22p  .a..
    ├─FONTWARE       ⬇  buren   .doc   2,048   7-05-90   3:23p  .a..  ⬇
```

┌─────────────┐   ┌─────────────┐ ┌─────────────┐
│   Print   │   │   Display   │ │   Done   │
└─────────────┘   └─────────────┘ └─────────────┘

F1=Help   Select directory to view file selections

265

Figure 11.15   The View Catalog screen shows a list, or catalog, of directories on the drive.

The Display box at the bottom of the screen is identical in function to the Display box on the Select Files screen. Selecting the Print option takes you to the Printer dialog box. Here you select your printer port (LPT1 is the default), continuous feed or single sheet paper, the number of lines to print per page (60 is the default for 8-1/2" x 11" paper), and if you want to print to a text file on disk instead of to your printer (enter a name for the text file in the brackets). When you have completed your printer setup, select Start Printing. When printing is complete, the program returns to the View Catalog screen.

The **Show Versions** option lets you display all versions of your files since your last full backup, if there *are* different versions of the files and if you have selected a master catalog for viewing. Each version of the file is differentiated by the date or time of its creation. On the Versions List, which appears when you select this feature, you can select which version of the file you want to restore.

Retrieving and Rebuilding a Catalog

If the program does not find the catalog file on your hard drive (if, for example, your entire hard disk has been erased), you can retrieve it from its second location—on the last of your backup diskettes. Select

Retrieve from the Select Catalog dialog box. In the Retrieve Catalog dialog box, select the floppy drive for the backup diskettes, then insert the last backup diskette when prompted.

You can also use this option to select a different drive and directory on your hard disk from which to load a catalog. This is useful if your hard disk is undamaged, but you have stored your catalog files in a separate directory.

If disaster has truly struck (your hard disk has been erased and the last backup diskette has been damaged), all is not lost. As long as some of your backup diskettes are readable, the program can rebuild at least a partial catalog file from special files that are stored on each backup diskette. Select Rebuild from the Select Catalog dialog box. On the Rebuild Catalog dialog box, select the floppy drive for your backup diskettes, and insert the backup diskettes when prompted.

If your last backup was to your hard disk and the hard disk itself is undamaged but the catalog file is gone, specify the drive and path containing the backup files on the Rebuild Catalog dialog box.

When a catalog has been retrieved or rebuilt, remember to Load it before returning to the Norton Basic Restore screen.

Selecting Restore Options

When you select Options on the Norton Basic Restore screen, the Restore Options dialog box appears, as shown in Figure 11.16. This box contains seven options, which you can turn on or off.

Verify Restore Data (Read and Compare) verifies that the data restored to your hard disk matches the data on the backup diskettes. As in the backup operation, verification slows down the restore process somewhat.

Prompt Before Creating Directories informs you during the restore operation if the drive to which you are restoring does not contain a directory that you've selected to restore. You may then choose to Create Directory or Skip Directory.

Prompt Before Creating Files similarly informs you if the drive to which you are restoring does not contain a file that you've selected to restore. You can choose whether you want to Restore the file anyway, Skip that file, or Cancel Restore.

Figure 11.16   The Restore Options dialog box lets you customize the way Norton Basic Restore operates.

Prompt Before Overwriting Existing Files warns you when an existing file on your hard disk is about to be overwritten (erased) by a file that you've selected to restore. You can choose from `Overwrite`, `Do Not Restore` (keep the existing file), or `Cancel Restore`.

Restore Empty Directories lets you restore directories that contain no files—for example, a \TEMP directory that is used for temporary files.

Audible Prompts (Beep) accompanies each prompt during restore with a beep.

Quit After Restore returns you to the DOS prompt, rather than to the Norton Backup main menu, when the restore is complete.

Selecting Files To Restore

You can select all files that have been backed up in the current drive by right clicking on the drive (or pressing the space bar) in the `Restore To:` box. You must do this *after* making any catalog selections, because exiting the Select Catalog dialog box erases any file selections.

> ⊘ **Caution:** If you select ALL files to restore, you run a
> greater risk of overwriting a newer version of a file with
> an older version. Unless you are restoring all files to a com-
> pletely erased hard disk, it is better to take the time to select the
> files you want to restore, or perform an Advanced level restore
> where you can select from more overwrite options.

If you do not want to restore all files, the `Select Files` box takes
you to the Select Restore Files screen, shown in Figure 11.17. This
is nearly identical to the Select Backup Files screen, except for the
Show Versions option at the bottom of the screen. This option works
the same on the Select Restore Files screen as it does on the View
Catalog screen.

Drive
Last
Backed
Up

Current
Drive

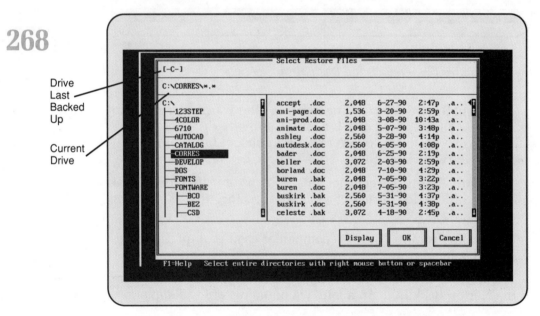

*Figure 11.17   The Select Restore Files screen is similar to
the Select Backup Files screen.*

The directories and files shown on the screen are those listed in
the backup catalog file selected. You select directories and files to be
restored from this list, exactly as you selected directories and files to
be backed up. The Display option also works the same as on the
Select Backup Files screen.

Starting the Basic Restore

After you have selected files to be restored and have returned to the Basic Restore screen, you start the restore operation by selecting the Start Restore box. This box is not available until you load a catalog file and select files to restore.

After you start the restore, a message prompts you to insert the first backup diskette (if you backed up to a floppy drive). After inserting the disk, select Continue and the progress screen shown in Figure 11.18 appears.

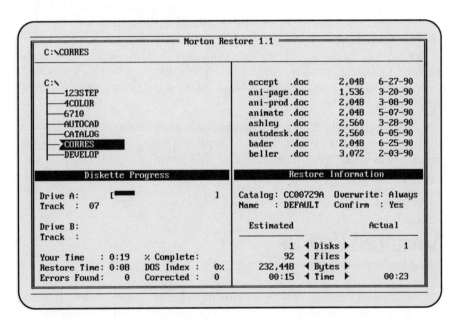

269

Figure 11.18   The basic restore progress screen provides prompts and statistical information about the restore.

During the restore process, screen prompts let you know when to insert diskettes and when you need to make restore decisions (based on the restore options you set). Files change color as they are restored, and a moving bar in the lower left window of the screen tracks the progress of the restore operation. A prompt informs you when the restore is complete. Select OK at the prompt to return to the Norton Backup main menu or the DOS prompt (depending on whether you selected the Quit After Restore option).

The Start Verify Option

Although Start Verify appears as a feature on the Restore screen, it may also be thought of as part of the backup process. Start Verify compares the backup files to be restored with the corresponding files on your hard disk. It performs essentially the same function as the Read and Compare Data Verification option, and can be used as such if you perform a backup or restore without this option set.

If you want to use Start Verify for data verification after a backup or restore operation, you need to do so before writing to your hard disk again; otherwise, the files may not match. Also, you cannot use this feature if you have selected either the Restore To Other Drive or Restore To Other Dir(ectories) option in an Advanced restore. These options make it impossible to compare the original backup files with the restored files because they are on different drives or directories.

When you select Start Verify, a screen message prompts you to insert the backup diskettes. Another prompt tells you when verification is complete. Select OK at this prompt to end the process and return to the main menu.

Advanced Restore

An Advanced restore offers additional control that makes it considerably more powerful than the Basic restore. Like the Advanced backup, it offers additional data verification options, file selection criteria, the Setup File: option, plus overwrite control and the capability of restoring to a drive or directory other than the one last backed up.

Select an Advanced restore from the Configuration screen. When you return to the main menu, select Restore. The Norton Advanced Restore screen appears, as shown in Figure 11.19.

As in the Basic restore, the Restore To: drive is the drive last backed up. Select the Restore From: drive and the catalog as described in "The Basic Restore." Advanced options and file selection are described in the next two sections.

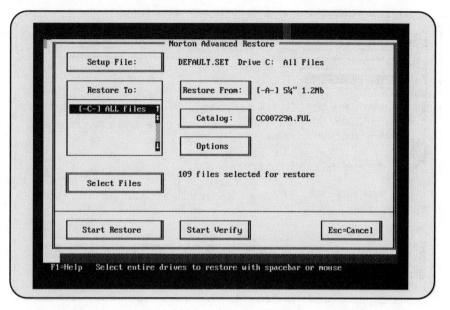

```
┌─────────────────── Norton Advanced Restore ───────────────────┐
│                                                                │
│  ┌──────────────┐   DEFAULT.SET  Drive C:  All Files           │
│  │ Setup File:  │                                              │
│  └──────────────┘                                              │
│  ┌──────────────┐  ┌──────────────┐                            │
│  │ Restore To:  │  │ Restore From:│  [-A-] 5¼" 1.2Mb           │
│  └──────────────┘  └──────────────┘                            │
│  ┌──────────────┐↑                                             │
│  │ [-C-] ALL files │  ┌──────────────┐                         │
│  │              │  │   Catalog:   │  CC00729A.FUL              │
│  │              │↓ └──────────────┘                            │
│  └──────────────┘  ┌──────────────┐                            │
│                    │   Options    │                            │
│                    └──────────────┘                            │
│                                                                │
│  ┌──────────────┐   109 files selected for restore             │
│  │ Select Files │                                              │
│  └──────────────┘                                              │
│                                                                │
│  ┌──────────────┐  ┌──────────────┐      ┌──────────────┐      │
│  │ Start Restore│  │ Start Verify │      │  Esc=Cancel  │      │
│  └──────────────┘  └──────────────┘      └──────────────┘      │
│                                                                │
└────────────────────────────────────────────────────────────────┘
  F1=Help   Select entire drives to restore with spacebar or mouse
```

Figure 11.19   The Norton Advanced Restore screen is similar to the Norton Basic Restore screen, but offers the Setup File: *option.*

Advanced Restore Options

There are nine advanced restore options, as shown on the Restore Options screen in Figure 11.20. Of these nine, three options are exactly the same as in the Basic restore: Data Verification:, Restore Empty Dirs, and Quit After Restore. The remaining six advanced options offer choices that greatly increase your control over the restore procedure.

Restore Prompts lets you choose the situations in which you are informed of a restore activity and given the option to continue that activity or skip it. The two options are Prompt Before Creating Directories (if a directory to be restored does not exist on your hard disk) and Prompt Before Creating Files (if a file to be restored does not exist on your hard disk).

Overwrite Files lets you avoid accidentally overwriting a new version of an existing file with an older backed up version. Your choices are Never Overwrite Files (files with the same name as an existing file are not restored), Always Overwrite Files (backed up files overwrite and erase, any existing version of the files on your hard disk), and Overwrite Older Files (only overwrites files prior to the last backup). A fourth option—Prompt Before Overwriting

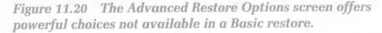

Figure 11.20   *The Advanced Restore Options screen offers powerful choices not available in a Basic restore.*

`Files`—can be selected in combination with either Always Overwrite Files or Overwrite Older Files. This option informs you during restore that you are about to overwrite an existing file and gives you the option to `Overwrite`, `Do Not Restore`, or `Cancel Restore`.

The **Archive Flag** option lets you choose how a restored file is flagged. When a file's archive flag is on, the Norton Backup sees the file as not backed up. When the archive flag is off, a file is seen by the program as backed up. `Leave Alone—Do not change` leaves the archive flag as it was before the restore. `Clear—Mark as backed up` turns the archive flag off. `Set—Mark as NOT backed up` turns the archive flag on.

The **Audible Prompts** option sets the volume of the beep that accompanies prompts during the restore process. The choices are `Low` and `High`.

Restore To Other Drive lets you restore files to a different drive than the one from which they were backed up. With this option on, you are prompted for the drive to restore to when you select `Start Restore`. This feature is useful for restoring older versions of a file without overwriting a newer version.

Restore To Other Dir(ectories) is a similar feature that lets you restore files to a different directory than the one you backed up. You actually select the directory to restore to after you select `Start Restore`. A prompt asks you for the new directory name.

Advanced File Selection

File selection is the same in Advanced level as in Basic level, except for the Special feature. When selected from the Select Restore Files screen, this feature gives you additional criteria for including or excluding files to restore. `Date Range` lets you include all files within a range of dates. `Copy Protected Files` lets you select up to five files to mark as copy protected and exclude from the restore. `Exclude Read Only Files`, `Exclude System Files`, and `Exclude Hidden Files` let you exclude all files with Read Only, System, or Hidden attributes.

Preparing Setup Files for PreSet Backup or Restore

You can create your own setup files for each type of backup or restore you want to run, name the files, save them, use them to run quick and easy PreSet backups or restores, and even copy them for others to use. The process is very easy, but must be done from the Advanced Backup or Restore screen.

Creating a Setup File

To create a setup file for a PreSet backup or restore, you must first go to the Advanced Backup or the Advanced Restore screen. Select the drives, options, files, catalog (for a restore) that you want, then select `Setup File` at the top of the screen. This takes you to the Setup File dialog box, shown in Figure 11.21.

From this dialog box, you can name and save a setup file that contains all the backup or restore information you just set. Highlight the bracketed name next to `Setup File` and type in a new setup file name. The name can be up to 8 characters long—for example, `C-BACK`. An extension of .SET is attached automatically to the name when you save the file.

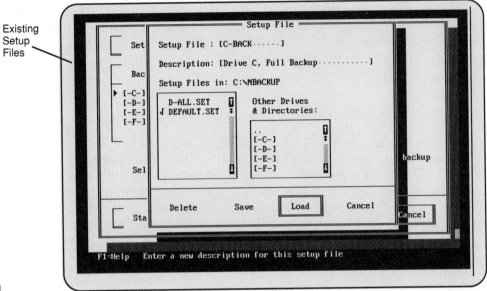

Existing
Setup
Files

*Figure 11.21   The Setup File dialog box is accessed from the
Advanced Backup or Restore screen.*

Next, highlight the bracketed text to the right of Description:.
Type in a brief description of the setup file you are creating, up to 24
characters—for example, Drive C, Full Backup. If you press Enter
at this point, a prompt warns you that the setup file is about to be
created and asks if you want to Create or Cancel the setup file.

The Setup File dialog box stores your setup file in C:\NBACKUP
unless you select a different drive and directory. To do so, select a
drive from the Other Drives & Directories list. The list will
change to display the directories in that drive. Select the directory
you want from that list. The new drive and directory will replace C:\
NBACKUP next to Setup Files in:.

Finally, select Save. That's all there is to it. You return to the
Advanced Backup or Restore screen, where you can create another
setup file under another name if you wish.

Changing a Setup File

You can just as easily change a setup file that you have already
created. From the Advanced Backup or Restore screen, select Setup
File. From the list of existing setup files on the Setup File dialog
box, select the file you want to change. Then select Load. You return

to the Advanced Backup or Restore screen, with the settings contained in that file displayed. Make your changes, select `Setup File` again, then `Save`.

If you want to use an existing setup file as a starting point to create a slightly different file, load the existing file, make your changes, then save it under a different name. The file you used as a starting point will still exist under its original name.

Installing a Setup File for Others

If you want to share a setup file with other, less experienced users, you can transfer it to the other person's NBACKUP directory using a floppy diskette. You must transfer two files for the setup file to work: the file you created with the .SET file name extension and another file that the program creates automatically with the same file name and an .SLT extension. Use the DOS `COPY` command to copy both files onto a floppy diskette.

275

Say you want to transfer setup file C-BACK, which is stored on your hard disk in C:\NBACKUP, to another user's \NBACKUP directory on his D: drive. Your floppy drive is A:. First, make sure you are on the C: drive. Then use the following commands to copy the files to a blank floppy diskette:

```
copy \nbackup\c-back.set a:
copy \nbackup\c-back.slt a:
```

Insert the diskette containing the copied files into the other user's floppy drive and type:

```
copy a:*.* d:\nbackup
```

This copies both files on A: to D: in the \NBACKUP directory.

PreSet Level Backup and Restore

Once you have a setup file, you can perform backups and restores in the PreSet level. This involves fewer keystrokes and less time, because your drives, options, catalog (for restore), and files (for backup) are already set.

The Quick Steps in the next two sections take you step-by-step through the PreSet backup and restore. First, select the PreSet level from the Configuration screen. When you return to the main menu, select either `Backup` or `Restore`.

> ▶ **Tip:** If you want to start the Norton Backup with a particular setup file already loaded, type the name of the setup file after NBACKUP; for example,
>
> `NBACKUP  C-BACK`

The PreSet Backup

When you select a PreSet backup, the screen shown in Figure 11.22 appears. In a PreSet backup, you do not have to select the drive to back up from, the backup options, the files to be backed up, or the backup type (and in fact, you don't even have the option). This information is all stored in the setup file.

You do have to select a setup file from the list in the PreSet Backups box. You *can* (but don't have to) select a drive to back up to. The default drive is part of the setup file, but you can change it if you wish.

Running a PreSet Backup

1. Select `Backup` from the main menu.

   The Norton PreSet Backup screen appears.

2. Select a setup file from the `PreSet Backups:` list.

   A checkmark appears next to the selected file.

3. Select `Backup To:` if you want to back up files to a different drive than the default shown. Select a new drive from the list in the resulting dialog box, then select `OK`.

   The new drive appears on the PreSet Backup screen.

4. Select `Preview Backup` if you want to see which files have been selected for backup. Select `Done` to return to the Norton PreSet Backup screen.

The Preview Backup screen appears, containing the same information shown in the Select Files screen in a Basic or Advanced backup. You cannot make changes to this screen.

5. Select `Start Backup`.

The Backup screen prompts you to insert diskettes and tracks the progress of the backup. A message informs you when the backup is complete.

6. Select `OK`.

You return to the main menu or to the DOS prompt. □

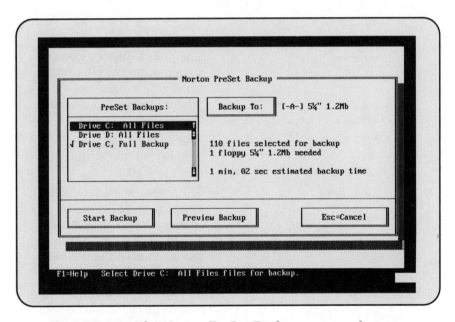

Figure 11.22   The Norton PreSet Backup screen asks you for the name of the setup file.

The PreSet Restore

The PreSet Restore screen is similar to the PreSet Backup screen with the addition of a Select Files box. Unlike a PreSet backup, you must select the files to restore, because this information is likely to have changed since the setup file was created.

In a PreSet restore, you do not need to select restore options. These are contained in the setup file. You can (but don't need to) set a drive to restore files from. This information is also contained in the setup file. The setup file for a PreSet restore is the setup file used for the last PreSet backup.

Q Running a PreSet Restore

1. Select Restore from the main menu.

   The Norton PreSet Restore screen appears.

2. Select a setup file from the Restore Type (Catalog) list.

   A checkmark appears next to the selected file.

3. Select Restore From if you want to restore files from a different drive than the default shown. Select a new drive from the list in the resulting dialog box, then select OK.

   The new drive appears on the Norton PreSet Restore screen.

4. Select the Select Files box.

   The Select Restore Files screen appears. This is the same as the Basic Select Restore Files screen (refer to Figure 11.17).

5. Select the files to restore, then select OK.

   The number of files selected appears on the Norton PreSet Restore screen.

6. Select Preview Restore if you want to see which files have been selected to restore. Select Done to return to the Norton PreSet Restore screen.

   The Preview Restore screen appears, with the same information shown in the Select Files screen. You cannot make changes to this screen.

7. Select Start Restore.

   The Restore screen prompts you to insert diskettes and tracks the progress of the restore procedure. A message informs you when the restore is complete.

8. Select OK.

   You return to the main menu or to the DOS prompt. □

Using Macros with the Norton Backup

A macro is a mini program that automates a process. The Norton Backup allows you to create such a program by recording the keystrokes you use to complete a process. Then when you run the macro (with a keystroke or two), it "replays" all of the keystrokes you recorded. The result is a significant savings in time.

The setup file that allows you to run a PreSet level backup can itself be thought of as a macro. Once you create and save the setup file, you "replay" your original selections when you choose a PreSet backup. In fact, when you create a macro, you store it in a setup file. You can create as many macros as you wish, but you can only store one macro in a given setup file.

Recording a Macro

Before you record a macro, it is a good idea to map out the process that you want to automate, keystroke by keystroke (you cannot use a mouse when recording a macro). Note that special keystrokes must be substituted for keystrokes that make certain types of selections. This prevents you from actually running a backup or restore operation when all you want to do is set up a macro to run a backup or restore. These special keystrokes and other keys used in macros are listed in Table 11.2.

Table 11.2   Macro Keystrokes

Keystroke	Description
Ctrl + Enter	Use instead of Enter when you don't want the recorded keystroke to activate a process during recording
Insert	Use instead of space bar to turn an option ON when recording
Delete	Use instead of space bar to turn an option OFF when recording
F7	Start/stop recording a macro
Alt + F7	Pause during recording (inserts a pause to allow input when the macro is replayed)
F8	Replay a macro

To record a macro, you must first load the setup file where you will store the macro. After loading the setup file, return to the main menu. All macros must start from here. Follow the Quick Steps below to record the macro.

Q Recording a Macro

1. From the main menu, press F7.

   The word Recording replaces the F1=Help message in the lower left corner of the screen.

2. Perform the keystrokes needed to complete the process you want to automate. (Refer to Table 11.2 for substitute keystrokes for Enter and the space bar.)

   You see the action resulting from each keystroke, as if you were actually completing the process, unless you use substitute keys.

3. Press Alt + F7 to insert a pause in the macro, whenever you want the user to make a menu selection or enter information. Select OK from the menu or press F7 to resume recording.

   The word Waiting replaces Recording during the pause.

4. When you are finished recording, press F7.

   The macro is saved automatically in the setup file currently loaded. □

Playing a Macro

When you want to replay a macro, first load the setup file containing it. Then press F8. The message Working appears in the lower left corner of the screen, unless the macro is pausing for input. Then the message is Waiting. While the Working message is visible, you cannot use either the keyboard or mouse because the macro is in control of the program.

280

What You Have Learned

▶ You can choose from three levels of backup and restore: Basic, Advanced, and PreSet. You choose the program level from the Configuration screen.

▶ Five different types of backups are possible: full, incremental, differential, full copy, and incremental copy. Copy backups do not use the DOS COPY command, and must be restored using The Norton Backup.

▶ The data verification option affects the speed and accuracy of a backup. The greater the degree of verification, the slower the backup.

▶ The data compression option affects the speed and number of diskettes used in a backup. The greater the degree of compression, the fewer diskettes are used and the slower the backup becomes.

▶ Overwrite options let you choose whether the program prompts you before overwriting (and erasing) previous files on a diskette or on your hard disk.

▶ The Start Verify option is offered on the Restore screen, but can be used immediately after a backup to verify that the backup data matches the original data.

▶ A catalog contains an index of the files backed up in a particular backup session. Each catalog has a unique name and is stored both on the hard disk and on the last diskette of the backup set.

▶ The catalog for a particular backup is necessary to restore those backed up files. If a catalog is lost from your hard disk, it can be retrieved or rebuilt from the backup diskettes.

▶ The settings for a backup or restore are saved in a setup file named DEFAULT.SET. In the Advanced level, you can create your own setup files, to save backup or restore settings for use by yourself or others in PreSet level.

281

Index

Symbols

/DEMO parameter, 14
80286 microprocessor, 21
80386 microprocessor, 21
80386SX microprocessor, 21
80486 microprocessor, 21
8088 microprocessor, 20

A

Address Book (Commander Mail), 230
Advanced backup *see* BACKUP, Advanced
    backup
Allow Hard Disk Formatting option
    (SFORMAT), 129
Alt-F7 (Commander Find File) key, 198-200
American Standard Code for Information
    Interchange *see* ASCII character set
ANSI.SYS device driver, 91
applications, running from Commander, 217-
    220
archive file attribute, 52, 209
ASCII character set, 118, 163-165
ASK BE subcommand, 94

B

BACKUP
    Advanced backup
        Audible Prompts Option, 259
        Data Compression Option, 258
        Data Verification Option, 257
        Full Backup Cycle Option, 258
        Overwrite Warning Option, 258
        selecting files, 259-260
    Advanced restore
        Archive Flag option, 272
        Audible Prompts option, 272
        Overwrite Files option, 271
        Restore Prompts option, 271
        Restore To Other Dir(ectories) option, 273
        Restore To Other Drive option, 272
        selecting files, 273
    Basic backup
        Always Format Backup Diskettes option, 251
        Audible Prompts (Beep) option, 251
        Backup From option, 247
        Backup To option, 247
        Compress Backup Data option, 250

Differential Backup option, 248
        Full Backup option, 248
        Full Copy option, 249
        Incremental Copy option, 249
        Keep Old Backup Catalogs on Hard Disk
            option, 251
        Prompt Before Overwriting Used Diskettes
            option, 250
        Quit After Backup option, 251
        Select Backup Files screen, 251-253
        Use Error Correction on Diskettes, 250
        Verify Backup Data option, 249
    Basic restore, 260-262
        Audible Prompts (Beep) option, 267
        Prompt Before Creating Directories option, 266
        Prompt Before Creating Files option, 266
        Prompt Before Overwriting Existing Files
            option, 267
        Quit After Restore option, 267
        Restore Empty Directories option, 267
        Restore From option, 262
        Restore To option, 262
        selecting files, 267-268
        Start Verify Option, 270
        Verify Restore Data option, 266
    catalogs, 262-266
    configuring, 239
        configuration tests, 241-242
        Direct Memory Access (DMA) test, 241
        mouse settings, 240
        video settings, 241
    differential backups, 248
    exiting, 245
    help, 243-245
    incremental backups, 248
    incremental copy backups, 249
    installing, 237-239
    macros, 279
        playing, 280
        recording macros, 279-280
    Preset backup or restore
        preset level, 275-278
        setup file, 273-275
batch files
    conditional execution, 86-87
        IF statement, 86-87
    creating, 80-81
    interactive, 94

283

looping, 85
    FOR loop, 85
    parameters, 83-84
baud rate, 43
BE (Batch Enhancer), 7, 88-90
    ERRORLEVEL variable, 94-95
    subcommands
        ASK, 94
        BEEP, 95-96
        BOX, 95
        CLS, 91
        DELAY, 96
        ROWCOL, 93
        SA, 91-92
        WINDOW, 92-93
BEEP BE subcommand, 95-96
Benchmarks menu (SYSINFO), 31-33
bits, 22, 118
blanking screen with Commander, 190
boot record, 121
boot sector, 121
bootable disks
    creating with DISKTOOL, 153
BOX BE subcommand, 95
bytes, 22, 118

C

cache, 173-174
    installing, 174
    NCACHE-F, 173-174
    NCACHE-S, 173-174
CALIBRAT (Calibrate), 7, 174-177
catalogs (BACKUP), 262-266
CD (DOS) command, 101
Central Processing Unit (CPU) *see* micropro-
    cessors
changing directories, 100-102
    Commander, 187
clock, setting, 47-48
CLS BE subcommand, 91
clusters, 60, 118
    marking with DISKTOOL, 156
CMOS Status screen (SYSINFO), 28
colors, screen, 36-38, 91-92, 190
COM serial ports, 222
Commander, 180
    as a memory resident program, 184-185
    changing directories, 187
    configuring, 189-194
        File Panel options, 190
        panels, 190-191
        Screen Colors option, 190
        Tree Panel options, 190
    copying files, 203-205
    deleting files, 207-208

DOS prompt, 186
editing files, 211-213
exiting, 196
F3 (View File) function key, 210-211
F4 (Edit File) function key, 211-213
F5 (Copy) function key, 203-205
F6 (Move/Rename) function key, 205-207
F8 (Delete) function key, 207-208
filtering file list, 193-194
finding files, 198-200
function key bar, 186
hard disks, 184-185
help, 194-196
installing, 182-184
keyboard, 188
Left Panel menu, 190-192
Link, 221
    connecting computers, 222-224
    terminating link, 225
    transferring files, 224-225
Mail
    Address Book, 230
    creating messages, 231-232
    File menu, 230
    hardware requirements, 225
    installing, 226-229
    Mail menu, 230
    modem settings, 228-229
    receiving messages, 232-233
    sending messages, 232-233
    setting up accounts, 227
    Setup menu, 230
mini status box, 186
mouse, 188-189
moving files, 206-207
pull-down menu bar, 186
renaming files, 205-206
right panel, 185
Right Panel menu, 190-192
running applications, 217-220
    point-and-shoot feature, 219-220
Screen Blank Delay option, 190
selecting files, 199-203
setting file attributes, 208-209
sorting files, 193
switching drives, 193
viewing files, 180, 210-211
    formats supported, 181-182
commands, DOS
    CD, 101
    DEL, 65-67
    DIR, 82
    ECHO, 82
    EDLIN, 80
    FDISK, 24

FORMAT, 127
LABEL, 107
MD, 100
NLSFUNC, 46
PAUSE, 82-83
PROMPT, 101
RD, 100
RECOVER, 154-155
REM, 82
TYPE, 80, 161
VER, 20
communications protocol, 43
compressing backup data, 250
conditional execution in batch files (IF statement), 86-87
CONFIG.SYS file, 91
Configure menu (NORTON), 15-16
configuring
BACKUP, 239
Direct Memory Access (DMA) test, 241
mouse settings, 240
video settings, 241
Commander, 189-194
File Panel options, 190
panels, 190-191
Screen Blank Delay option, 190
Screen Colors option, 190
Tree Panel options, 190
serial ports, 42-44
connecting computers (Commander Link), 222-224
master/slave computers, 222-224
terminating link, 225
copying files with Commander, 203-205
Country Info option (NCC), 46-47
CPU *see* microprocessors
CPU Speed screen (SYSINFO), 31-32
Cursor Size option (NCC), 35-36
Custom Message option (NDD), 142
customizing Norton Utilities with NORTON Configure menu, 15-16
cylinders, 119

D

data area, 123
data bits, 43
Data Encryption Standard (DES), 159-160
date, setting, 47-48
date/time stamps, FILEFIND, 62-64
dBASE files, repairing with FILEFIX, 72-73
decrypting files, 160
defragmenting hard disks, 171-173
DEL (DOS) command, 65-67
DELAY BE subcommand, 96
deleted files

preserving, 68-72
recovering, 64-67
recovering manually, 167-170
deleting files
Commander, 207-208
permanently, 74-77
DES *see* Data Encryption Standard
device drivers, ANSI.SYS, 91
Device Drivers screen (SYSINFO), 30
differential backups, 248
DIR (DOS) command, 82
Direct Memory Access (DMA) test (BACKUP), 241
directories
changing, 100-102
with Commander, 187
creating, 100, 106
NCD, 216
DOS directory structure, 99-101
recovering erased, 108-111
removing, 100, 106
NCD, 216
renaming, 104
root directory, 100, 121
searching for with NCD, 214-216
disk cache, 173-174
installing, 174
NCACHE-F, 173-174
NCACHE-S, 173-174
Disk Characteristics screen (SYSINFO), 124-125
Disk Light option (DISKMON), 151
Disk Park option (DISKMON), 151-152
Disk Protect screen (DISKMON), 150-151
Disk Speed screen (SYSINFO), 32-33
Disk Summary screen (SYSINFO), 123
DISKEDIT (Disk Editor), 7
ASCII character set, 163-165
hexadecimal notation, 162-163
text view, 165
viewing File Allocation Tables, 165-167
viewing files, 161-163
DISKMON (Disk Monitor), 148-150
Disk Light, 151
Disk Park option, 151-152
Disk Protect screen, 150-151
DISKREET (Diskreet), 8
Data Encryption Standard, 159-160
decrypting files, 160
encrypting files, 157-158
Disks menu (SYSINFO), 28, 123-126
disks *see* hard disks or floppy disks
DISKTOOL (Disk Tool), 8
creating bootable disks, 153
marking clusters, 156

reformatting defective diskettes, 155
rescue diskettes, 156-157
undoing DOS RECOVER command, 154-155
display modes, 38-39
displaying file attributes, 52-54
DOS
addressing memory, 22
commands
CD, 101
DEL, 65-67
DIR, 82
ECHO, 82
EDLIN, 80
FDISK, 24
FORMAT, 127
LABEL, 107
MD, 100
NLSFUNC, 46
PAUSE, 82-83
PROMPT, 101
RD, 100
RECOVER, 154-155
REM, 82
TYPE, 80, 161
VER, 20
directory structure, 99-101
root directory, 100
ERRORLEVEL variable, 94-95
versions, 20
DOS Colors option (NCC), 36-37
DOS mode (SFORMAT), 130
DOS prompt (Commander), 186
Drive options (SFORMAT), 128

E

ECHO (DOS) command, 82
editing files, Commander, 211-213
EDLIN (DOS) command, 80
encrypting files, 157-158
Data Encryption Standard, 159-160
decrypting files, 160
erased files
preserving, 68-72
recovering, 64-67
recovering manually, 167-170
erasing files, Commander, 207-208
ERRORLEVEL variable, 94-95
exiting
BACKUP, 245
Commander, 196
expanded memory, 23
extended memory, 23

F

F1 (NCD help) function key, 103
F2 (NCD Rescan) function key, 103-104
F3 (Commander View File) function key, 210-211
F3 (NCD Switch Drive) function key, 104
F4 (Commander Edit File) function key, 211-213
F5 (Commander copy) function key, 203-205
F6 (Commander Move/Rename) function key, 205-207
F6 (NCD Rename) function key, 104
F7 (NCD MkDir) function key, 106, 216
F8 (Commander Delete File) function key, 207-208
F8 (NCD Delete) function key, 106
F8 (NCD Remove Directory) function key, 216
F9 (NCD Set Line Display) function key, 107
F10 (NCD Quit) function key, 107
Fast Wipe option (WIPEINFO), 75
FAT *see* File Allocation Table
FDISK (DOS) command, 24
File Allocation Tables (FAT), 121-122
viewing with DISKEDIT, 165-167
file attributes
archive, 52, 209
displaying, 52-54
hidden, 52, 209
modifying, 54-55
from command line, 56-57
read-only, 52, 209
setting with Commander, 208-209
system, 52, 209
File menu (Commander Mail), 230
File Panel options (Commander), 190
FILEFIND (File Find), 8
date/time stamps, 62-63
setting from command line, 63-64
disk space, 58
displaying file attributes, 52-54
file size, 58
file storage information, 60-61
modifying file attributes, 54-55
from command line, 56-57
searching for file names, 111-113
searching for text strings, 113-115
wildcards, 57
FILEFIX (File Fix), 8
dBASE files, 72-73
Lotus 1-2-3 files, 72-73
Symphony files, 72-73
files
CONFIG.SYS, 91
copying with Commander, 203-205
decrypting, 160

deleting
    permanently, 74-77
    with Commander, 207-208
editing with Commander, 211-213
encrypting, 157-158
erased
    preserving, 68-72
    recovering, 64-67, 167-179
finding with Commander, 198-200
fragmentation, 122
moving with Commander, 206-207
preserving erased, 68-72
recovering erased, 64-67
    manual recovery, 167-170
renaming with Commander, 205-206
searching for with FILEFIND, 111-113
selecting with Commander, 199-203
size, 58
sorting, 193
storage information, 60-61
transferring with Commander Link, 224-225
viewing, 161-163
    with Commander, 180-182, 210-211
FILESAVE (File Save), 8
preserving deleted files, 68-69
TRASHCAN file, 69-70
    purging files from, 71-72
    recovering files from, 70-71
filtering file list (Commander), 193-194
finding files with Commander, 198-200
floppy disks
formatting with SFORMAT, 127-128
installing Norton Utilities, 4-5
storage capacity, 23-24
testing with NDD, 137, 140-144
unformatting, 132-135
volume labels, 107-108
FOR loop in batch files, 85
FORMAT (DOS) command, 127
formatting floppy disks with SFORMAT, 127-128
fragmentation, 122
correcting with SPEEDISK, 171-173
full backups, 248
full copy backups, 249
function key bar (Commander), 186
function keys
Alt-F7 (Commander Find File), 198-200
F1 (NCD help) function key, 103
F2 (NCD Rescan) function key, 103-104
F3 (Commander View File) function key, 210-211
F3 (NCD Switch Drive) function key, 104
F4 (Commander Edit File) function key, 211-213
F5 (Commander copy) function key, 203-205
F6 (Commander Move/Rename) function key, 205-207
F6 (NCD Rename) function key, 104
F7 (NCD MkDir) function key, 106, 216
F8 (Commander Delete File) function key, 207-208
F8 (NCD Delete) function key, 106
F8 (NCD Remove Directory) function key, 216
F9 (NCD Set Line Display) function key, 107
F10 (NCD Quit) function key, 107

G–H

Government Wipe option (WIPEINFO), 75-77
hard disks
bits, 118
bytes, 118
clusters, 118
Commander, 184-185
cylinders, 119
data area, 123
fragmentation, 122, 171-173
installing Norton Utilities, 3-4
interleave factor, 174-177
logical drives, 24
parking, 151-152
partition size, 24
platters, 119
sectors, 118
slack space, 60
space
    FILEFIND, 58
    slack, 60
storage capacity, 24
system area, 121
    boot record, 121
    boot sector, 121
    File Allocation Table (FAT), 121-122
    root directory, 121
testing with NDD, 137, 140-144
tracks, 119
unformatting, 132-135
volume labels, 107-108
hardware
microprocessors, 20-21
requirements for Commander Mail, 225
requirements for Norton Utilities, 2-5
Hardware Interrupts screen (SYSINFO), 27
help
BACKUP, 243-245
Commander, 194-196
specific utilities, 16-17
syntax help, 17
hexadecimal notation, 162-163
hidden file attribute, 52, 209

I

IMAGE, 8, 131-132
incremental backups, 248
incremental copy backups, 249
installing
    BACKUP, 237-239
    Commander, 182-184
    Commander Mail, 226-229
        modem settings, 228-229
        setting up accounts, 227
    disk cache, 174
    Norton Utilities
        floppy disk installation, 4-5
        hard disk installation, 3-4
        hardware requirements, 2-5
        INSTALL program, 3
interactive batch files, 94
interleave factor, 174-177

K

Keyboard Speed option (NCC), 40-41
keys *see also* function keys
    delay before repeat, 40-41
    repeat rate, 40-41

L

LABEL (DOS) command, 107
Left Panel menu (Commander), 190-192
logical drives, 24
looping batch files, 85
looping in batch files (FOR loop), 85
Lotus 1-2-3 files, repairing with FILEFIX, 72-73

M

macros (BACKUP), 279
    playing, 280
    recording, 279-280
Mail menu (Commander Mail), 230
marking clusters with DISKTOOL, 156
master/slave computers, 222-224
MCI Mail, 225
MD (DOS) command, 100
memory
    addressable by DOS, 22
    bits, 22
    bytes, 22
    expanded, 23
    extended, 23
    RAM, 22
    ROM, 22
    TSRs, 23
Memory Block List screen (SYSINFO), 30

Memory menu (SYSINFO), 28-30
Memory Usage Summary screen (SYSINFO), 28-29
messages (Commander Mail)
    creating, 231-232
    receiving, 232-233
    sending, 232-233
microprocessors, 20
    80286, 21
    80386, 21
    80386SX, 21
    80486, 21
    8088, 20
mini status box (Commander), 186
modems (Commander Mail), 225
modifying file attributes, 54-55
    from command line, 56-57
mouse
    BACKUP, 240
    Commander, 188-189
Mouse Speed option (NCC), 41-42
moving files with Commander, 206-207

N

NCACHE-F (Norton Cache), 9, 173-174
NCACHE-S (Norton Cache), 9, 173-174
NCC (Norton Control Center), 9
    County Info option, 46-47
    Cursor Size option, 35-36
    DOS Colors option, 36-37
    Keyboard Speed option, 40-41
    Mouse Speed option, 41-42
    Palette Colors option, 37-38
    Serial Ports option, 42-44
    Time and Date option, 47-48
    Video Mode option, 38-39
    Watches option, 44-46
NCD (Norton Change Directory), 9, 101-102
    creating directories, 106, 216
    deleting directories, 216
    F1 (Help) function key, 103
    F2 (Rescan) function key, 103-104
    F3 (Switch Drive) function key, 104
    F6 (Rename) function key, 104
    F7 (MkDir) function key, 106, 216
    F8 (Delete) function key, 106
    F8 (Remove Directory) function key, 216
    F9 (Set Line Display) function key, 107
    F10 (Quit) function key, 107
    removing directories, 106
    renaming directories, 104
    searching for directories, 214-216
    Speed Search, 102-103

TREEINFO.NCD file, 104
volume labels, 107-108
NDD (Norton Disk Doctor), 9
  Custom Message option, 142
  skipping tests, 143
  Surface Test Options screen, 140-142
  testing disks, 137, 140-144
  Tests to Skip option, 143
  undoing repairs, 144
Network Information screen (SYSINFO), 27
Network Performance Speed screen
  (SYSINFO), 33
NLSFUNC (DOS) command, 46
NORTON (Norton Integration), 9, 11
  Configure menu, 15-16
  selecting other utilities, 11-14
Norton BACKUP *see* BACKUP
null-modem cables (RS-232), 222

O–P

Overall Performance Index screen (SYSINFO),
  33
Palette Colors option (NCC), 37-38
panels (Commander), 190-191
parameters in batch files, 83-84
parity, 43
parking hard disks, 151-152
Partition Tables screen (SYSINFO), 125-126
partitioning hard disks
  FDISK command, 24
  partition size, 24
PAUSE (DOS) command, 82-83
placing text on screen, 93
platters, 119
playing macros, 280
preserving erased files, 68-72
PROMPT (DOS) command, 101
pull-down menu bar (Commander), 186
purging files from TRASHCAN, 71-72

Q–R

Quick mode (SFORMAT), 130
quitting Commander, 196
RAM *see* memory, RAM
Random Access Memory *see* memory, RAM
RD (DOS) command, 100
Read Only Memory *see* memory, ROM
read-only file attribute, 52, 209
receiving Commander Mail messages, 232-233
recording macros, 279-280
RECOVER (DOS) command, 154-155
recovering
  erased directories, 108-111
  erased files, 64-67

manually, 167-170
files from TRASHCAN, 70-71
formatted disks, 132-135
REM (DOS) command, 82
removing directories, 100, 106, 216
renaming
  directories, 104
  files
    Commander, 205-206
Report menu (SYSINFO), 34
rescue diskettes, creating with DISKTOOL,
  156-157
restoring backed up files *see* BACKUP, Basic
  or Advanced
Right Panel menu (Commander), 190-192
ROM *see* memory, ROM
root directory, 100, 121
ROWCOL BE subcommand, 93
running applications from Commander, 217-
  220
  point-and-shoot feature, 219-220

S

SA BE subcommand, 91-92
Safe mode (SFORMAT), 130
Save IMAGE Info option (SFORMAT), 130
Screen Blank Delay option (Commander), 190
screen colors, 36-38, 91-92
Screen Colors option (Commander), 190
searching for
  directories (NCD), 214-216
  files with FILEFIND, 111-113
  text strings with FILEFIND, 113-115
sectors, 118
selecting files with Commander, 199-203
sending Commander Mail messages, 232-233
serial ports, 222
  configuring, 42-44
Serial Ports option (NCC), 42-44
Set Custom Message screen (NDD), 142
setting system clock, 47-48
Setup menu (Commander Mail), 230
SFORMAT, 127
  Allow Hard Disk Formatting option, 129
  DOS mode, 130
  Drive options, 128
  formatting floppy disks, 127-128
  Quick mode, 130
  Safe mode, 130
  Save IMAGE Info option, 130
  System Files option, 129-130
  Volume Label option, 130
SFORMAT (Safe Format), 10
skipping NDD tests, 143

slack disk space, 60
Software Interrupts screen (SYSINFO), 27
sorting files, 193
Speed Search (NCD), 102-103
SPEEDISK (Speed Disk), 10
  correcting fragmentation, 171-173
stop bit, 43
stopwatches, 44-46
storage capacity
  floppy disks, 23-24
  hard disks, 24
Surface Test Options screen (NDD), 140-142
switching drives in Commander, 193
Symphony files, repairing with FILEFIX, 72-73
SYSINFO (System Information), 10, 25
  Benchmarks menu, 30-33
    CPU Speed screen, 31-32
    Disk Speed screen, 32-33
    Network Performance Speed Screen, 33
    Overall Performance Index screen, 33
  Disks menu, 28, 123-126
    Disk Characteristics screen, 124-125
    Disk Summary screen, 123
    Partition Tables screen, 125-126
  Memory menu, 28-30
    Device Drivers screen, 30
    Memory Block List screen, 30
    Memory Usage Summary screen, 28-29
    TSR Programs screen, 30
  Report menu, 34
    Report Options screen, 34
    View AUTOEXEC.BAT screen, 34
    View CONFIG.SYS screen, 34
  System menu, 25-28
    CMOS Status screen, 28
    Hardware Interrupts screen, 27
    Network Information screen, 27
    Software Interrupts screen, 27
    System Summary screen, 26
    Video Summary screen, 27
system area, 121
  boot record, 121
  boot sector, 121
  File Allocation Table (FAT), 121-122
  root directory, 121
system clock, setting, 47-48
system file attribute, 52, 209
System Files option (SFORMAT), 129-130
System menu (SYSINFO), 25-28
System Summary screen (SYSINFO), 26

T

telecommunications *see* Commander Mail
Terminate-and-Stay-Resident programs *see*
  TSRs
testing disks with NDD, 137, 140-144

Tests to Skip option (NDD), 143
text
  placing on screen, 93
  searching for with FILEFIND, 113-115
time, setting, 47-48
Time and Date option (NCC), 47-48
time stamps, FILEFIND, 62-64
tracks, 119
transferring files with Commander Link, 224-225
TRASHCAN file, 69-70
  purging files from, 71-72
  recovering files from, 70-71
Tree Panel options (Commander), 190
TREEINFO.NCD file, 104
TSR Programs screen (SYSINFO), 30
TSRs, 23
TYPE (DOS) command, 80, 161

U

undoing NDD repairs, 144
UNERASE, 10
  Prognosis column, 67
  recovering erased directories, 108-111
  recovering files, 65
  recovering files manually, 167-170
unerasing files, 64-67
  manually, 167-170
UNFORMAT, 10, 133-135
unformatting disks, 132-135

V

VER (DOS) command, 20
verifying backup data, 249
Video Mode option (NCC), 38-39
video settings (BACKUP), 241
Video Summary screen (SYSINFO), 27
viewing files
  Commander, 180, 210-211
    formats supported, 181-182
viewing files with DISKEDIT, 161-163
  ASCII characters, 163-165
  hexadecimal notation, 162-163
  text view, 165
viruses, 148-150
Volume Label option (SFORMAT), 130
volume labels, assigning with NCD, 107-108

W

Watches option (NCC), 44-46
wildcards in FILEFIND, 57
WINDOW BE subcommand, 92-93
windows, creating with BE, 92-93
WIPEINFO (Wipe Information), 11, 75
  Fast Wipe option, 75
  Government Wipe option, 75-77
  wiping entire disks, 136-137